Heart for the Fight

Heart for the Fight

A Marine Hero's Journey
from the Battlefields of Iraq
to Mixed Martial Arts Champion

Brian Stann with John R. Bruning

ZENITH PRESS

First published in 2010 by MBI Publishing Company LLC
and Zenith Press, an imprint of MBI Publishing Company,
400 1st Avenue North, Minneapolis, MN 55401 USA.

Zenith Press titles are also available at discounts in bulk quantity
for industrial or sales-promotional use. For details write to Special
Sales Manager at MBI Publishing Company, 400 1st Avenue North,
Minneapolis, MN 55401 USA.

Front cover image: AJ Photography

Cover designed by Simon Larkin

Maps by: Patti Isaacs

Library of Congress Cataloging-in-Publication Data

Stann, Brian, 1980-

Heart for the fight : a marine hero's journey from the
battlefields of iraq to mixed martial arts champion / Brian Stann with
John R. Bruning.

p. cm.

ISBN 978-0-7603-3899-5 (hb w/ jkt)

1. Stann, Brian, 1980- 2. United States. Marine Corps—Officers—
Biography. 3. United States Naval Academy—Biography. 4. Iraq
War, 2003—Campaigns—Iraq—Anbar (Province) 5. Marines—
United States—Biography. 6. Martial artists—United States—
Biography. 7. Mixed martial arts. 8. Scranton (Pa.)—Biography.
I. Bruning, John R. II. Title.

VE25.S73A3 2010

956.7044'345092—dc22

[B]

2010007360

Printed in the United States of America

"It is not the critic who counts; not the man who points out how the strong man stumbles, or where the doer of deeds could have done them better. The credit belongs to the man who is actually in the arena, whose face is marred by dust and sweat and blood; who strives valiantly; who errs, who comes short again and again, because there is no effort without error and shortcoming; but who does actually strive to do the deeds; who knows great enthusiasms, the great devotions; who spends himself in a worthy cause; who at the best knows in the end the triumph of high achievement, and who at the worst, if he fails, at least fails while daring greatly, so that his place shall never be with those cold and timid souls who neither know victory nor defeat."

—Theodore Roosevelt, speech at the Sorbonne, Paris, France, April 23, 1910

Contents

Prologue

Fear and I became acquainted very early in my life. As a kid, I went to South Scranton Intermediate School, a graffiti-scarred hell hole built sometime before the Second World War. With barred windows and shit-brown paint that gave the place a jailhouse sort of vibe, the gangs roaming the hallways seemed like the natural order of things. In those halls, you joined a gang for self-protection, became a perpetual victim, or tried to steer a path between the two. I chose the latter, mainly because I didn't want to lose my individuality. It was the only thing I had at that age, and I found, like almost everything in my life, I had to fight to hold onto it. Being an individual in a world of conformity and violence made me a target. I grew up fast and learned how to use my fists when I needed them.

The gang that ruled our school came from the nearby federal housing projects. Known as the Valley View Terrace boys, these pre-teen gangbangers grew up in a disjointed world of drugs, violence, and poverty. It united them, and they controlled our school through strength of numbers and liberal doses of terror.

I ran afoul of these guys in seventh grade. My best friend, Jake, was dating a girl from the projects, and we'd all gone to a church dance one Friday night. Afterward, we walked home past Vince the Pizza Prince, a greasy joint that the Valley View boys used as their weekend hangout. Jake had the bad judgment to say goodnight to his date right in front of the place. Their goodnight peck turned into a thirty second eyeball-popping make out fest.

I knew we were in trouble as soon as we turned and left Jake's girl behind. A block up from the pizza place, I ventured a glance over my shoulder and saw that we'd picked up a tail of almost a dozen Valley View Terrace boys. A few of their girls trailed along excitedly, smiling and whispering to each other.

"Jake. We're about to get jumped," I said to my best friend.

"What? No we're not, Bro. Are we?"

We walked another block. Another quick look behind us and I could see the Valley View boys had closed the distance. They were nonchalantly moving in for the kill, trying hard to look innocent and harmless as they did so.

"Hey Jake!" one of the girls called from behind us. Jake made the unforgivable mistake of turning around.

"Huh?" he asked as a lean, white girl with overdone makeup and bright red lipstick strutted his way.

"Yo Jake? Why'd you go an' grab ma' ass?" asked the girl. This befuddled both of us. We didn't know the girl, and hadn't seen her at the dance. Behind her, the Valley View Terrace boys started to laugh. A few made rude comments as they enjoyed the show.

"What are you talking about? I didn't grab shit!"

The girl answered with her fist. She punched Jake so hard he reeled backward, blood dripping from a split lip. Before he could get his hands up to protect himself, the street vixen landed two more solid punches.

Even the Valley View Terrace chicks liked to kick ass.

While Jake and I concentrated on the girl presently thrashing him, the rest of the gang fanned out around us. Her attack was a ploy to distract us, pure and simple. These guys knew how to deliver a beating, and they fought without rules. There was no escape. I knew we could either fight or beg for mercy. I was never one to beg, and mercy was not what the Valley View Terrace boys were about anyway.

There was no way to win this fight. Maybe in a Jackie Chan flick, we'd be able to demolish these dead-enders with cool moves, flips, and kicks. But on the street, those celluloid heroics just don't work. So when you can't run, and you can't win, you can give up or fight for the sake of honor and pride. For respect.

Might as well go down fighting.

It was in moments like these that I gained my intimate knowledge of fear. Would I panic and try to run? Would I scream for help and get hysterical? If I tried to fight, would I even be able to defend us? Or would I feel those blocks of ice suddenly form on my nervous system, clogging all my brain's commands and leaving me frozen and helpless.

The Valley View Terrace boys tightened the noose. The vixen kept landing blows. Jake covered his face, but her fists still connected. I watched it all unfold, each second ticking off like an hour, everything moving with interminable slowness.

One beefy proto-gangbanger came straight at me. The fight was on.

Fear. It starts in the pit of your stomach, then travels up and down your spine, making every movement an effort. Raising fists, dodging a punch. To do those things, first I had to break through those terror-spawned blocks of ice that jammed my nervous system.

Some kids never got through those ice floes. They'd freeze up in a fight. Eyes wide, fists half-balled, they looked like deer caught on a back county road. Their terror rooted them in place. Unable to move, they were meat on the table. I'd seen more than one kid get turned into a bloody pulp this way. Even worse, you freeze in a fight at South Scranton, and you became marked forever, punching bags for every bully, gangbanger, and skate punk with something to prove. With every fight, I saw their sense of self-worth slough away until they had nothing left. I swore I would not let this school and these people destroy who I was.

That's what always broke the ice inside me. They weren't going to own me, even if it meant taking a beating because I was outnumbered or overmatched. The fact that they would even try sent a surge of indignation into me. In a flash, that would morph into rage, and I'd feel my fists clench and my muscles go taut. The fear would always remain, but I used it. It kept me alert and vigilant, sometimes almost paranoid.

On that night, I felt the ice melt before my rage. I charged the beefy kid and slammed into him with a line-backer's embrace. I caught him in mid-stride. Off-balance, he staggered backward. I kept pumping my legs and drove him right through a nearby hedge. He tripped and we both went down, fists flailing. Moments later, Jake came flying over the hedge, four Valley View Terrace boys in his wake. Before he could get to his feet, they pounced on him. One kid kicked Jake in the face hard, and I saw more blood spew from his lip.

The beefy kid and I rolled, kicked, and punched. Another kid jumped in, and pretty soon, I had three on me while the others pounded on my best friend. Somehow, I managed to get up on my feet again. I pushed one of the Valley View Terrace boys through the hedge, then I slugged and kicked my way to Jake. Just as I reached him, a passing motorist stopped her car and shouted, "Hey! I'm callin' the cops, like right now!"

Most of the Valley View Terrace boys already had rap sheets and parole officers. A night in juvenile hall did not appeal to them. They bolted into the night, hurling invectives our way as they ran.

I wasn't badly hurt, just a swollen eye and a bloody nose. I'd get worse—a lot worse in the months to come.

I helped Jake up. His face looked like hamburger, with cut cheeks and two black eyes. He wiped some of the blood and dirt away as he said, "What the hell did we ever do to them?"

"Oh my God Jake, do I have to spell it out for you, buddy?"

He looked the picture of despair. Heart racing, blood flowing, he'd been thumped on good.

"Whaddya mean?" he asked.

"Listen up, brother: Don't date gang chicks."

He nodded ruefully. Together we walked through the bitter Pennsylvania night to my mother's house. Lesson learned. On our streets, the Valley View Terrace boys made the rules. Cross them and no matter how tough you were, they'd figure out a way to beat you down. Sheer numbers usually worked just fine.

A few months later, Jake and I ran afoul of the skater punks. These kids were skinny, acne-prone little twerps who worshipped Kurt Cobain and decided personal hygiene was not for them. They hated their lot in life, so they threw in a hint of Goth to their gang attire, which complemented their overall grunge affectation. They also despised the Valley View Terrace gang, since they were way tougher and far more feared.

That didn't stop the skate-punks from trying to carve a niche out for themselves. They traveled in a pack and like jackals would descend upon the weak at our intermediate school. By seventh grade, about a third of them had already dropped out. They spent their days on the school's fringes, waiting for their buddies to finish class so they could all go skate and get high together.

When the bell rang, they'd hop on their boards and slalom through the throngs of escaping kids looking only to get home for the day. In the crowd, they would select their target: always a smaller, younger kid. They specialized in the ones who let fear own them.

One day in February 1995, three o'clock rolled around and I rendezvoused with Jake in the filthy hallway by our lockers. At South Scranton, you survived by surrounding yourself with as many pals as possible, so we always walked home with the other kids from our immediate neighborhood. Within minutes, we had our normal gaggle present and were ready to depart. Out the school we went, ducking into an alley that emptied out next to a mini-mart. No Valley View Terrace boys lurked, but we kept moving fast.

A minute later, we reached the mini-mart. This was a favorite after-school pit stop, a place where we could buy a snack and chat before making the final dash for home.

On this afternoon, the skater punks filled the small parking lot. Some were trying to look cool, grinding their boards, or jumping off curbs. The others had surrounded a sixth grader. They'd found their target for the day.

I didn't know the kid, but he looked meek and terrified and that was more than I could stand. This had to stop. Jake saw me suddenly veer for the circle of stringy-haired skaters and said, "Got your back. But, Brian, what are you doing?"

"This is bullshit, man!" I said, a swell of anger rising in me.

The king of the skate punks was a thirteen-year-old named Justin. His long, unwashed hair and sickly complexion made him look a little like a tweaker. Within the year, he'd be just another junior high drop out.

"Hey Justin, get the fuck outta here!" I roared.

The skate punks turned to see Jake and I coming. Behind us, our neighborhood posse watched silently.

"Piss off Stann, or we'll fuck you up," Justin spat back.

The skate punks formed a phalanx, their target forgotten. I could see fear in their pasty faces. They knew my reputation. Not long before, I got jumped by the older brother of one of the Valley View Terrace boys. The crowd drawn by the drama expected him to make short work of me. Before he matriculated to reform school, he had become something of a legend at South Scranton. Known to his classmates as ruthless and violence prone, he especially loved to prey on the weak. He sealed his legendary status one day after he beat another kid senseless with a monkey wrench. That incident, forever known as the "wrench fight" became part of the school's oral tradition, one of the many sordid moments in its history that got passed down from grade to grade every year. Even the teachers still talked about it.

Fortunately, he didn't have a wrench the day he attacked me. It turned out he didn't have much skill with his fists, and he lacked my determination. By the time a neighbor finally broke up the fight, put me in a headlock, and dragged me to the principal's office, I was covered in the kid's blood. When our principal found out who I'd fought he said, "Off the record, I'm glad you kicked his ass."

The skate punks had seen the fight, and they had no stomach for that sort of one-on-one action. They looked uncertain, posturing there in the parking lot of the mini-mart.

"You guys are small fucking change. Get outta here," I sneered.

"We're gonna get you Stann." Justin said, not noticing that their sixth grade target slipped away while they faced me.

"Come on, guys, they're not worth it," I said and derisively turned my back to the skate punks. They made no move. We left the parking lot unhindered and made our way home.

The next day, as we left the school after the three o'clock bell, Justin and three or four of his lackeys were waiting for me in the alley. This time, they'd brought armament. Justin sported a lead pipe. The guy next to him hefted a two-by-four like a baseball bat.

I walked past them, and one of the skate punks called, "As soon as our two other buddies show up, you're fucking gonna get it, Stann."

I started laughing at them. They didn't like that, but they made no move for me.

"You don't have the balls," I said to Justin as I locked eyes with him. Once again, he hesitated. I sensed his fear. For a long moment, we squared off, a few feet of gang-tagged sidewalk between us.

"You guys are pathetic," I sneered. The skate punks said nothing, but I could see I had dealt a blow to their pride. I called their bluff, and everyone would know it at school tomorrow.

I walked away and didn't bother to look back. I imagine Justin and his pals just stood there, looking foolish and cowardly with their backstreet weapons in hand.

I had humiliated them again, and while I didn't know it, I pushed it too far with my loose mouth.

About a week later, Jake and I met at our lockers as soon as the bell tolled three o'clock. It was cloudy and a little chilly, so I put on a forest green suede jacket that was a hand-me-down from my high-school-aged sister. In my household, we had to make use of everything as much as possible. We didn't have the luxury to be fashionable, my mom barely kept the household afloat on her meager salary.

I strapped on my backpack. A few more of our neighborhood pals gathered with us. We were ready to run the gauntlet. A moment later, we piled out of the school's side exit and found the alley deserted. This was a good sign, and I think we all relaxed a little bit. We pushed on for the mini-mart. We were thirty feet shy of the parking lot when a beat-up white van suddenly swung into the alley and squealed to a halt right in front of us. The side door slid open and two men jumped out.

They came straight for me. Shock and surprise collided with an onslaught of fear. Those ice floes blocked every movement. I struggled to break through it, get my fists balled and my legs in a fighting stance. But I knew that even if it took me a moment to shake this off, I had my posse to back me up. We'd fight and stand together. I just needed to set the example.

Before I could unfreeze my system, Jake bolted. As he plowed through our friends and dashed down the alley, his panic spread to everyone else. Soon, everyone else had turned tail like gazelles fleeing a cheetah.

My friends had abandoned me to my fate.

The two men rushed me. There would be no escape this time. I couldn't run, paralyzing fear still controlled my nervous system. Even if I had full use of my body, they were too close to me to avoid them now. I would have to fight, but they were almost twice my age and had almost a hundred pounds on me. I knew I wouldn't last long.

I had to focus on something to get my body to work again. Dimly, I realized I had my backpack on, which was not a good thing in a fight. I tried to get my arms to move. I'd slipped this backpack off my shoulders countless times. The muscle memory was there, but the neurons still wouldn't fire.

Still fumbling for the strap, I never saw the first blow coming. A fist slammed into my right jaw with such force that my head snapped backward. I freed one strap off my shoulder. Now my backpack hung half on, half off. I never got free of it.

Another hard blow rocked me backward. My face burned with pain. A kick and two punches drove me to one knee. Blood splattered the graffiti-covered sidewalk, and through blurry eyes I caught a glimpse of my friends scattering down the alley.

Cowards.

The two men battered away at me. Fists slammed into my head and face. One of them gut kicked me. I tried to get to my feet. They beat me back down. I tried to get my arms up to defend myself and protect my face. They swung even harder, and I took a vicious hit to the eye. My brow split open, and I could feel my eye swelling shut.

A kick to the head knocked me senseless. I sagged to the sidewalk, feeling dizzy and disembodied. A moment later, I felt nothing at all.

I don't know how long I lay sprawled in the alley. I do remember that when I finally got a handle on my spinning head, my attackers had disappeared. Both eyes were so blackened and swollen that I looked like the Elephant Man. A concussion made my head ring and my vision unfocused. My face was cut and gashed. My lips were split and bleeding. I'd never been beaten this badly by anyone, ever.

I later found out that Justin had cut a deal with two eighteen year olds to "put me in my place." My attackers were already wanted on assault and armed robbery charges. When the police took them down a few weeks later, they ended up doing hard time for their prior felonies.

I staggered home, escorted by two passing neighborhood girls who found me in the alley. I barely said a word to them. Instead, my mind fixated on the sight of my best friend leaving me at the moment I most needed him. When it came to crunch time, my posse had deserted me.

It took me months to forgive Jake, and I spent the rest of the year isolated from my supposed friends. In some ways, I don't think I ever got over what happened that day.

Loyalty and courage are not automatics in life, even with close friends. That was a hard lesson to learn at twelve years old. But as I tried to make sense of what happened in the nights that followed the attack, I realized that if I was going to survive and get anywhere in life, I couldn't depend on anyone but myself.

Night after night my mind replayed those final seconds before the two thugs reached me. I'd feel that sudden chill of fear spike down my spine. I'd see my arms and fists useless at my sides. I didn't fight back. I couldn't. That one time, fear owned me just as totally as those broken-spirited kids I'd tried to protect. In that one instant, I saw what life was like for them. I swore fear would never control me again.

PART I

Confidence

CHAPTER ONE

The Man in the Arena

Fight Night, Las Vegas, August 2008

*T*heir *screams are the worst. We're more than a hundred meters away, on the other side of the river, but I can hear Marines dying. Their armored vehicle hit a land mine. It caught fire with fifteen men aboard.*

They scream as they burn alive. The radio chatter is desperate, almost hysterical. Nobody can get to them. There will be no salvation, only a torturous death in the flames. From our position across the river, we hear every agonizing moment and can see their funeral pyre rising over the riverbank.

I can do nothing. It is the most helpless, enraging feeling I've ever experienced. I have no way to get across the water to those burning men.

It takes forever for the last screams to fade away.

My eyes flick open. I'm instantly alert. For a second, it feels like I'm back in western Iraq.

Travis Manion, one of my closest friends, stares at me from across the makeshift locker room, as if he senses I've relived that day in 2005 all over again. He knows I always do.

You gotta have heart for the fight, Bro.

Travis says that before every bout. He's a wrestler with butt-ugly, battered jug ears that he had to drain after every match at the Naval Academy. Fighters break their fingers so often that they frequently become useless digits. Wrestlers get their ears boxed until they're bloated and fluid filled. It's just part of the game. We understand that sacrifice, and respect each other for it. It is who we are—Marines driven to win at whatever cost.

I am the WEC light heavyweight champ. Tonight is fight night. Steve Cantwell and I are the main event.

I won the belt with heart and a hell of a lot of work, not with my technique or my skills as a fighter. On that front, I'm still raw, a fact my new coaches repeatedly remind me about. I haven't had the years to develop like other fighters have. While my opponents have been training, I've been in combat. Every time I go into the cage, I face that disadvantage.

At least everyone else says it's a disadvantage. It has never bothered me before. I'm not the kid who couldn't get his backpack off anymore. I won't be caught off guard, and I'll be damned if there's another fighter out there with more heart than I.

Besides, after days like that one in 2005, everything seems a hell of a lot easier than combat.

At the moment, I have time to kill. I'm in the lull, that dreadful space between arriving for the fight and actually getting in the cage. Here at the Hard Rock Casino, they put us fighters into a cramped storage room near the loading docks. The hotel staff divides the room with a curtain, and our opponents can be heard warming up on the other side. We've also got 8x10 mats on the floor so we can warm up when it's time. Flanking the mats are folding chairs with our names taped to them.

I've been here for over an hour now. My fight isn't until seven, and it is just after five. Around me, the undercard boxers are suffering through the same lull. Some sit and stare at the ceiling, lost in thought. Others listen to music. A few join their coaches on the mats and start to warm up.

The tension here is like no other locker room I've ever experienced. Football at the Academy was intense, but never like this. At times, the tension borders on quiet desperation. For us fighters, our careers hang by a thread. One loss and we will see our contracts torn up, our endorsement deals vanish. That's just the start. A loss can send you back down to the local venues where a fighter's lucky to make two grand per event. Many of the WEC fighters have families. If they lose, they've got no way to cover next month's house payment. One wrong move, one punch not blocked, and it is over. The dream of becoming one of those few who can make serious money at this game will evaporate, and it'll be back to living on a relative's couch between bouts.

Tonight, careers will be destroyed, fortunes won and potential ones lost. Our destiny resides in our fists.

I have two major endorsements riding on tonight's championship fight. If I lose, they'll stop courting me. Nobody wants a loser as a shill.

I sit back in my metal chair and listen to my iPod. Travis leaves me alone. So do my corner men. Frank, my brother-in-law, knows my routine and stays out of my way. My new coach, Rory Singer, has another fighter on the undercard named Brian Bowles. He taps Brian on the shoulder and tells him to warm up. Together, they walk over to the mat and get to work.

My other corner man, Thierry Sokoudjou, is a fighter of great reputation and skill. He's been with me in one other fight. He keeps his distance, but I know he's watching to make sure I stay relaxed—or at least as relaxed as I can. The worst thing a fighter can do is get his heart rate going prematurely. That's a hard thing to avoid when you've got a three hour wait for the biggest five minutes of your life. I don't tell him about my recurring memory. For some reason, it always pops into my head on fight nights. I guess it serves as a reminder of who I am and what I went through.

I don't fight for myself. I fight for my Marines, for the kids I lost in Iraq and the friends I helped lay to rest at home. The bonds we sealed at the Academy? They are stronger than death, but it doesn't make their loss any easier.

I do know this: Every time I put my gloves on, I feel them at my side. Their presence and memory guides and drives me. I cannot let them down.

I will justify their faith in me with every strike.

Thumbing through the tracks on my iPod, I search for a song that captures the moment. Nothing seems to fit. In past fights, I've always found a song that clinches my mood, one that sparks my final mental preparations before the fight. When I took the belt from Doug Marshall in the spring, I listened to rap. I hate rap, but it just felt right. When I took on Craig Zellner, I played Bullet for My Valentine's *Tears Don't Fall* over and over. It reminded me of Iraq, and it filled me with cold fury.

Tonight, I try out some classic Guns N' Roses. *Paradise City* does nothing for me. I move on to *Night Train*, but that's a dud as well. It makes me feel unsettled. Something's not right. A fighter's mental state is critical. A ripple in his psyche can mean the difference between victory and the cold kiss of the mat.

In the final moments before a fight, I bundle up all the grief and rage and turn it into fuel for the battle ahead. When I step into the cage, I unleash all of it on my opponent. It explodes out of me and becomes a force of its own. One of my pro fights lasted just sixteen seconds. So far, nobody has been able to go more than one round against me. I am 6–0. The undefeated Marine.

I represent the Corps every time I climb into the cage. I've said that to the media many times during the pre-event hype. On camera, I've talked about the people I've lost, the friends I've seen die and how their memory propels me forward. The truth is, fighting is how I cope. It is my release, and it keeps my life in balance outside the cage.

How many friends have you lost?

Too many.

Trav knows. He's been through it with me.

There's no way to escape the grief. Instead, I pour it out through my fists and feet.

I hear them screaming. I can almost see their faces.

Cantwell hasn't seen these things. He didn't smell burning flesh. That motherfucker on the other side of the cage—he didn't go through that. And I'm going to show him. I'm going to make him feel the pain I live with every day.

My gym bag sits nearby. I reach down and rummage through it until I find my wallet.

By now, we're well into the undercard. The clock reads six-thirty. Two fights to go, then I'm up. Bowles leaves for his bout, Rory trailing after him. I hold my wallet and watch Brian climb into the cage on one of the flat-screen televisions mounted on the wall.

I clutch my wallet and feel that ripple in my psyche again. It flows across the rage I've been trying to create and feels even more unsettling than before.

Brian wins his fight. He returns to the locker room all smiles. Rory is pumped. He slaps my shoulder and says, "Cantwell can't handle ya, Brian. No way. He's all yours."

"Thanks, Coach."

Burt, one of the WEC organizers, enters the locker room. "Hey, the card's moving quick now. You got about twenty minutes, Brian."

From my wallet, I extract a small business card. On the back, below an embossed anchor, are words first shared at a classmate's funeral. I glance up at Travis, then back down at the card. He's not smiling any longer. He knows the score.

Make my lonely grave richer
Sweeter be,
Make this truly the land of the free
And the home of the brave.
I gave my life to save
That I might here lie
Eternally
Forever free.

The spirit of the Corps. These are the words that sealed and bonded our brotherhood. It exists beyond the realm of this life. Nothing breaks it. It is stronger than death. That's what makes the Corps unique, and why we Marines have accomplished so many historic things.

Travis watches over me. Those words have guided his life as well. They are what made him rush to the sound of gunfire in Iraq and try to save a wounded comrade. They are the reason why he received a Silver Star.

My brother-in-law, Frank appears next to me. "Let's get your gloves on."

I stand up, and Frank slides them onto my hands. These are my weapons now. In Iraq, I carried an M16 and could call down laser guided bombs, artillery, and tank fire on my opponents. Here, in the cage, it will be my fists and feet against Cantwell's.

I step onto the mat. Rory comes over, holding pads. Time to warm up.

Another ripple rolls through me. This is my first fight with Rory. I'm not used to him holding the pads I'll soon be striking. Travis used to do that, like several of my Marine training partners since. We've worked together for years now. I remember nights where we didn't even have a gym to practice in, so we dragged our pads onto a lawn and worked out in the dark as best we could. We did whatever it took to get better.

Tentatively I strike the pads. Rory encourages me. I push a little harder. It still doesn't feel right. Whatever it is that's bothering me, it is too late to fix. I just have to make the best of it. I get to work.

Fighters know that the warm-up before a bout is almost as important as the bout itself. Stepping into the cage cold shocks your system. Your heart rate spikes to 180 and your body loads up with lactic acid. You get stiff quickly and lose your wind. The best warm-ups are the ones that get you all sweaty and tired. The fight itself becomes your second wind. Your body has time to adjust to the exertion and abuse it will take.

"Okay," Rory says at last. "Now, let's go out there and get it done."

"Roger that, Coach."

Burt arrives and tells us it is time to go. We follow him out the Casino's back door, around the corner to the front entrance. We walk through the main floor, surrounded by gamblers and cocktail waitresses. Rory, Frank, and Thierry stay protectively close to me. I can't see Trav, but I know he's close too.

We pause at the staging door. On the other side is a small room that then opens onto the arena. Steve Cantwell waits inside. As the challenger, he'll be introduced first tonight, which means I have to wait.

I bounce on the balls of my feet, trying to keep my heart rate up. The wait continues. A drunk wanders up to me and asks, "Who ya fightin'?"

Somebody else asks me for my autograph, which was kind of silly since I'm wearing gloves and can't sign anything. In the past, I've been able to focus during these final moments, but now, I'm distracted by the people around me. Travis appears, and I see he looks unusually serious, borderline worried. In a different situation, I know he'd take me aside and ask me what the hell was going on. Our friendship starts and ends with blunt honesty. We never pull our punches because we know whatever we say to each other is designed to make us better. Better men. Better officers. Better warriors.

More looky-loos gather until I'm in the eye of a mini mob scene. I look around and see we're ringed by drunks, all of whom are shelling me with slurred questions. Some cheer me on. A few try to pat me on the shoulder to wish me good luck. One with liquid legs wobbles up to me and exclaims, "Who the fuck are you?"

The staging room doors open at last and I'm led inside. We leave the chaos behind us. A few final seconds of silence and then I'll be Teddy Roosevelt's man in the arena once again.

"We're at commercial. Stand by," says Burt.

Brian. You're not a Marine anymore.

The ripple just became a tidal wave. I try to ignore it.

You're not a Marine.

I will always be a Marine, even if I did leave the Corps earlier this summer. This is my first fight as a civilian.

Who are you?

Oh come on. Don't even start. I'm a veteran of Iraq. I'm the Light Heavyweight Champion of the WEC.

You aren't a fighter. You don't have the skills. You brawl. You strike. But your technique is weak. And now, you're not even a Marine. You gave that life up for your wife and daughter.

I have no answer for this. This summer, after I left the Marines, I moved my family down to Atlanta. When I did, I left my sparring partners and coaches behind. I had always trained with other Marines; now I had to find a new home. I ended up training at two different gyms, relying on four different coaches. It was so decentralized that I learned things from one coach that canceled out the things another one was trying to teach me.

My coaches all agreed on one thing: I don't have the skills yet. I have the heart, plenty of that, but at this level, they told me, heart ain't enough.

Travis doesn't buy that. Neither did I, and that's how I got this far.

You gotta have heart for the fight, Bro.

Another wave crashes over me.

A jolt of fear jabs my gut.

Oh hell no. Not this. Not now.

I have always had confidence in myself. I've never doubted my heart. Another shock of fear courses through me. For a second, I feel like I'm in Iraq again, getting ready to sortie on a mission with my platoon.

Brian, you have never let fear get the best of you. Don't start now.

That's what Travis would tell me if I had time to talk to him about this. But any second now, that other set of double doors will open, and I'll walk into the arena alone, thousands of fans cheering or booing, millions more watching on television. It's too late for talk.

Okay, what am I going to do?

As I wrestle with that question, I realize my body has cooled off. The wait on the casino floor went longer than I thought. I'm not sweaty anymore, which is a bad thing. I'm going to climb into the cage cold.

Frank gives me a quick hug. "I love you, brother. Kick his ass."

"Okay, we're back and live," Burt announces.

The second set of double doors fling open. The crowd screams and howls. A camera waits just across the threshold.

I step forward and pass through the doors like a man in a dream. No, not a dream. A nightmare.

I'm going to lose this fight.

CHAPTER TWO

Rematch

I step into the octagon, the WEC's version of the venerable boxing ring. Cantwell's already there, mugging to the crowd. They're eating it up. He trains and lives in Las Vegas, so this is his home turf.

Steve Cantwell's a young up-and-comer in the business. He left school at age sixteen and took up residence in a gym. He's been training ever since I graduated from the Academy.

He bounces around the ring, shouting out to his fans. I stand quietly and watch. I notice he's cultivated the same sleepy-eyed tough guy look Stallone made famous. The first time we met, I knocked him off his feet in the first round. During the media events this past week, he's flapped his gums about revenge and payback.

I try to get pissed at all this showmanship, but I'm still hung up on the ripples in my pond.

Still think you're gonna lose this fight?

Fuck. I don't know.

Charge the guns, Marine. Hold nothing back.

There's only one way to go out. Fighting to the end.

25

The announcer introduces Cantwell, who flexes for the camera and then throws a few jabs at the folks watching on television. He's a spectacle, and he loves the attention. At the same time, I can tell he's focused and completely zoned in for the fight ahead.

I feel Travis at my side. I want to turn and look him in the eyes. I want to hear whatever pearls of wisdom he has for this moment. But I can't do that. Instead, the announcer shouts out my name. I bounce back and forth on the balls of my feet, trying to stay loose. I'm no showman, so I don't mimic Cantwell's stunting for the crowd and camera. Instead, I stay within myself, head down, lost in last thoughts.

Time to fight. We meet at the center and tap gloves, and round one begins. The first few seconds of a fight are always near out-of-body experiences for me. I train for months for each fight. I visualize this moment every night for weeks on end. When it finally arrives, it seems surreal, as if I'm caught between reality and my own vision of this moment, unsure of what is real or simple daydream.

Keep your feet moving.

We size each other up. Cantwell looks laser-focused. Intense. Cocky. His gloves are up, he's watching my movements, matching what he's seen on tape to what I'm doing now in the octagon.

He bounces forward and launches a jab. I block it easily with my own gloves. As quick as he attacked, Cantwell bounds backward out of range. A test, or recon by fire. He's wanting to see how I'll respond to aggression. Last time we fought, it was a slugfest, and I pressed him until he went down.

I surge forward on my left foot and jab a second later. He dodges and slides to the right.

Charge the guns.

I launch a head-on attack. Nothing fancy, just sheer power, like a Marine division hitting a beach. I come at him swinging. He's seen this before. Heck, I did this to him last time we fought. And he's waiting for me. My blows glance off his arms. He holds his ground and tags me with a sharp right uppercut. As I back away, I hook my right into his head to score a small victory. Then we're apart, both fighters looking for an opening while bobbing and weaving.

Cantwell's an expert in Brazilian jujitsu. He also started kickboxing at age sixteen, and he's integrated that into his game. He's flexible, with long, powerful legs that have done serious damage in previous fights. Now, he takes a shot at me. He kicks with his right, and his foot brushes my gloves as I back away from the blow.

Pour it on him. You've got nothing to lose.

I've got everything to lose.

Before I can respond, Cantwell comes after me again. This time, he ducks low and jabs for my stomach. He connects but does no damage. As he retreats, I swipe a fierce right hook at him. He stays under it, and my glove whiffs through empty air.

I follow him, jabbing with my right. Cantwell bounds out of range.

He's a lot tougher to hit this time. He's moving, and he's quick.

Get on him. Just go straight after him.

I try another head-on attack. Cantwell's waiting. I deliver a kick to his left side, then jab away at him. I miss, and he punishes me with a solid punch to the face. It drives me back on my heels, and Cantwell stays on me. He closes and unloads a roundhouse kick to my left side. I break contact and slide to the right. That buys me a couple of seconds.

Brian, you're being tentative. Where's your aggressiveness? Where's your killer instinct?

Fuck it. I throw caution to the wind and bull rush Cantwell. Nothing fancy, just a left-right combination and keep pressing forward. I feel my gloves make contact, but he doesn't seem fazed. Instead, he holds his ground and our arms get tangled before I back away to try something else.

We come at each other again, Cantwell kicking as I jab and hook. We both land some hits, but they do no damage. The fight falls into a rhythm. I charge. We exchange flurries. We back up, look for an opening until I bull rush again. Cantwell tries to slide right. When I need to, I edge left.

We circle, close, and beat on each other through the middle of the first round. He's tough, far tougher than our first match-up, a fact that eats away at my remaining self-confidence.

Suddenly, Cantwell charges. He's lightning quick, and before I can respond, he's hammered me with multiple punches. He drives me back against the cage. The fight turns vicious, and we unload on each other at point-blank range. I hammer Steve's head with furious combinations until he finally backs away. I slide away from the ropes and Cantwell charges me again. Left hook, right hook. I reel backward, battling the entire way.

This is not how my fights go. Nobody is more aggressive than I am in the octagon. But Cantwell's got fury in his soul tonight, and he doesn't fear me.

He drives me against the cage again, then ducks low and tries to take me down. I counter that and we clench.

We've got several minutes to go in the round, but already I can feel my energy's been sapped by the intensity of the last thirty seconds. We hang on to each other, both looking for a way to do more damage. I knee him. He lands a few weak punches. I feel blood dripping on my right cheek. Cantwell's cut me.

We grapple against the cage, both of us trying to find a way out of this clench. Finally I slide left and we break contact. I fire a jab at him as I back up, just in case he was thinking about charging me again.

Okay. That was bad. He scored some points, did some damage. Now what?

Center octagon, we clash again. This time, we exchange flurries. When I jab with my right, I drop my left just slightly. Cantwell takes advantage of that and hammers me with sharp rights to my head and face.

And then, he attacks again. This time, he half-leaps into the air, as if he's about to deliver a *Matrix*-like gut kick. He lands on his right foot and starts jack-hammering me with left-right jabs. In a flash, he's got me against the cage again. I dart to the right just as he launches another punch that hits the side of the cage as I maneuver away.

He doesn't let up. He's like Grant on Lee right now. He spins left and we pound each other mercilessly. Blow after blow slams into our heads and faces, but neither of us budge. Two-thirds of the way through the first round, and we're toe-to-toe in a street fight slug fest.

What do I do? Nobody's withstood my striking power like this before. He's also dodging my hardest punches and punishing me in return. His technique is incredible.

We clench again. Exhaustion assails both of us now. There's less than a minute fifty left in the round. We hang onto each other, kicking, kneeing, and punching whenever we get an opening.

We break clear and once again, we kick and jab our way in circles around the octagon.

Cantwell storms forward and winds up for a superman kick. Instead, he slips. It is his first serious mistake. I lash his head with quick jabs, and he goes down on his back. This isn't boxing, so I don't have to back away and wait for Cantwell to get on his feet.

Close and finish him! This is your chance!

Before he can recover, I get between his legs, pull his right hand away from his head and start raining punches onto his face. I'm punishing him, and he can't last. No way. I throw everything I've got into each punch, and Steve's totally defenseless.

A few more seconds of this, and he'll be unconscious.

I batter away at him. Then, cat-quick he flips over on his knees. His back and head are exposed still, but he covers up with his gloves. I slam my fists down on him again and again. His eyes roll back. I have him. I can feel it.

He springs upward into me. It catches me off guard. I thought he was done. He has all the leverage, and I can't keep him pinned on the mat. I punch and jab until he's back on his feet.

The bell rings. We break apart and head for our corners, as he passes me, I see his eyes are unfocused. He's dazed and rocked.

I had him. I fuckin' had him.

CHAPTER THREE

Reality Check

I reach my corner feeling a little woozy myself. Nobody's dished out that amount of punishment on me in any of my fights. But I know Cantwell's hurting too.

Rory Singer, my coach, gets in my ear. Over the crowd noise, I hear him urging me to change things up. I'm predictable. I'm relying too much on my striking. He tells me to stop going straight at him. Use angles, surprise him. Use my feet and legs.

I process all this. Right now, I just want to pound my way to victory. Rory wants me to finesse Cantwell in round two. Okay. Coach knows what he's doing.

The bell rings, and I head off to finish this fight.

Right away, Cantwell attacks. He's slower and a bit uneasy on his feet. He's still reeling from the shots I delivered at the end of round one. Now's the time to wade in, guns blazing.

Rory's words hold me back. Okay, I'll change it up. I'll snipe from the angles and use my feet. We trade flurries again, then Steve tries to take me down. I slip from his grasp and hammer him for the effort. I feel the fight going my way again.

I close in, looking for an opening. A split-second chance presents itself, and I unleash a vicious kick to the sciatic nerve. Cantwell sees it coming and has just enough time to dodge. My foot grazes his crotch. I've struck him in the balls.

The ref steps between us and stops the fight. Cantwell reaches for himself, then remembers he's being watched by millions of people. He backs up and takes several deep breaths.

The ref keeps us separated, giving Steve time to overcome the accidental crotch shot. In a fight, each second is precious. Time ticks off the clock. I stare across at Cantwell, whose eyes regain focus.

Oh shit. He's coming back from the brink.

I've made a terrible mistake with that errant kick. I've given him time to recover from the head-shots he endured in round one. The ref goes and checks on Cantwell, who nods. The ref clears us. The fight resumes.

We collide in a fury of punches, kicks, and knees. Toe to toe, neither of us breaks contact. But I'm facing a different man. The break gave Steve his second wind, and I feel his strength start to dominate our battle. He pins me to the cage ropes again, and we clench after a series of brutal exchanges.

It's slipping away.

My head's swimming, my thoughts move through my mind in slow motion. Every movement becomes effort. My vision blurs, then tunnels. All I see is Cantwell, his fists flailing, gloves slamming home.

I strike back, but my punches have no power behind them. Suddenly, Steve nails me with a Brazilian kick that throws me back against the cage. I go defensive, keeping my gloves up to protect my face. His blows rain down. I strike when I can, but by now, I have nothing left.

He hammers me one more time, and my world flips inverted. I stagger, fling one last desperate punch, then the mat hits my face.

When the world stops spinning, I open my eyes and see my corner men all looking devastated. My eyes wander across Rory, Thierry, and Frank. My brain registers that Travis is gone.

Make my lonely grave richer
Sweeter be,
Make this truly the land of the free
And the home of the brave.

He was one of my closest friends and one of my biggest supporters. He gave everything for me. He trained with me rain or shine, outside or indoors in mold-covered Marine Corps gyms. Travis was all heart. He's with me every fight. But now, his image I cannot see.

I lie on the mat, the magnitude of the defeat slowly seeping into my battle damaged brain. I blink and search my corner. Travis is nowhere to be seen.

Of course he's not there.

Don't go there. Not now. I fought for Trav. I fought for all the Marines I lost in Iraq. But now, I've disgraced them with defeat.

I gave my life to save
That I might here lie
Eternally
Forever free

Those were the words spoken at Travis' funeral. I read them before every fight. He earned that Silver Star with his life. Every fight since his death, I feel him with me. I see him at my side. I speak to him. I love him like the brother I never had.

But now, his image is gone, replaced by the twin realities of defeat and death. I'm left humiliated, tilting toward despair, five million eyes witnessing my fall. Grief, long suppressed, leeches into me like a toxin.

My eyes close and the arena vanishes into never-ending blackness.

PART II

Resolve

CHAPTER FOUR

I-Day

United States Naval Academy, July 1, 1999

We all have our dividing lines in life, forged by decisions we make, or experiences we endure. Sometimes, they are self-evident in the moment; sometimes they only become clear in hindsight. Some of these events we control through behavior and choices we make. Others happen to us, created by external forces beyond our control. Either way, these milestones cleave life into distinct chunks that, when stacked together, form a confluence of will and Fate that ultimately creates our path through the world.

My first and biggest dividing line came on July 1, 1999, the day I arrived on campus at the United States Naval Academy. From that day forward, my life became a two act play: pre-Academy and post-I-Day.

I-Day, short for Induction Day, is a tradition that stretches back for generations. Every year on the first of July, the new Plebe class arrives at Annapolis, fresh from high schools across the country. They line up at Alumni

Hall, the historic gymnasium on campus, to begin the transformation from undisciplined civilian to naval officer and leader of men.

The day of my dividing line, I queued up in front of Alumni Hall with hundreds of other eighteen-year-olds, male and female. We wore our civilian clothes, and we looked like a motley collection of teenagers, not so different from the young crowds waiting to see the next summer blockbuster at the local theater.

Our families stood in little halos around us, enduring the wait. The air was electric: all of us were excited at the prospect of starting our new lives here at Annapolis. Beneath the anticipation, I felt uncertain and nervous. How would I be received? My senior year in high school turned into an ordeal after even my closest friends on our football team rejected my seriousness and commitment level. I flat out tried too hard and put way too much pressure on myself, which became a huge turnoff to my peers. They wanted to party and enjoy their last year before setting out into the real world. I wanted to win and was willing to sacrifice to do it.

The line moved slowly that summer day in Maryland as we were fed a few at a time into Alumni Hall where our transformation would begin. My mother and sister stood with me, gawking at the beautiful setting the Navy chose for its leadership mill. We did not speak much, but the few words my mother did find for the moment reflected her pride in this path that I had chosen.

During my senior year, I had been recruited by several Division I and IAA schools, as well as Yale and Harvard. I played quarterback, had a good arm and instincts. I could move around in the pocket, scramble when necessary, and hit a receiver on the fly. On the down side, I was still pretty raw on some fundamentals. I also lacked the size and height of the modern prototypical quarterback. Didn't matter, I loved the game because it had become an escape from the dark side of South Scranton. Early in high school, I recognized that if I worked at it, the game could be my ticket to an education and a brighter future.

When it came time to decide, I wanted to go to one of the Ivy League schools. Problem was, they don't offer athletic scholarships, and my family could not afford the cost of tuition. Then a friend from the track team, Clint Cornell, who'd been two years ahead of me, came home from the Naval Academy. He told me how much he loved it. He described the discipline, the devotion it required, and the bonds that developed between fellow Midshipmen. All of that appealed to me. I'd wondered if my ultra-serious, focused personality would clash at a civilian college where drinking and partying were the norm and perhaps more important to some than tangible achievements. That side of life wasn't for me. I wanted to achieve, excel, drive myself to secure something significant in life. The Academy offered that atmosphere. I jumped at the chance, much to the relief of my stepdad, who appreciated the fact that I would not saddle the family with massive debts to pay for my education.

Hours passed. At last I reached the front doors of Alumni Hall, and I parted company with my family. They went off to tour the campus. I went inside to become a Plebe. Set up around the gymnasium were various stations. As if on a production line, we moved from one to another, gradually gaining all the equipment and clothing we would need for the year ahead. At one of the first stations, gruff men took our measurements. With those in hand, we moved on to receive our uniforms. Socks, shoes—nicknamed

"Go-Fasters"—T-shirts, sweats, shorts, and pants were doled out and stuffed into oversized duffel bags.

And then we came to the barber station. One by one, we sat down to have our heads unceremoniously shaved. Hair we'd agonized over for hours before high school dates and proms ended up in piles on the gym floor. It was the biggest step yet away from our old lives into the new one we'd selected.

Finally, after further stops to learn how to salute, gather up more gear, and strap a canteen full of water to our new belts, we were processed through another set of doors and led to our company area. This would be our living quarters as we went through "Plebe Summer"—a six week boot camp run by U.S. Marines. All incoming freshman, whether they play sports or not, endure this naval rite of passage.

Sweating in the heat, I hauled my bags of gear up the stairs of our dormitory and into a hallway, where I found the other members of my company standing shoulder to shoulder. Unsure of what to do, I moved next to the last guy in line, dropped my duffels, and said loudly, "Man, what a whole lotta shit that was, eh?"

The guy next to me, whose name I later found out was Mark Hughes, didn't even look at me. His face remained expressionless, his eyes locked straight ahead.

First day and I'm already being ignored? What the hell is that guy's problem?

Before I could puzzle over this any further, three Detailers descended on me like vultures. A Detailer is the naval equivalent of a drill instructor. For Plebe Summer, the Detailers are hand-picked Midshipmen going into their junior years.

"Ok, we've got our first trouble maker!" one Detailer screamed in my face.

Another joined in, nose almost against my cheek, "Stann, that's your name, eh? Well, there's one in every class. Now we know who it is in this one!"

"Wait," I protested. "Time out!"

"You think you're funny! Stand at attention! Eyes front!" The third one shouted at me. I now had one in each ear and one eyeball to eyeball with me. I was being berated in stereo.

"You've gotta be kidding me. Time out! I didn't know we were playing yet!" I said, making a *T* with my hands.

This sent them into a frenzy of screaming. I shut up, put my eyes front, and stood as rigid as a bronze statue until the ass-chewing mercifully ended.

Lesson learned. Much chastised, and not a little shaken, I followed Mark Hughes as the Detailers led us to Bancroft Hall, another storied landmark on campus. Inside, we formed up in Tecumseh Court. There, our families watched as we shed the last vestiges of our civilian lives. Heads shaved, all of us now in white sailor uniforms that made us look a little like Popeye, we stood shoulder to shoulder, raised our right hands, and swore our oath to the United States and its Constitution.

Amid this tranquil, almost antebellum setting, I said the final words completing the dividing line in my life. This new phase had begun, and I was relieved the old life I knew in Scranton was at last behind me.

After the daily battles and back alley brawls that characterized my time at South Scranton Middle School, my mother moved mountains to get me enrolled at a private high school. She could not really afford this, but she did it anyway. The tuition was a stretch for our family.

Once, I showed up at the start of a term to get my course schedule. Surrounded by friends, the secretary behind the desk refused to give it to me. When I demanded to know why, she said that the school had decided to withhold it until my mother paid the overdue tuition bill.

Somehow, she scraped the money together to make it happen. Most of my peers came from wealthy families. Money never seemed to be an issue. For us, we worked for every dollar we got. I was the blue collar middle class kid at a school full of scions of business and industry. If I didn't already have a chip on my shoulder, that did it. I worked harder, practiced harder, studied longer, and tried to prove I belonged at the school with sheer energy and determination. The intensity ended up turning some of my peers off. To some of them, life came easy and it was to be enjoyed to the fullest. For me, it was a daily challenge to prove I belonged.

My sophomore year I turned sixteen and found at job at a tomato processing plant. They paid me six bucks an hour under the table and I worked alongside illegal immigrants, convicted felons, and lifers who could find no other employment. It was hard, physically taxing work in stifling hot conditions, but it paid for my insurance, uniforms, and part of my tuition every semester.

I worked every night and double shifts on most Wednesdays. In between, I studied, lifted weights, practiced, and played football.

Nothing came easy for me. In one sense, this was good. I learned to appreciate and take pride in everything I earned. At the same time, it made me ultra-serious, and that isolated me from my peers. I never quite shook the black sheep stigma. When I became team captain my senior year, I wanted the team to match my intensity. Instead, they rebelled, and I didn't handle it well. I wasn't ready to be a leader and didn't know how to deal with it. We had a mediocre year, and I left the field for the last time feeling bitterly disappointed with my own performance both during and between each game.

I came to the Academy wanting to play ball, desiring the fine education every Midshipman receives, but most of all, I came to the Academy wanting to learn how to be a leader.

Late in the afternoon on I-Day, we finished reciting the oath. Our right hands fell to our sides, and the Detailers dismissed us so we could say goodbye to our families. Once again, we Plebes found ourselves ringed by loved ones. My mother cried. My sister hugged me. We snapped photos of each other, and then it was time to say goodbye. "I know you'll make it," my mother said to me as she held me in one final, farewell-to-childhood embrace. This was her moment. She'd spent eighteen years guiding me, sacrificing for me, and fighting for me when necessary. Now, her work was done. It was time to hand me off to the Navy.

It dawned on me that this was it for us. We'd spent almost two decades together, but now my ship was launching. Midshipmen don't get much time at home, even during the summers. This woman, who had been the only constant in my life, would always be present in it, but now I'd see her only during brief interludes between terms. The thought that this relationship I'd depended on so much for so long would be totally transformed never occurred to me until this moment. I held her close, feeling her tears on my cheek, and told her how much I loved her.

In retrospect, I wish I had thanked her too. She prepared me well for the trials that lay ahead.

I turned away from my old life and joined my fellow Plebes. My sister and mom walked out of Tecumseh Court and vanished from view.

CHAPTER FIVE

Plebe Summer

The next morning, the Detailers woke us up long before dawn by throwing a tire iron into our hallway. The sound of it clattering past my door is one that I'll always associate with those first six weeks at the Academy.

With the tire iron thrown, our clock began ticking. We had ten minutes to shave, make our beds, and line up for the morning's abuses. All the while, our Detailers screamed at us.

We operated in squad-sized units—about a dozen of us incoming freshmen—and had to do everything together. If one of us screwed up, the whole squad suffered. We learned to rely on each other, to work as a team and make our unit function as smoothly as possible.

First order of the day was a regimen of jumping jacks, flutter kicks, sit-ups, mountain climbers, and push-ups. With those out of the way, we'd start our morning run. The Detailers never told us how far we were going to go, but we were guaranteed at least three miles.

During our initial runs, the Detailers timed us, then grouped us according to our speed and abilities. The idea here was to get us into better shape, not drive us into the ground with a pace we couldn't keep.

Jessica van Norman, one of the members of my squad, was grouped with me. She was a volleyball player, an outstanding athlete and a driven, Type A personality. No matter how far we went each morning, she never fell out during a run. For me, she was both an inspiration and a challenge. I'd never done much long distance running. As a football player, we were "fast twitch" sprinters, well-practiced at running with short, intense bursts. The morning "slow twitch" marathons demanded endurance, the ability to conserve and mete out energy as needed, and the ability to understand the depths of our personal reservoirs of determination and strength.

Jessica handled all of this in stride. She made it look easy. For me, staying with Jessica stretched me and helped me grow as an athlete.

After our morning run, we'd head to the chow hall for breakfast. Everything was strictly regimented and timed. We had to ask permission to "rig the table for chow" before we could sit down and eat. Once we'd obtained permission, we learned to eat in the same manner: eyes straight, crisp motions from plate to mouth with each serving properly squared with our lips.

After breakfast, we spent the morning doing course-work. We had classes on navy terminology, history, and etiquette. We learned to sail. If we missed even one question on a test, we had to write the General Orders of the Century out as punishment later in the evening.

After noon meal, we underwent basic rifle drills and marching under the tutelage of Marine Corps instruc-tors. For two and a half hours each afternoon, we drilled on the parade ground until each platoon became precise, disciplined, and razor-sharp. At the end of Plebe Summer, there is a traditional review where the incoming Midshipmen get to showcase their new marching skills. We spent hours honing those until we could move as one.

After evening meal, we'd assemble at Alumni Hall for a two hour lecture or briefing. By this point, everyone was exhausted, and it became a struggle just to stay awake. The Detailers were all over that. They prowled around searching for anyone who nodded off. When they found their victim, his or her entire squad suffered.

The group punishment forced us to take responsibility for each other. In the first week at Annapolis, we grew adept at keeping our neighbors awake. If somebody's eyelids grew heavy, we made a point of seeing it before the Detailers did. We'd nudge each other in the ribs and give quiet encouragement.

After the evening lecture, we returned to our hall by 2030 to assemble on the quarter deck. This was where all the discipline meted out during the day took place. After the physical training, the running, the drilling, we faced another round of flutter kicks and push-ups for various transgressions the Detailers witnessed.

Finally, twenty minutes before lights out, we received brief personal time. Even then, we couldn't just break out a book and read, or watch television or listen to a radio. For our first year at Annapolis, we were prohibited from watching TV or having radios. During Plebe Summer, we couldn't make phone calls either.

Instead, those twenty minutes before our sleep cycle began were crammed with basic things like showering, brushing our teeth, and squaring away our living areas. If any of us had missed a question during the day's lectures, we also had to pay the price for that by writing the General Orders of the Century longhand thirty, forty, and sometimes fifty times.

In twenty minutes, this was impossible for one person to do. Again, the system forced us to work as a team to overcome an obstacle. My squad split up the General Orders and wrote them out together for whoever received the punishment.

With all our day's work finally done at 2230, we dropped like stones into our bunks and slept the sleep of the dead until that goddamned tire iron woke us up to start the whole routine over again at oh-dark-thirty.

For the athletes in our class, the physical challenges and discipline were not the issue. The loss of freedom that we'd enjoyed all our lives just proved too much for some of us. Gone were the easy-going days of watching TV, parties, and dates with our girlfriends. It was not long before the regimen and its demands inflicted casualties on my platoon of about forty young men and women. Four quit before the end of Plebe Summer.

About a week and a half into our ordeal, the schedule changed and we received a couple of hours of sports time in the afternoons. Designed to foster further fitness as well as the competitive spirit so cherished at the Academy, I loved these afternoons of basketball or baseball.

It was during one of those sports periods that those among us recruited to play football gathered to meet our coach, Charlie Weatherbie. Coach Weatherbie had turned Navy's program around in the mid-1990s, going 9–3 during his second year. The team beat Cal in the Aloha Bowl that year, the last time we'd been to post-season play. In '97, the team finished 7–4, but there the turn-around became a slide into mediocrity. That would be the last time the team broke the .500 mark in the '90s. As a result, Weatherbie was coming under increasing scrutiny by the school, and he knew that if he couldn't get a winning record in the next couple of years, he'd be looking for a job.

Coach Weatherbie greeted all of us incoming players with a quick prayer and a quip. "It's a great day to play by the bay!" In the months to come, we'd hear that quip a lot. We'd also do a lot of praying. Weatherbie was a man of faith, and he had us take a knee before and after every team meeting, every practice and game.

That first day's speech was short and to the point: "I know you guys are probably wondering why you've come here to endure all this. Trust me, you've made a great decision. Keep with it. Plebe Summer ends in a few weeks. There is light at the end of the tunnel. Soon it'll be football season and you'll be doing what you all love to do. Remember that in the days ahead."

The truth is, Navy football will always suffer from a serious disadvantage compared to the other Division I schools. Where incoming freshman at your typical public university will endure the dreaded two-a-days of August, come September they're also students who get to sample freedom for the first time. There are fraternities, parties, girls, and fun to be had. Here at the Academy, Plebe Summer and the near-monastic existence the incoming players face during their first year are huge turn-offs for some recruits. Coach Weatherbie had seen too many quit during that first summer and go play ball somewhere else where they could have fun and get a little wild. His speech was meant to reassure us and keep us from bailing on the program.

But then, he dropped a bombshell. "Twenty-two of you will be invited to practice with the varsity team in

August. Those of you selected will dress for our opening game against Georgia Tech."

The first flutter of concern resonated through me. There were close to eighty of us incoming freshmen football players. This meant only a quarter of us would make the cut. I reassured myself with the memory that Coach Weatherbie had personally recruited me. I'd been a damned good run-and-shoot quarterback in high school. I possessed a strong arm and could move around and scramble when needed. No worries. I'd be one of the twenty-two.

Coach Weatherbie turned the floor over to a couple of the upperclassmen on the varsity team. They reinforced Weatherbie's main point: it gets better, just keep plugging away and you'll be through Plebe Summer in no time.

We prayed again as the meeting came to an end. For the rest of the afternoon, we got to be football players at last. It felt glorious, as if we'd received a furlough from prison. We started in the weight room and did some lifting. After all the PT, all the physical punishment and running we'd endured already, most of us had dropped weight. This tends to be a real problem at the Academy. Where freshmen at other Division I schools bulk up going into August two-a-days, the Navy players can lose upwards of forty pounds during Plebe Summer. Linemen who were recruited at two-eighty end up weighing in as the season starts at two-thirty or less.

On the other hand, we'd been broken down and were in the process of being built up into something more than just your average eighteen-year-old college player. None of us forgot that in coming to the Academy, we'd become naval officers. Discipline would be our watchword for the rest of our lives. And on the football squad, discipline was the only advantage Navy had over its rivals.

In the weight room, I noticed right away that a lot of the players already knew each other. The Academy runs a prep school for those who didn't have the grades to get in the first time around. These recruits spend a year at NAPS—Naval Academy Prep School—undergoing a vigorous academic program that prepares them for their first year at Annapolis. At the same time, the NAPS football team is a mirror image of the Academy's. They run the same system, coach the same philosophies, and that extra year helps these prospects develop into seasoned veterans within the program.

As the NAPS players congregated into their previous year's cliques, I sensed that I was an outsider in a community that had already bonded.

Later that afternoon, we jogged out onto our practice fields. The day was gorgeous. The football team has two practice fields, one turf, one natural grass. Both stretch along the west bank of Chesapeake Bay. Sailboats tacked and jibed in the distance, seagulls floated on the air currents overhead. The afternoon sun stood high above us, and the lushness of our surroundings seemed truly a blessing.

We jogged to the turf field, where we saw the bulk of our coaching staff sitting in the stands, notebooks and clipboards in hand. They were here to get a first look at the new recruiting class. Most of what they knew about us came from game film they'd watched. Now was their chance to assess us in the flesh.

We were quickly organized into stations. The quarterbacks and wide receivers worked together against a basic defensive package in non-contact seven-on-seven drills. As I walked over to meet my competition, the NAPS players stood together, sizing us up. No doubt they were taking the measure of the competition as well.

Each of us received a card with basic plays drawn on them. Nothing fancy, just straight drop-backs with one or two receiver patterns. From this, I inferred that the coaches wanted to assess our arm strength, accuracy, and basic throwing mechanics.

The drill began. The receivers bolted off the line. One by one, the new quarterbacks took their turns. Within minutes, it was evident who had some serious talent with the ball and who did not.

One quarterback really stuck out. His name was J. P. Blecksmith, and he had a 155mm howitzer for an arm. Time after time, he'd drop back and nail a receiver in full stride forty yards downfield and make it look effortless. He was fast, his footwork was outstanding. I deemed him my toughest competition.

When my turn came, I lined up with a Texan as my wide receiver. Before our first play, we introduced ourselves. Garret Cox was his name, and he was one of the NAPS players who already knew the system used here at the Academy.

I took the snap and dropped back. Cox lunged off the line and blew past the defensive back in man coverage on him. When he separated, I saw our chance. Five steps back, I planted and fired the ball. Cox broke toward the center of the field as he ran a deep post. The ball landed right in his hands and he never slowed.

The crowd of players and coaches applauded. My confidence soared. Cox trotted back to me grinning and said, "Hey, we just made each other look good! Let's keep it up!"

And we did, too. Dropping back, I hit Cox and the other receivers time after time. My arm felt good, my feet were light and agile. I could break tackles and move around in the pocket and scramble. The future looked bright.

But in the days following that first practice on the field, the coaches exposed us to the triple option system Coach Weatherbie ran. I had known Navy ran the option before coming to the Academy, but I had not realized just how different it would be from what I'd run in high school. Option quarterbacks aren't pocket passers. They don't drop back and hurl the ball downfield. Instead, they're shifty and small and extremely quick. The best ones have incredible agility and unbeatable acceleration. They can change directions in a heartbeat and slip through the narrowest holes in a rival's defense.

That wasn't me. As we learned the Navy system, I started running full speed again for the first time since the previous spring when I tore my hamstring during track season. That injury robbed me of the acceleration and extra gear I had my senior year on the football field. I never got it back. That first summer at the Academy, as I got my chance to run the option, I found myself always a heartbeat out of position. Not enough acceleration, not enough shiftiness. Not enough raw physical talent for a running offense, just acres of heart and a refusal to quit.

At the end of Plebe Summer, the coaches ran a two-a-day practice for us new recruits. This gave us one last chance to showcase our skills. As pure passers, J. P. Blecksmith and I had no peer. J. P.'s arm was simply incredible—NFL caliber for sure. As we competed against each other, I wondered why he didn't go to another Division I school that wasn't allergic to the forward pass. When I finally asked him, he told me that his dad had been a Marine officer. During Vietnam, he'd fought in the Tet Offensive.

He wanted to follow in his father's footsteps. J. P. and I turned up the heat and we fought hard right down to the last snap to be one of the twenty-two who'd make the varsity team.

At the end of the freshman two-a-days, the coaches huddled up to make their decisions. When Coach read the list of players who made the cut, my name was not on it. For the first time in my life, I'd come up short. I could not have been more devastated.

Our position coach took me aside and put it bluntly, "You're not a fit in our system. If you stay at quarterback, you'll get cut from the team. If you contribute at another position, you better start doing it now."

Division I ball is not about who has the most heart, who practices the hardest and toes the company line the best. It is about performance and nothing else. The coaches have to field a winning team, or at least at the Academy a competitive one, lest they lose their jobs and livelihoods. Sentimentality plays no part in the decision making process. It comes down to one thing: can this player help us win at his position. Any other factors are not even considered.

All around me, players who had been heavily recruited by Coach Weatherbie and his staff failed to make the list of twenty-two. A few were even cut from the squad, which was both a shock and a wake-up call to all of us.

Garret Cox made the cut. J. P. and I did not. We took a hard look at what we could do to contribute in the months ahead. For the time being, we were sent to the scout team, the tackling dummies for the varsity squad who labor thanklessly during the week to help the first string prepare for the next game.

I knew I'd come to a crossroads. I could leave the

Academy and go play ball in a system that could utilize my skills. That would be quitting, and that was something I had never done.

I could leave the team. Some of the players had already done that. One of the advantages about the Academy is that athletes who either leave their team or get cut can continue with their education. They will become Navy officers should they want to stay and graduate.

I loved football. It had been a major part of my life since middle school. I wanted to contribute, I wanted to stay with the program more than anything. I just needed to find my niche. Somehow, someway, I'd erase the sting of this first failure and claw my way onto the field.

CHAPTER SIX

No Effort without Error

Fight Night, Las Vegas, August 2008

Silence. Darkness. Pain. My head swims, I feel like I'm tumbling end over end through some yawning void. The darkness seems all consuming, and I am lost in its endless depths.

A strange sensation assails my cheek. It is cold and hard, and I cannot fathom what has touched me. There's pressure there, as if someone were holding a slab of meat against the side of my head.

Dazed and dizzy, I spin through the void like an untethered astronaut. I want to test my body, find out where I am, but my nerves aren't firing. Arms won't move. Legs are limp. Nothing functions. I lay in the silence and try to piece together what has happened. Is this a dream?

No, your worst nightmare.

Fragments of thoughts and images swirl around

me. I try to catch them as they flit through my brain, but nothing makes sense. I glean bits and pieces, like a garbled radio transmission sent across a distant sea.

I see Cantwell, his gloves flailing. Then he's gone, replaced by Travis holding pads for me under a halo of light from a nearby lamp post. He's egging me on, and I want to hammer those pads with quick jabs. My arms and fists fail me.

Fail.

Two-a-days at the Academy. Sweat pouring down as we had another "great day by the bay." Such a picturesque place right there on the water. It was really a shame we never could enjoy our venue. We were always too pissed off, too hot and wound up and focused on beating our competition to appreciate it.

The Academy field vanishes, replaced by a bridge across a desert river. Mortar shells explode silently around my men while they scan for targets. I yell into the radio, trying to call in air support. Words form, but no sound emerges from my lips.

And then I'm back at the Academy, staring at a list of twenty-two names, searching in vain for mine. Despair and desperation well up inside me, flowing from the dark corners of the heart where self-loathing resides.

I have failed. Now what?

I open my eyes. The mat is flush against my cheek. The ref bends down to look at me. His mouth moves. He's asking me something, but the silence drowns out his words.

The world slow rolls. I see Cantwell, upside down, fist raised, celebrating victory. Celebrating my defeat.

A wave of shame strikes me. Failure on a grand stage. Defeat in the arena. A humiliation watched by millions.

Cantwell hasn't just knocked me out. His fists have battered away my pride.

I have failed my Marines, my family, and my friends. I fight for them. And now I have sullied the memory of the men I lost. That realization is pure anguish.

I lay on the mat, letting the world spin around me. Fighters don't fear getting hit. We don't fear getting hurt. Injuries and pain are just part of the game, like football. But this humiliation is the worst. It robs us of our identities.

I look over at Cantwell. His euphoria ignites his hometown crowd. Suddenly, the silence washes away, replaced by thousands of cheering voices. I haven't heard such fan noise since my days on the football field.

I watch Steve reveling in the moment. It occurs to me that when he first started out, he lost one of his first pro fights and endured the same humiliation I am experiencing now. He picked himself up and went on to the climb the mountain. Tonight, he's reached its peak.

I must honor that with him. I sit up. The world tilts. The spinning grows worse. Slowly, I ease myself up onto my feet. With deliberate steps, I walk across the pinwheeling cage until I'm next to Steve. I put my hand on his shoulder, which is still slick with sweat.

"Congratulations, Bro. You earned this."

From the announcer, I take the light heavyweight championship belt and hold it in my hands one final time. It was mine, but now it rightfully belongs to Steve. I wrap it around his waist. It is my homage to his own struggle in this sport, but the act robs me of the last shreds of pride.

The crowd roars. I congratulate Steve again and climb out of the octagon. My corner men speak words of consolation that fall on deaf ears. Nothing can balm this wound right now. I still have to walk up the aisle flanked by screaming fans before I can escape from this disaster.

Steve sees that I'm about to leave. He comes over to me and gives me a sweaty bear hug. "You know I love you, Bro."

Fighting is a brotherhood. We experience the same emotions, the same drive to succeed propels us forward and the same fear of failure pushes us forward when our motivation flags. Steve's been in my shoes. More than anyone in the arena tonight, he understands. His compassion is appreciated. No matter what happens in the future, we will always share this bond.

We make for the door, the world still wheeling around me. Each step becomes a challenge, a matter of focus and intensity. My brain is lean on both and continues to short circuit. I stagger and weave. Then I see the security guards have allowed my wife to meet me in the aisle. She rushes for me. I see her dark eyes brimmed with tears and full of pain. Her arms slip around me, and for a moment I'm lost in the comfort of her embrace.

"I love you. I love you. Love you. Love you," she says again and again as we enfold each other. The fans disappear. The screaming fades away. In that fleeting moment, I feel safe.

And then, she pulls away. We must clear the venue. I escape through the double doors that only minutes ago had opened with me plagued with self-doubt.

In the locker room, Frank sits in front of me and untapes my hands and pulls off my gloves. "Brian. This is nothing. Nothing, remember that. Family—that's what matters."

I nod but cannot speak. Frank intuits that I need space, so he stands up and whispers a few more words of consolation before leaving me to my own thoughts.

I sit in a metal hardback chair, my gear bag at my feet, head down, eyes closed. I cannot stop the tears. They pour out of me as the full magnitude of what just happened sinks in.

Every fighter sobs at some point in his or her career. My manager has told me time and again that this sport has the highest highs and the lowest lows. In these past two years, I've known only the highs. Part of me understands that hitting rock bottom like this is all part of the process, but that doesn't make it any easier to handle.

A thousand thoughts assault me at once. Questions, self-doubt, agonizing over decisions made and effort expended—they all strike simultaneously. And swirling through it all, one question keeps resurfacing: *What next?*

I am a part-time fighter, always have been. Up until this summer, if someone asked me who I was, I'd tell them I was a Marine infantry officer who sometimes fought professionally. That identity is in my past. I'm an office worker now, whose day job has nothing to do with my fighting career.

How can I continue like this? Guys like Cantwell—they don't have day jobs. They live in their gyms and prepare every day for the next fight. How can I compete with that?

I always thought Travis had it right. You gotta have heart for the fight. And I refuse to submit that anyone's got more heart than me. That was my secret weapon, the great equalizer that balanced the rawness of my skills and gave me the edge in every fight.

I can't give up my day job. Fighting alone won't cover the house payment. It won't provide for my wife and daughter. At the same time, I need the sporadic income from these events to help pay the bills. My expenses straddle both jobs, making them indispensable without a major life change.

But, do I have a future in the WEC? I've heard rumors that they are going to abolish my weight class. If they do, after a defeat like this, will the UFC pick me up? Or will I be relegated to the Siberia of our sport—local venues that pay a grand or two a fight?

My manager comes over. I wipe my face as he reminds me, "Brian, like I've always said, it's a marathon, not a sprint. Don't forget that, okay?"

His words evoke memories of those long runs along the bay at the Academy. I'd been so used to fast twitch sprints that those distance runs initially challenged me. Jessica helped me adapt. I've seen my pro fighting career as a sprint all along. When I kept winning, it just seemed to all tumble together at once in my favor.

Not anymore. The fast ride ended on the mat a few minutes ago.

Who are you?

I can't answer that.

Is it time to walk away? The run was good while it lasted, but has my career run its course? Will I be scraped off the sport like every other yesterday's news?

Even if I stay and battle my way back, do I have what it takes? My mind probes my past for answers. It falls on my freshman year at the Academy. Once again, I see that list of twenty-two names. The sense of defeat, that failure to achieve my heart's greatest desire burns hot once again.

I've been here before. This time it feels worse.

My body aches. My head throbs. Some officials from the WEC appear around me. They regard me with sympathy. I flare inside from that. I don't want pity. I want to win.

All I want to do right now is stagger to my hotel room, shut the lights off, and wallow in this cascade of shit. I want to flay myself over and over, second-guess every decision I made and beat myself up for fighting as I did. I was too stiff. Too convinced of my own upcoming defeat. I should have stood and fought harder. I shouldn't have come at Steve with that same frontal assault. Rory was right. I should have worked the angles.

Shoulda. Coulda. Woulda. The three amigos of defeat.

I can't lock myself away, much as I ache for solitude right now. There is a series of post-fight rituals I must endure. Plus, my friends and family will be waiting for me at a party already scheduled.

The last thing I want to do is attend a party.

First things first. I rise to my feet and follow the WEC officials. Certain fighters must randomly submit to a urine test both before and after his bout. The post-fight urine check determines if the athlete ingested anything immediately preceding his match.

I piss in the cup, an indignity that I understand but still have trouble accepting. As a Marine officer, honor and personal responsibility are everything. In a perfect world, my word that I haven't taken any performance enhancing drugs should be enough.

Everything feels bitter at the moment.

Next, the docs check me over. Since I was knocked out, they want to send me to the hospital for some tests. I can't think of a worse place to end up tonight, so I lie and tell them I feel fine. They grow insistent. I entrench. Nobody is sending me to the ER.

I talk my way out of their presence and gingerly head for my hotel room. Inside, the silence seems golden. No cheering fans. No bright lights. Just me and my wife. I flee even her for the solitude of a shower.

The water cascades over me, and in the steam that fills the air, my thoughts return to the question of the moment.

What next?

A plague of self-doubt follows a defeat. That much I understand. Right now, I feel like everything I've worked for has just crumbled around me. Leaving me—with what?

The road ahead I cannot see. I've always planned. I've always known where my future will take me. And while there have been surprises along the way, the road map has always been right there in my lap to guide me to my destination.

Now, I don't even know what the destination will be, let alone how I'll get there. I feel so lost, the path I sought now nowhere in sight. I put my head against the shower wall and just try to breathe. The pain only gets worse.

Maybe I'm not good enough. I've peaked. I have no doubt that come morning, the MMA boards will be full of Monday morning comments. They'll say I've been exposed, which in the sport means the hype around me has been stripped away to reveal what I really am: a green fighter with limited skills. I was overhyped, my Marine background used as the hook the WEC needed to market me.

Maybe the chat room pundits are right. Is it time to walk away? Should I give up this dream and settle down, be the father and husband my family needs? I'd live out my days as a commuting cubicle dweller, attend reunions when I could, and grow old in the cradle of the middle class. There is honor to be found in an ordinary life lived with principles and decency. I would become a small part of the bedrock that forms the soul of this country—hard-working, family-focused, with values shared with the generations that forged us into a superpower.

There is nothing wrong with that life. It will be devoid of these devastating lows. The highs won't be as high, traded for a more stable course that surely will please my wife.

I step out of the shower and dry off. I put on a fresh set of civilian clothes and open the bathroom door.

Joey Fay stands on the other side, waiting for me. He grins that Puckish smile of his and I don't see even a hint of disappointment on his face.

"Brian, don't let this shit get to ya, Bro. You've gone farther than any of us ever could. Hell, you don't see any of us even trying this shit!"

"Thanks, Joey."

"Hell, we're all fucking proud of ya!"

Suddenly, he bear hugs me. Right then, consoled as I was by this old friend, I knew the past could be my guide.

CHAPTER SEVEN

Great Devotions

Naval Academy, Summer 1999

"What are you going to do?" Garrett Cox asked after we learned our fate with the team at the end of Plebe Summer. Garrett, the eternal Texan, had become a rising star in our recruit class with his performance on the practice field. He was stocky and strong, built like a brick barn, which served him well in the triple option where receivers are less pass catchers and more like blocking fullbacks split to the outside. Not only did Cox have soft hands, he loved knocking linebackers on their asses. The coaches loved that.

"Work harder. Find a niche where I can contribute," I told him. Quitting was never an option. I loved football too much, and I hadn't come all this way to let failure stand in my way. Instead, I used that humiliation as a motivator.

In Cox's circle of friends, a defensive back named Joey Fay and a fullback named Bryce McDonald both failed to make the list of twenty-two. Together with J. P.

Blecksmith, we ended up on the scout team. For most of the freshman recruits, the scout team was the only way to make a contribution.

Day after day we showed up to do battle with the varsity team. Talk about a thankless task. We were part of the team, but nobody would know it come Saturday afternoon, since we couldn't even be on the sidelines with our fellow players. Instead, we sat in the stands, sore from the week's beatings, cheering like the rest of the Midshipmen.

At times, it was hard not to be discouraged. Yet, at the same time, there was a silver lining. As we endured and fought to be noticed by the coaches during every practice as we imitated that week's opponent, my first true connections to my fellow Midshipmen blossomed.

Joey Fay was the spark for much of that. Always laughing, quick with a joke and a sly prank every now and then, he kept me from getting broody. By nature, I am a very serious individual. Joey made it his mission on the scout team to loosen me up. An odd couple sort of friendship grew between us. I bottled my emotions inside me; Joey wore his on his sleeve. I walked a straight and narrow line; Joey liked to break rules and skirt authority. Later in his career at the Academy, he'd sometimes stuff his bunk then sneak off campus to see his girlfriend and future wife. He never got caught—not once.

Even when he did get on somebody's radar, his silver tongue usually saved his bacon. At times, I'd shake my head in wonder at all he managed to get away with, especially since I knew if I tried to hang with him on this front, I'd go down for sure.

While Joey prided himself as a free spirit, he was all business on the practice field. At NAPS, he'd started at safety. Not making the list of twenty-two burned him as deeply as it had me. That failure brought us together, but it was how he handled that setback that bonded us for life. It became the main common thread in our lives together at the Academy.

We simply refused to quit. Each day, we suited up and went out there to compete. When discouraged, we bucked each other up. When we succeeded and got noticed by the coaches, we celebrated those moments together. When my seriousness drifted toward melancholy, Joey was there with a joke or a prank designed to remind me that life needed to be enjoyed, not just conquered.

And then there was Bryce McDonald. He came from a military family of some distinction. His father had served in the Marines during Vietnam as a helicopter pilot, earning a Navy Cross with his valor under fire. Just before Bryce went to the Academy, his dad succumbed to cancer. He'd been exposed to Agent Orange during the war, and decades later it finally claimed his life.

Bryce had gone to NAPS with Joey and Garret Cox. Academically, he struggled at NAPS, and then again at the Academy. This was just another mountain for him to conquer. His work ethic was his greatest asset. Nobody studied harder, or played on the scout team with his intensity and dedication. He fought for everything he earned.

On the field, we all saw his talent. He was a hulking fullback, cut from the mold of such greats as Tom Rathman. He was in his element when he could just put his head down and deliver a crushing blow. When given the ball, he didn't monkey around with elegant moves or shiftiness. He ploughed ahead and flattened anyone who tried to tackle him.

To survive on the scout team, everyone had to have faith their skills and effort would be noticed by the coaches. The goal was to get on the field come Saturday, but we also set more general personal goals that helped us stay the course. For Bryce, he resolved that first fall never to be outworked by anyone on the team. He stayed longer on the field, practiced harder, studied with more intensity, and never gave anything less than his last full measure.

Through the battles on the practice field, Joey and Bryce not only became my friends, they set the example I always strived to match. We were driven, Type A's who loathed failure and would do almost anything to succeed.

That first fall, Bryce's mother moved to Annapolis to be close to her son. On Saturdays, the freshmen were allowed to be off-campus from ten in the morning to just after midnight as long as we wore our uniforms. Most of us had no connection to the area. Bryce's mother opened her doors to us. Her place became our home-away-from-home, and on any given Saturday she'd have upwards of a dozen Midshipmen to feed. In time, she got to know our families and organized tailgate parties for them before our games.

During the weekday afternoons following class, we'd dress and hit the practice field. Each week we simulated the varsity team's opponent, running their plays and their system. At first, I tried to stick with the quarterback position, but it clearly wasn't going to work out. I took my position coach's advice and switched to wide receiver. All year long I ran pass patterns, blocked the first team's defensive backs, and ran the occasional reverse. I hadn't played receiver in high school, and I didn't really like it. Aside from the scout team beatings, I didn't get any reps at the position.

I refused to give up. I just needed to find my niche.

Meanwhile, on the field come game day, the varsity squad had its own issues. We went 5–7. The one bright spot in the season came in the final game of the year when we beat Army 19–9 at Veterans Stadium. No season is a total loss at the Academy if the team wins that game.

The failure on the gridiron exacerbated some of the divisions within the student body. From day one, we sensed from some of our classmates underlying resentment about our presence at the Academy. The non-athletes were there to become Navy and Marine Corps officers. For some, they had coveted such a career since they were kids. In us, they saw carpetbaggers who'd come to Annapolis to play ball first, serve their country second.

Perhaps there was some truth in this stereotype, but that didn't mean we took our future roles as military leaders any less seriously than the non-athletes. Looking back, some of the best officers I served with in the Marine Corps had also played ball at the Academy. The pressure-cooker atmosphere within the team fostered by the fierce competition for starting jobs actually prepared us well for the level of stress we faced as combat leaders.

The divide between the football team and the rest of the Midshipmen grew deeper as we continued to lose. Every student is required to attend home football games. Thus, instead of enjoying their one day off campus, the students must stick around to watch the game. The more we lost, the more that sacrifice of precious freedom engendered bitterness.

As the divide grew, it pushed guys like Joey, Bryce, J. P., Cox, and others closer together. We became our own insular unit, tempered in the battles on the practice field and drawn together by our shared experience in the face of peer hostility on the part of the non-athletes.

By the start of spring ball in 2000, I could not even imagine life at Annapolis without football.

Unfortunately, that's what I faced.

CHAPTER EIGHT

Seventy to Seven

That spring of 2000, I gave up trying to play offense for the Academy. In high school, I had occasionally played linebacker. I loved the physicality of the position that allowed me to unload some good hits and tackles on our opponent's offense. Quarterbacks rarely get to put the hurt on anyone, unless something has gone drastically wrong. Being a linebacker let me release pent-up aggression.

Spring ball is the first opportunity to gain attention and have the coaches re-evaluate you for the new season. After a record of 5–7, Weatherbie had to turn things around. The pressure he faced flowed downhill to us, and the intensity of the practices increased.

I threw my heart into every play, but again it wasn't enough. Spring ball came and went with the coaches lukewarm on my new switch. Come summer and the two-a-days, I failed to make the cut again. I ended up on the scout team as a sophomore, something that doesn't happen often. I'd worked hard all year only to end up in the same place. It took discipline and focus not to let the disappointment turn into bitterness.

For some, it became increasingly harder to stave off that bitterness. J. P. Blecksmith realized at the end of his freshman year that playing quarterback at the Academy—even with his golden arm—would never become a reality. Like me, he switched to linebacker. We ended up competing against each other again. Tall, with blue eyes, his athleticism earned him a spot ahead of me on the scout team. But that didn't satisfy him. He wanted to play offense, and not just on the J.V. or scout teams. He switched to wide receiver and threw himself into the role. At times, I could see his frustration and admired him for his remarkable composure. He was a talented player who didn't fit the system. Had he gone anywhere else, he'd have been riding his arm all the way to the NFL.

Joey Fay and I started our sophomore year on the scout team again. Bryce kept plugging away, and his growing skills drew increasing attention. He'd made the cut that summer and was dressing for games now. His stock was red hot.

Oddly, for some reason, the coaching staff had gone cold on Garret Cox. His future with the team, once bright and promising, suddenly tanked. By the end of the year, it was clear the coaches weren't going to use him on the field. Cox quit the team but remained tight with all of us. Other players who left sometimes drifted away, but Garret had always been the center of our clique. Even without the shared misery of daily practice, the bond between us never faded.

For me, my sophomore year blended disappointment with coming of age. Though I'd been relegated to tackling dummy status again, I'd been noticed by one of the senior defensive backs: Mike Wiedle, a redheaded former enlisted Marine who took me under his wing and mentored me.

"Look Brian, you've got to make a statement out there," he told me time and again. "Go onto the practice field every day and make things so hard for the offense that the coaches have to pull you out and use you."

Joey and I adopted that as our mantra. Every day that fall, we busted our asses to prove to the coaches that we belonged on the field come Saturday. I started all of the J.V. games, and a few times the coaches encouraged me with, "Keep it up Brian, you're being noticed."

Once the team's offensive coordinator confessed during a coaches meeting, "We're having a hard time stopping Brian Stann."

I was becoming a serious prospect, and I set my sights on a breakout junior year.

Unfortunately, when the regular season came, the team struggled on the field. Out of the gate, we lost to Temple 17–6. The next week, Georgia Tech scored 40 points on our defense. That set the tone. The week after, Boston College crushed us 48–7. As the defense collapsed, the offense— hamstrung by the run-heavy triple option—had no ability to win a scoring battle. Week after week our opponents routed us. Notre Dame, Tulane, and Wake Forest all scored forty or more points against us. Going into the Army–Navy game, we were 0–10. It proved small comfort that we edged Army 30–28 to avoid a winless season.

The beatings we took further cleaved us apart from the rest of the student body. If our freshman year was bad, our sophomore year saw the divide grow to a chasm. Nobody wanted to sit in the autumn rain on his or her one day of liberty to watch the team disgrace the Academy with another blowout.

Discipline suffered. The coaches began to panic. Discord riled the ranks. And for us, there was no escape.

Until the end of the season, we couldn't go off campus. As lowerclassmen, we were not allowed out on Friday nights. On the Saturdays we did get to leave the Academy, we still had to wear our uniforms. There wasn't much to do when we weren't playing football or studying. We took to watching DVDs on our computers, but that grew old fast.

The sophomore blues set in. It became our worst year at Annapolis.

That spring of 2001, when the team gathered for its yearly practices, Coach Weatherbie had fired both the offensive and defensive coordinators. Gone was the old 5–0 scheme, replaced by a standard 4–3 defense. This totally changed the complexion of the linebacker corps, and just as I thought I had a chance to dress with the squad, I suddenly found myself frantically learning a new scheme.

I made the team, though, and went through the two-a-days with everyone else that August. So did Joey and Bryce. We'd fought for two years, and now we'd earned the right to wear the uniform on Saturday.

Bryce was the star of our group of overachievers. During our season opener, the coaches called his name only once. He took the handoff and rumbled for 13 yards, defenders hanging off him. He finished the year with 29 carries, 123 yards, and a touchdown. He'd come a long way from the freshman who failed to make the list of twenty-two.

Joey Fay and I had mixed success. I flirted with second string but rarely made it on the field at my position. Instead, I played on special teams with J. P. Blecksmith and Joey. J. P. had grown so frustrated that at the end of our sophomore year, he submitted his letter of transfer.

He wanted to go play somewhere else where he could be a drop-back quarterback. Coach Weatherbie sat him down and talked him out of it. He saw J. P.'s talent and didn't want to lose it. Unfortunately, Coach never figured out how best to tap J. P.'s natural skills. He caught one pass for 13 yards that season and threw another pass for 16 yards.

While my circle of friends had battled their way onto the field, the team's overall performance collapsed. Discipline issues in the locker room appeared. The team's defensive line and linebacker corps were too undersized to run the 4–3 effectively, and the offense never jelled. Our second game drove a stake through the team's heart when Georgia Tech pummeled us 70–7. The season was lost right then, and we never recovered. After Toledo beat us 21–20 in game seven, Coach Weatherbie was fired. We didn't win a game that year. To add misery to heartache, Army manhandled us 26–17 to cap the worst season Navy football had endured in decades.

Even though I wasn't on the field much, I took these losses hard. I hated defeat. After each game, I grew increasingly sullen and quiet. My teammates and I would usually go out somewhere after the games, and I'd be the stick in the mud. I brooded more than usual, which Joey and Bryce took as a challenge. Week after week, they were the only ones who could lift my spirits after the pounding we took on the gridiron.

We had one last shot to make something of our football careers. Spring ball came in April 2002, and I caught the new coaching staff's eye. I went into the August two-a-days second on the depth chart at my position.

Two-a-days are brutal ordeals, detested by every player who has stepped onto a football field. That summer, our new coach, Paul Johnson, used the two-a-days to make a statement.

He made us start practicing before dawn every day at 0445. We reported to the field and Johnson's new coaching staff beat us half to death with repeated fourth quarter drills. We ran, we hit. None of this no-contact drilling. Johnson spared no one. By midmorning, guys were puking where they stood.

"No wonder why you pussies went 0 and 11!" he shouted more than once as we gasped and suffered. During a brief, but blessed, break, my friend Pete Beutenmueller staggered over to me and said, "Today I have met Death, and he kicked my ass."

"Why do I get the sense that football's gonna suck this year?" I replied.

Joey shook his head. "One thing's for sure. He's getting his point across."

"What's that?"

"That we were not well conditioned."

No doubt.

Coach Johnson showed no mercy. When he evaluated the team, he concluded that we lacked discipline and motivation. He made our two weeks in August a crucible designed to test our toughness and our commitment to the team. At one point, a wide receiver went down with a phantom injury. Under Weatherbie, some of the starters would sometimes do this to get out of practicing. Johnson had no time for this bullshit. After the team doctor examined the wide out and found nothing wrong with him, Coach Johnson demoted him on the spot.

That was the day that all the distractions stopped. Those who survived the two-a-days became hard, tempered, and focused. Johnson demanded discipline and intelligent play. "Come on, you guys are taking thermodynamics and economics!" He'd shout at us, "Use your heads. Be smarter. Be tougher. Be more disciplined."

We practiced through pain, stayed on the field with injuries. At one point, I vomited all over myself right in front of our new offensive coordinator. Later that summer, I switched spikes and the new footwear caused quarter-sized blisters to form on my feet. They slowed me down, affected my quickness, but I never left the field. In fact, I was the only linebacker who didn't go down from an injury.

We had a very talented crop of young linebackers that season. Remembering how Mike Wiedle had taken me under his wing the previous year, I did the same for two of our underclassmen. I taught them how to read defenses and react to different formations and game situations. I helped them with their mechanics. In the end, I coached myself out of a job.

Johnson and his staff went with the younger guys. Whenever there was tight competition for a roster slot, they went with the underclassmen for two reasons. First, they assumed the younger guys would have a bigger upside and could grow into the roles as they played. Second, they wanted fresh blood, players without the taint of the previous regime who didn't bring with them the old culture that Johnson was trying to remake.

We could feel the tide turning, and when we stepped onto the field for our first game that season, I knew Johnson had forged an entirely new team. The chemistry and attitude were vastly different. That year, 2002, became the season that laid the foundation for success through much of the rest of the decade.

We beat SMU in our opener 38–7. I don't think we scored thirty-eight points in any previous game during my time at the Academy. J. P. was used on offense more, mainly for gimmick plays. He had 88 yards passing on three attempts. Bryce carried the ball forty-two times and ended the season with a 6.2 yard per carry average. Of all of us, Bryce was the one who made the most of every opportunity he had to touch the ball. He stayed in the rotation the entire season and made a living out of crushing defenders with his broad-shouldered blocking ability.

Joey and I played on special teams. We stayed true to the concept that loyalty to the team matters above everything else, even if it means subordinating what's best for yourself at times. J. P. became the embodiment of that selflessness for us. Anywhere else, he would have been a starting quarterback, bound for the NFL. He stayed with Navy and made his father proud.

We played competitive ball that year but lost all except our first and final games. Nevertheless, with each play we could feel the team growing into what Coach Johnson wanted us to become. At the end of the season, we demolished Army 58–12 and my circle of overachievers ended their college football careers on a high note.

Things hadn't worked out as I intended when I first stepped onto the practice field by the bay in the summer of '99. Back then, I had dreams of Saturday afternoons spent throwing deep balls to Garret Cox and juking linebackers out of their jocks while scrambling for a first down.

That never happened, but I didn't quit, didn't give up. I found a way to contribute. While my career went in a totally unexpected direction and I never started, a funny thing happened. All that effort, pain, and misery made me a more disciplined human being. It prepared me for the trials ahead as a Marine infantry officer. In fact, many of the lessons I learned helped me better prepare my platoon, and later my company, for combat in Iraq.

In football and in a rifle company, there is no substitute for discipline, hard work, and commitment. If any of these three elements are lacking, the team is going to lose. The company will get shot to pieces in combat and men will die. I learned there is no margin for error in both, and the only way to be perfect is to demand perfection and never brook excuses.

Most importantly, when I didn't give up that first summer, I earned the respect of those around me. The friendships that I formed with guys like Bryce and J. P., Joey, Garret, and many more grew deep and permanent. Long after our Academy days were behind us, we remained as close as brothers.

I never started at quarterback. I never started at linebacker. But in the end, I gained so much else—things I could never see or fathom that first summer—that when I emerged from the Academy, my experience with the team had largely defined my character and values. Had I walked off the field in '99, I would have lost out on so much that I could not even see at the time. In the end, it wasn't about who started. It was about shared experience, the value of throwing your heart into something larger than yourself, and the bonds that are forged in the fires of competition.

Lesson learned. Quitting would never be an option for me.

CHAPTER NINE

Stumbles

Fight Night, Las Vegas, August 2008

"Don't let this shit get to ya, Bro," Joey Fay says to me as we break our man-hug.

"How can I not?" I ask my brother-friend.

"Look, win or lose—none of us care. Your fights give us all an excuse to get together again."

I nod silently. He's right in that regard. I look forward to fight night for more reasons than the ones that drove me into the cage in the first place. My circle of friends and family always come to see my bouts, and these weekends end up being welcome reunions we otherwise never would have.

I finish getting ready, then Joey, Frank, my wife, and I head down to Lucky's, the grill in the Hard Rock Café we selected for the post-event festivities.

I'm not feeling very festive.

This is the first time in my professional career that I have lost a fight. Sooner or later, it had to come. But I've never been in this situation, and I don't know how I'll be received downstairs.

We step into the elevator. Joey hits the button for the main floor. Teressa, my wife, holds my hand. Her touch is a comfort.

As we stand there, waiting for the elevator doors to close, I'm struck by the symmetry of this moment. At my side is my wife, my future. At my other side is an old and dear friend, bound to me forever by the intensity of our experiences at the Academy. Past and future, with me lost in the misery of the present.

We stand silently in the elevator. I almost wish Joey would fart. At least it would lighten the mood. Instead, I focus on Teressa's hand. It is soft and warm, and she squeezes mine periodically, just to let me know she's thinking about me. We haven't been married long, but already we have our nonverbal shorthand down pat.

The doors open and we step out into the hotel's main floor. The last thing I want right now is to be recognized, but it happens as we thread through the casino. It starts with the eyes. I can feel them on me, gazing from every compass point. How will I be received?

Fuck it. I have nothing to prove after Iraq.

A fan crosses our path. He stops and regards me. "Hey, Brian! Shake it off! You'll get 'em next time!"

"Thank you," I manage, wanting to look away as he reaches to shake my hand.

A minute later, another one comes up. "Don't worry, dude! You'll grow from this and be better for it."

At least they're not telling me I suck, or that I'm a poser, or that I've been exposed. Those fans are the ones who lurk on the MMA chat forums and hide behind anonymous nicknames like Nutcruncher38 while typing from their mothers' basements. They are the cold and timid souls, the ones who don't even have the courage to criticize and put their own names to their words. There's no place for victory or defeat in momma's basement.

Another fan spots us and approaches me. "Brian, you've given so much. Thank you for everything you've done." His words are heartfelt. He asks for a photo, and I pose with him.

A minute later, we find our group inside Lucky's. As we arrive, Bryce McDonald stands up and limps over to give me a bear hug. My old roommate from the Academy, Cameron Lickle, follows suit. I haven't seen him since graduation, and finding him here raises my spirits. He served as a nuclear surface warfare officer in the Navy after we left Annapolis. Now, like Joey and I, he's left the military for a civilian's life.

We find seats and I find myself surrounded by those who love me most. Teressa's at my side, my mother across the table. Frank's here, along with my Uncle Matt and Uncle Joe. My cousins also came, as did my sister.

And then there are the ones who aren't here. I think of Travis again, and how he loved being with me on fight night. The man in my corner. I feel him on my shoulder.

Drinks and food are ordered. There's an electricity here that transcends victory and defeat, created by the mere presence of so many people who share common pasts and ideals. These fights bring us all together again, and nothing will stop the celebration born from this reunion.

The merriment draws me out, little by little. Most of it is for show. Underneath the smiles and the recounting of stories, my brain can't let go of what happened tonight.

As Marine officers, we defined ourselves through our performance and dedication. The reason for that was clear: if you fucked up, people you loved died. We operated on a razor's margin, a place where excuses go to die.

But you're not a Marine anymore.

Yeah. There is that.

The memory of Cantwell's last punch stings me again. For a second, I am flooded with a sense of shame again. I let him take my pride.

Around me, everyone's talking and spinning yarns. My silence doesn't surprise my Academy buddies. After games our junior year, I usually ended up appearing sullen and moody. Really I was turning within myself, searching for ways I could have helped the team more.

I am no longer an active-duty Marine. I work in a cubicle. I have a day job that I must return to come Monday morning. I'm not a full-time fighter. Besides, fighting skills do not define me as a man.

Then what does?

Well, that's the problem. My life's in transition now. No longer on active duty, I'm not a full-time anything— employee, fighter . . . husband and father. I've got to sort out just who I need to be in this new path I've charted for myself.

Across from me, Joey Fay recounts a story from our Academy days. He's got everyone hanging on his words, laughing and smiling as the yarn unfolds in dramatic fashion. Joey looks over at me, his face a picture of mirth. His eyes tell the bitter truth: he's with me all the way. He knows what I'm going through, and it hurts him to see it.

Bryce McDonald sits next to Joey, laughing in all the right places. He swore he'd never leave anything on the field when we played for the Academy. He practiced with the same intensity he brought on game day, and he never let anyone down. He set the example for all of us. Before we graduated, one of Coach Johnson's assistants said, "I have a three-year-old son. If I could pick anybody that I'd like him to be like, it would be Bryce McDonald."

He carried that example into his battalion. After graduation, he and Joey Fay stayed on with the Navy football team, serving as general assistants for the 2004 season. They went to a bowl game that year, the first since the mid-1990s.

Now, after a tour with 2/4 Marines in the Western Pacific and another in Iraq, Bryce serves as the liaison officer to the Navy football team. Once this tour's up, though, he'll be medically retired.

He and Joey present a perfect comedic pair. Joey's outgoing and loud and loves to tell stories. Bryce balances him with his butter-smooth voice, gentle demeanor, and soft-spoken words. If you hadn't seen him in combat, or on the gridiron, the casual observer would never know he is the toughest and most rugged SOB I've ever known. I remember times at the Academy where any other man would have held himself out of a game. Not Bryce. The coaches had to keep him on the sidelines after he broke a hand, then later a foot.

In Iraq, he was tasked with protecting his commanding officer as the head of his personal security detail. While on the road one day, his armored Humvee got hit with an improvised explosive device (IED). The blast broke his leg in multiple places. It also broke his arm and nose.

Those are the kinds of friends I made at Annapolis. No matter where our lives go from here, our connections will never fade. Not even separation and war can affect them.

Our food arrives, and everyone digs in. I look at my plate and stir its contents listlessly. I have no appetite.

What are we now? Joey's set to get out in a year. Bryce, maybe two or three. Soon we'll all be civilians again with the Academy and football as the common links between us.

Right then, it hits me. There is one other thing that binds us. It is the one common feature that we can all take forward into our uncertain futures. Our time at the Academy was more than the hazing, the rigorous coursework and conditioning. It was more than football and the adversity we tried to overcome everyday on the practice field.

Annapolis forged us into leaders. We learned the moral courage required to lead men into battle. It also showed us the responsibility that comes with command. These are skills we will always be able to use. Hell, I use them every day in the office back in Atlanta.

My fighting career cannot define me as a man. But my leadership and ability to battle through adversity always will.

CHAPTER TEN

The Leadership Factory

All the academic classes in the world will never teach anyone to be a leader. The Academy recognized that long ago, and while we all had to take courses on the subject, we learned by doing. Those four years at Annapolis became our opportunity to develop our own leadership style, learn from our mistakes, and grow into our roles as young officers soon to be out with the fleet, or in the field with the Marines.

The Academy is structured to provide leadership opportunities in a variety of places and levels from the very first day we start our Plebe year. Each class is organized into squads, platoons, and companies. There are leadership slots in each unit that must be earned and kept with consistent outstanding performance. Above the company level, there are also a variety of school-wide leadership positions available to upperclassmen. Within the extracurricular activities, there are also leadership roles to be filled.

You cannot go through your four years at the Academy as a sheep. One way or another, almost every Midshipman gets hands-on experience making decisions and handling that delicate balance required to both build respect and find effective direction.

During our first two years, the leadership slots available were limited to platoon level and below. This meant that those who became squad leaders and platoon commanders had to figure out a way to motivate their peers to get behind them. This proved far more challenging than dealing with lowerclassmen. A peer needs a reason to respect your authority, a reason to submit to the decisions you make. A junior who presides over a group of Plebes doesn't have that trouble. The authority of the institution, plus the upperclassman's own status and position, legitimize his or her orders.

When you combine peer leadership with the fact that most of our peers at Annapolis were Type A, alpha dog characters in their own right, those first two years become an intense atmosphere. You either learn to make it work, or you fall on your ass in front of men who will be in the field with you in a few years.

Nevertheless, the years at the Academy are the years to experiment, fail, and learn from those mistakes. By the time graduation rolls around and the Midshipmen receive their commissions, it is too late. From that moment on, there is painfully little margin for error.

My junior year provided my first real challenge of command. Within a Midshipman company, the roles of commander and executive officer are filled by seniors. For juniors, the most coveted slot is first sergeant. The duties of a first sergeant include training and mentoring the freshmen in the company.

I applied for the first sergeant slot and succeeded in receiving that appointment. I took on the job during a very tumultuous time at the Academy. The 9-11 attacks had taken place right at the start of the year, and the security changes transformed the school into a veritable fortress. The atmosphere changed as well. We were at war now, and we all realized that sooner or later, we would end up in the fight.

But underneath the added security procedures, the closing of the campus to civilians, and the other changes instituted, conflicts developed within the student body. It had started the previous year when the football team only won a single game. Junior year saw us getting blown out in every game—even at home in front of our fellow Midshipmen. The divide that existed between football players and the non-athletes in the student body grew increasingly wider and more hostile.

As the losing streak continued, resentment reached a boiling point. Who wanted to spend their precious time off on Saturday sitting in the rain watching the team disgrace itself? The mandatory attendance stoked the other resentments the non-players felt. They saw us as coddled members of the student body who got out of drill and other duties they were required to perform. Since we practiced every day, those things were impossible to expect of us on top of maintaining our academic grades. The non-athletes didn't see it that way. They saw it as favoritism. And then there was the stereotypical view that the football players weren't there to be officers above all else. There was a lot of talk that the members of the team were poor examples in this regard. Some of us were overweight, our uniforms were not as squared away, and our hair was longer than other students. Those exceptions became the stereotype hung on all of us.

Some of the football players made things worse. There was an arrogance that prevailed toward the non-athletes. The players generalized them as "nerds" who had no idea the extra effort and commitment required to be a member of the team—to say nothing of the additional pressure to perform. And what about the nerds as officers? How could they lead men better than the players who had been marinating in a pressure cooker environment that required a higher level of discipline and performance than they had ever experienced? How could they know what it took to sacrifice one's own self-interest for the greater good of the team?

The sniping grew louder as the fall continued and the losing streak persisted. When I became the company first sergeant, I noticed right away that the freshmen were absorbing from the upperclassmen this divisiveness.

We defined leadership as the ability to make a team better. To take a group of individuals and convince them to subordinate their own self-interest for a larger cause requires unity. To create that unity, especially when there's an atmosphere of conflict, requires forging a new culture within the team.

Sitting around, complaining about the situation without doing anything just encouraged the problem. So, I set about changing the culture. In the process, I learned my first key lessons in leadership.

In any organization, there are bound to be diverse individuals from a range of backgrounds and upbringings. It is all too easy to devote energy to those members of the team you understand the most. Those with common heritages and similar goals tend to form their own networks within the team. If left unchecked, the team simply becomes the sum of all these smaller social nodes.

I made a point of getting to know everyone within the company. Though I was a football player, my effort to spend time with every node in the unit let me develop a deeper understanding of my peers. It also gained me credibility throughout the company. I was not someone who played favorites or developed my own clique around my authority. Instead, I made a concerted effort to be a unifier. In the years ahead, this lesson served me very well. Once assigned to a Marine infantry battalion, I made a point of getting to know all the non-infantry officers and noncommissioned Officers (NCOs). Within a typical battalion, a division exists between the front line personnel and the rear echelon support types. The infantry tends to look down on everyone else. The infantry suffers the most, risks the most, and develops an esprit de corps based on the ability to withstand both. The rear echelon troops are seen as having cushy, safe jobs.

Taking that lesson from my junior year to heart, I made every effort to connect with the support personnel by treating them with the respect they deserved. I got to know them and periodically stopped by just to shoot the breeze.

In the end, it opened doors for me. When some infantry officers needed gear from the supply NCOs, they sometimes treated them harshly and with disrespect. In return, the NCOs wouldn't go the extra mile for these officers, and frequently their requests were never filled as a result. With a positive relationship, the story was totally different. If the supply NCO respected the officer bringing the request to him, he or she would call in favors, work the system, and get things done. In the end, the men under that officer's command benefited the most by getting what they needed to enhance their performance in the field.

Functioning as the company's first sergeant my junior

year also taught me another critical command lesson. Working with the freshmen allowed me to do something about the increasing divide between the athletes and non-athletes. As the freshmen witnessed the tension between the two groups, cracks appeared in their own class.

Here was an opportunity to change the culture. The basic issue behind the division was a lack of understanding, mainly because communication between the two camps had broken down. To fix this, I put several freshmen football players into positions of authority within their platoons. This forced them to interact with their fellow classmates as peer leaders. Within weeks, the dynamic began to shift. Communication improved, a better understanding developed between the two camps, and they found common ground from which to work. While it didn't erase the division completely, it certainly made a difference.

This experience underscored the important role subordinate leaders play in creating the culture that best fits the goals you set for your command. If they aren't on board with the program, nothing will change, and you'll never get the results you desire. That was a lesson I used many times in my career within the Marine Corps.

Discipline forms the cornerstone of any military team. And of course, punishment serves as one of the means to maintain discipline. During my junior year, I learned not to be afraid to mete out punishment. At the same time, doing so requires a balance of appropriateness and understanding. My first serious encounter with Travis Manion highlighted this nuance of leadership.

Travis came to the Academy our freshman year from Philadelphia. We were fellow Pennsylvanians and athletes—Travis was a wrestler—yet we didn't get to know each other very well that first year. Travis subsequently left, then returned a class behind the rest of us our junior year. When I became first sergeant, he was a sophomore within our company.

One Friday night, some of us gathered to watch the movie *Vanilla Sky* on Travis' computer. Everyone but the two of us hated the film. That Travis and I had a soft spot for movies like that one surprised us both. In the weeks that followed, Trav started coming around my room to chat.

Travis was a polarizing figure within the company. He was either extremely well-liked or thoroughly disliked. There was no middle ground. Most of it came down to understanding him.

Travis embodied that Philly toughness that's long since become legendary. He was hard-nosed and brooked no bullshit. He said what he felt and meant what he said. He was a straight-shooter, who worked phenomenally hard on the wrestling team while maintaining good grades.

Our sophomore year, Travis left the Academy and went to school in Philly. He missed Annapolis and returned the following year. His dad had served thirty years in the Marine Corps and retired as a lieutenant colonel. That year away convinced him that he really did want to follow in his father's footsteps. He returned, intent on becoming a Marine officer upon graduation.

Travis tackled each day as a new challenge and a new way to test himself. He pushed himself harder than almost anyone else. In the end, the pressure this put on him caused an outburst that almost led to serious trouble.

My senior year, Trav had a roommate who was a nonathlete. Wrestlers spend a lot of time cutting weight, a process that requires considerable self-discipline. They're hungry almost all the time, and that can make them edgy.

Travis' roommate didn't understand that.

One night while Trav was cutting weight, he turned in early. His roommate refused to turn his light off. Trav asked him repeatedly to shut it off so he could sleep. His roommate ignored him. Finally, out of patience, Trav told him to shut it off, or he'd do it himself. Again, his roomie blew him off.

That did it. Travis got out of bed, stepped over to his roommate, and punched him square in the face. As he went down, Trav reached over, shut the light off, and went back to bed.

The fallout from this egregious breach of conduct swiftly caught up to Travis. The company officers wanted to burn him. They perceived him as a bully who deserved to have the book thrown at him. He was looking at serious punishment and a blemish on his otherwise exemplary record at the Academy.

I knew Travis well enough to recognize that he was a promising Midshipman with plenty to offer. His drive and dedication were unmatched by most. And while what he did was clearly wrong, I thought Trav deserved a break. Punishment can be a balancing act: too little, it serves as no deterrent; too much, it simply becomes retribution. Neither extreme is good for discipline.

Along with another junior named Paul Fisher, I went to bat for Travis. I explained to the company's leadership that they misread Trav. He wasn't a bully. He was a young man under intense pressure in the middle of cutting weight for the wrestling season—a double stressor on top of everything else on his plate. That his roommate chose to ignore him and didn't try to work out a compromise also played in Travis' favor. In the end, the company officers agreed with Paul and me. Trav received a slap on the wrist. His roommate moved out.

Part of being a leader is serving as a buffer between high levels of command and those either in your peer group or below. How that relationship develops depends on how willing you are to stand up to those above your pay grade, and when you're willing to do it. If you don't back your troops to higher leadership, they'll lose respect for you. But, if you expend your prestige for somebody who ultimately lets you down, that can have a very dramatic effect on your ability to mesh with your superiors in the chain of command.

The incident with Travis became the first time I experienced this balancing act. I staked my own reputation on defending Travis. Had he screwed up again, it would have had direct consequences for me. Chances would have been good the company leadership would not have listened to my opinion on such matters again.

You've got to pick your battles and fight for those you know will not let you down again. Travis not only stayed out of trouble, his gratitude for what Paul and I did for him became the foundation of a very tight friendship. In the months ahead, Travis became an integral member of our circle of friends. The loyalty he showed for us never wavered. In time, he returned the favor tenfold when I faced my own potentially career-ending situation.

When we graduated from the Academy the following year, we joined the fleet imbued with the raw fundamentals of leadership. We had learned that leadership was an art, full of nuances. It required balance, understanding, and a measure of risk. Of course, discipline above all else, and setting a personal example form the cornerstone of military leadership.

Those raw skills gave us what we needed to become

officers. But to go from leading freshmen at the Academy to running an infantry platoon bound for combat requires a huge leap forward and a level of sophistication we were expected to develop between the Basic School—TBS—and our units.

It was there that we learned about command presence. For men to follow you into the heat of battle, a leader had to be calm and decisive. In the field, it became all about making effective decisions without hesitation while maintaining a coolness that seemed to defy the nature of the situation. It is never easy to act calm while bullets whine and zip around you. But the best leaders rely on their sense of self-discipline and pull it off.

After graduation, I learned quickly to depend on the wisdom and experience of the noncommissioned officers around me. Before taking my first command, I asked a lot of questions to the SNCOs I'd come to admire, including Gunnery Sergeant Marlow, whom I met at the Marine Corps' Martial Arts Center for Excellence. In time, I grew close enough with Gunny Marlow to use him as a resource and drew on his considerable experience for ideas about how to approach my first command.

"Who were the best second lieutenants you've served with? What made them the best? How about the worst ones? What did they do wrong?"

Gunny Marlow respected my sincerity and opened up. I listened to his stories, cherry-picking techniques he said worked and using his negative examples as cautionary tales to avoid.

There were common threads to both. Bad officers try to be buddies with their Marines. There's a fine line between getting to know the men under your command and bonding with them as friends. It is all too easy to make that mistake. At the same time, if a young second lieutenant doesn't make an effort to know his men, his aloofness becomes a drag and will hinder his ability to command in several ways. First, he won't understand the strengths and weaknesses in his squads. More important, he won't have the respect or the connection needed to motivate and lead in the worst of circumstances. Men will follow other men into the worst possible circumstances if they respect and believe in their leadership. Like all other aspects of command, it is a delicate balance.

The SNCOs highlighted another common mistake. A second lieutenant taking his first command cannot ignore the wealth of knowledge and experience resident in his own noncommissioned officers. This is particularly true of his platoon sergeant, part of whose job it is to mentor along the new officer. He can't do that if the second lieutenant won't listen to him.

At the same time, go too far and the SNCOs end up running the platoon with the officer along for the ride. That diminishes the second lieutenant's command presence and the respect the men have for him. After all, they'll know he's the figurehead and the real power in the platoon sits with the senior NCOs.

I concluded the proper balance here depended on the officer's ability to listen and accept input while still making it clear that he was the ultimate decision-maker. That was the key. A second lieutenant couldn't be afraid to engage in frank and productive dialogue with his key leaders.

Appearance was also another factor Gunny Marlow mentioned. The second lieutenants he didn't respect came into his platoons with sloppy uniforms and lacking in physical conditioning. The best ones tended to be in shape and willing to set an example with their uniforms and how they carried themselves. Truth was, this was rarely a problem for Marine officers, as coming out of TBS they are usually physical specimens.

A platoon becomes the reflection of its commander. He sets the example. If his uniform is jacked up, his men won't care about their own. That leads to disciplinary issues and becomes a very slippery slope. The only way a second lieutenant can have the moral authority to set a high standard for conditioning and appearance is to be the example himself. Without conditioning, a platoon cannot achieve its potential in the field. Aggressiveness suffers. Appearance breeds pride and reinforces discipline and esprit de corps.

One of the first mistakes a young second lieutenant can make stems from the way he introduces himself to his first platoon. In their enthusiasm, young officers tend to start things off with an overly long speech that dwells on their background. One of my instructors, Captain McClam, explained that the best second lieutenants never opened up about themselves to the platoon. They kept an air of mystery about them—the way Captain Miller, Tom Hanks' character, did in the movie *Saving Private Ryan*. If the platoon knows everything there is to know about their lieutenant, a certain familiarity sets in that can breed contempt. But, play your cards close to your vest, and that will keep them curious and interested in you. It will help maintain their focus, and in the end, it will help allow them to create in their minds a picture of who you are based on what you do within the platoon, not what you did before you got to it.

In early 2005, I took over a platoon in Weapons Company, 3rd Battalion, 2nd Marines. At the time, these platoons were being used as mobile assault units with other assets attached to them, such as tanks or additional vehicles. As a result, the billet was usually filled by an experienced first lieutenant. When I showed up, fresh from Infantry Officer Course (IOC), the Marines in my platoon were leery of their new green-as-grass commander. The other platoon commanders and lieutenants in the battalion also put me under the microscope. I needed to start off on the right foot.

The advice from the NCOs and instructors made all the difference to me. During our first platoon meeting, my introductory speech lasted less than two minutes. "We're going to be aggressive," I told my new command. "We're going to train our asses off. And we're going to work harder than anyone else in the battalion."

That was it. Short, to the point, all business. What's more, they quickly found out I wasn't kidding.

CHAPTER ELEVEN

Errors and Shortcomings

Las Vegas, Sunday, August 9, 2008

Alone in bed. Teressa's already up. The early morning light streams in through the hotel's drapes, bathing me in its golden glow. I peel one eye open and the room comes into focus. I've managed only to doze for a few minutes at a time since turning in last night after the party.

What's that foul taste in my mouth?

That's the taste of rock bottom.

I groan and roll over, away from the window, not yet ready to face the consequences of this day after.

Most of the night, I lay awake, my mind second-guessing everything I did during the fight. I replayed every step, every strike over and over, looking for reasons for my failure.

I cannot shake the truth. I lost the fight before I stepped into the ring when my sudden identity crisis robbed me of confidence. I've wrestled with it ever since. I haven't come to any conclusions yet, but at least I know I have a solid foundation. Joey, Bryce, Travis, and I—we were groomed to be leaders. Those skills are universal. And for now, I can rest at least some of my identity on them. Who I need to be for the months and years ahead I will have to work through once I'm beyond the hangover of this defeat.

I lay in bed for a while, indulging my mind and its desire to poke the wounds opened last night in the octagon. It replays those final punches that brought me to the mat. I hear the crowd cheering. I hear the hecklers. I see myself wrapping the belt around Steve's waist.

This is the first day beyond defeat. I can either wallow or get up and get dressed. We have a plane to catch, and Monday morning at eight o'clock I've got to be at the office.

I slip out of bed and step over to my laptop. Something inside me wants to see how the fans reacted to the fight. Did they see it as a stand-up duel between two promising fighters? Or did they see it as something else.

I should not have looked.

So much for the fighting pride of the marines. This foo straight up got owned.

At least the tool with the slipknot tattoo lost.

HE DIDN'T GET KO'd!!!!! Watch that shit in slo motion!!!!! He gave up avoiding more pain

I thought, okay. Let's watch the M-A-R-I-N-E. Then the guy showed his heart and warrior spirit by quitting.

I try to tear my eyes away from the computer screen, but part of me wants to flay myself raw. I read on.

He is nothing but hype.

Stann has no heart at all. He just gave up.

I guess seeing a former marine beat up a can is something

to be proud of compared to murdering innocent women and children like in Haditha.

Is Stann really a Marine. . . . I was in the corps for five years and didn't see a guy quit like that.

I hope this guy isn't the standard Marine material, because if it is . . . so much for the Marines.

One French fan from Paris wrote:

HAHAHA. Take that silly Marines

Finally, even my self-flagellating brain has had enough. I turn away, lost in a complete sense of despair. I pack up my laptop, feeling like a zombie. I stumble over to my bag and begin to stuff my clothes into it.

All this has to have meaning. It can't just be about the money. It can't just be about the one-on-one challenge, the constant test of myself against other talented fighters. Truth is, it never was about any of that for me, especially at first. Fighting became an escape from the worst period of my life. I was locked down, stuck Stateside awaiting a court martial that would have decided my fate as an officer and Marine. The JAG office had warned my friends to have no contact with me. I had nothing. Then I found my way to the Martial Arts Center of Excellence, went through the program, and found a way to keep myself together. Fighting became my outlet, the way I dealt with the adversity I faced.

Later, when I turned pro, I saw it as an opportunity to seize a bully pulpit that I could use to tell my fellow Americans about the men I lost in Iraq. If I could keep their memories alive by sharing their accomplishments every chance I had, it would be a way to honor them and ensure they were not just consigned to anonymity by a feckless nation.

Now, the way I've represented myself turns out to have another edge. I've lost my first pro fight. The antimilitary crowd and the opponents of the Iraq War within the mixed martial arts (MMA) fan base have come out swinging. Even some Marines have turned on me.

And then there's that fucking Frenchman. They haven't won a war on their own since Napoleon invaded Russia, but even he took a shot at the Corps because of me.

I want nothing more than to represent the men I served with as best I can. Each time I step into the octagon, I am paying homage to them.

And now, I've opened them to ridicule and disgrace. One post even accused me of profiting from my dead Marines by making them my marketing hook. Reading that one made me want to vomit.

I look over at my wife. I remember the night I proposed to her. I was between tours in Iraq. She was still on the Philadelphia Eagles' cheerleading squad. At the end of the last home game, which happened to be on New Year's Day, 2006, I proposed to Teressa on the fifty-yard line. She gives me balance. She keeps me grounded. In return, I am the strength of our union. In the worst situations, I'm there to hold the line for us both. Even after I came home from my second deployment, burned out and questioning the losses we'd suffered, that visage of strength has never cracked.

My eyes fall to my bag.

I hope this guy isn't the standard Marine material, because if it is . . . so much for the Marines.

The hype, the marketing. None of that matters to me. Honoring my men by telling their countrymen what happened—that matters to me. It is my greatest motivation. It is the penance that serves as Novocain to my guilt. I didn't bring them all home.

I couldn't bring them all home.

Second tour. Rene Martinez. October 2006. He stepped on a homemade bomb that blew him seventy feet into the air. I was not out on that patrol, but I raced to the scene as fast as I could. When I arrived, the platoon's corpsman was still working on his broken and faceless body.

I covered him up. We got him into my Humvee. We drove him back to the base. The doctors left me alone with him. I stood beside Rene, my hand on his shattered forehead. "I'm sorry. I'm so sorry. I should have been there."

LOL! I guess that six weeks in paris island SC didn't make him as tough as he thought he was. lets hope he doesn't quit in iraq like he quit in the ring tonight LOL!!!

My loss has allowed others to defile the memories of the very men I fight to memorialize. Everything I stand for has blown up in my face.

"Brian, are you okay?" Teressa says with alarm.

She's standing across the room. I feel her eyes on me, but I cannot meet them. I'm the strength, the one who holds it together in the maw of a storm. I have never cried in front of my wife.

Now, as the memories spill over me, I cannot stop.

PART III

The Wild West

CHAPTER TWELVE

360-Degree Firefight

Day 1, Operation Matador, with 3rd Battalion,
2nd Marines (Betio Bastards)
Al Qaim, Anbar Province, Iraq, 0400, May 8, 2005

"Okay, if War Pig One doesn't get into position by 0530, Brian goes."

Dawn had not yet broken over the western Iraqi desert, but already firefights had broken out all around al Qaim, which was what our train-station-turned-fire-base had been named. This morning marked the launch of our first major offensive since getting in theater in March. Dubbed Operation Matador, our regimental combat team—about a thousand Marines total—received the job of clearing one of the worst pockets of resistance left in Iraq. Around al Qaim, squirreled away in the hamlets and villages on both sides of the Euphrates River, Musab al Zarqawi's band of foreign fighters lurked. Since the '03 invasion, most of our area had not been well patrolled, which gave Zarqawi's men the breathing space they needed to develop their strength, smuggle weapons across the nearby Syrian border, and reinforce their ranks with volunteer fighters from all over the Muslim world.

These foreigners terrorized the local civilians. They established checkpoints on the roads, which they used to rob truck drivers and civilians just trying to get from one place to another. Anyone who resisted met a bloody and violent end. In the towns, they ruled through fear and violence. Anyone who showed overt defiance to their presence died horribly. Zarqawi's men would frequently also kill their families as a warning to others.

The blood-soaked reign had worked. Zarqawi's men moved about the countryside with near impunity. The villages along the Euphrates became havens and bases for attacks against us and the main supply route that ran east toward Baghdad and west to Syria.

We didn't have the strength in the province to stop them. Zarqawi's men and their allies controlled everything around our little outpost in al Qaim. The company we replaced in March told us not even to bother patrolling west to the Ramana Bridge, which served as the only crossing over the Euphrates in the area. They went up there once, only to get ambushed by a superior force. After taking casualties, they withdrew and did not try again.

Our battalion's operations officer glanced over at me. "Brian, are you ready to go?"

"We're ready now, sir." A half hour before, I'd briefed my mobile assault platoon's Bravo Section on what to expect. They were loaded up in our vehicles, waiting for the word to get moving.

The plan had a lot of moving pieces. North of al Qaim, the Euphrates River wound like a sidewinder through the desertscape. In one of the loops the river created sat a town called New Ubaydi. This was the start point for Matador's main effort. Regimental Combat Team Two would eventually clear part of the town as an Army engineer company threw a bridge across the Euphrates. Once completed, the main assault would flow across the bridge and push east to west through all the towns and villages on the river's north bank.

My company, call sign War Pig, received an unusual role. We were the offensive's left hook, tasked with rolling through previously unpatrolled terrain and securing the Ramana Bridge to the west. This was the only crossing point Zarqawi's men could use to reinforce their fighters on the north bank. If we controlled it, the insurgents would be split into two groups by the Euphrates and we could defeat them in detail. We would also be able to keep them from withdrawing south of the river as the main effort cleared the north bank. If the rest of the regiment was the hammer, War Pig One was to be the anvil.

When the plan was first briefed, I found myself disappointed with the mission assigned to my men. My Alpha Section—half my forty-two-man platoon—was detached and sent northeast to provide security for the units waiting to cross the river once the engineers finished their bridge. My other section received quick reaction force (QRF) duty. This meant we stayed behind at Camp Al Qaim as a reserve element, ready to intervene should any of our other units need help. I wanted to be out in front. Instead, we were sitting on the firebase out of the fight.

But no plan survives first contact—or initial movement. The left hook bogged down within minutes of getting underway. This was Lieutenant Leahey's first platoon— ten Humvees and about forty men. To avoid the main roads west of al Qaim, they had tried to get to the bridge by cutting through the desert and the south bank of the Euphrates. Instead of hard ground or sand, they stumbled into a bog and their rigs got stuck. By 0530, it was clear they wouldn't reach the bridge by their assigned time.

That's when our call came. Our battalion's ops officer, Major Day, turned to me and said, "Okay, Stannly, get to the bridge as quickly as you can."

"Roger, sir."

Captain Ford Phillips, my company commander, took me aside and gave me a few last minute instructions. I admired Phillips for being a blunt and honest man. He didn't have time for niceties. When I screwed up, he let me know. When I did well, he never failed to praise me. There was never any guessing where you stood with him.

"Brian, if I were you, I'd take Route Diamond," he said with his characteristic soft-spoken voice.

A quick glance at a map showed we didn't have many options. Diamond ran east–west along the south bank of the Euphrates, right through numerous towns. It then intersected with the only asphalt road going north to the bridge, which we called Route Emerald.

To the south of Diamond ran a parallel road, Route Jade. That was our other option to get to Emerald. Jade was closer to us and paved. But if the enemy was waiting for us, it would be there. The few times the battalion had probed west since getting in theater in mid-March, we had used Route Jade. Diamond, which was a wide, mostly dirt road, had never been traveled.

"Roger, sir." They wished me luck as I headed out to my men.

The sun hadn't yet come up over the sand-colored city. In the pre-dawn gloom, I found my men lounging in our armored Humvees, which Sergeant Peterson, my section leader, had already lined up next to the front gate.

For Matador, my section had been reinforced by a couple of M1 Abrams tanks. They belonged to an Idaho reserve unit under the command of Sergeant Luke Miller. I'd never worked with the tankers before, but in the few conversations I'd had with them, Miller and his other M1 commander, Staff Sergeant Plumkey, seemed like capable professionals.

"We're going!" I shouted over the idling engines. In the lead rig's turret, I saw Corporal Rene DeLatorre, a Floridian of Latino decent. He was Sergeant Peterson's gunner, and I judged him to be the best one in the company, if not the battalion. He was a virtuoso with an M2 heavy machine gun—so accurate that I used to call him our .50 caliber sniper. He waved to me and gave me a thumbs up.

I climbed into the second Humvee in our column— our company's standard position for the platoon leader to be—and we rolled for the Ramana Bridge. Since arriving here in March, the intersection between Diamond and Emerald was the farthest west we'd been. We took no contact that day. Maybe, we could surprise them and get through to the bridge before the enemy had time to mobilize against us.

We headed north out of al Qaim, passing the Jade intersection, then swung left onto Diamond. Not a soul was out on the street, and I wondered if the early hour was the reason or if the locals had been tipped off and told to stay inside. Either way, the houses and shops we passed looked shuttered and deserted. Few lights blazed from within.

A few minutes later, we sped into Saddah, a town we had yet to start patrolling. Within a minute, somebody opened fire on us.

"We're taking small arms fire, sir," reported Corporal Culver, my rig's gunner, in a matter-of-fact voice. This was his second tour, and he knew how to communicate in combat.

Remember what Gunny Marlow told you.

Stay calm. Leadership in combat is all about presence and quick decision making. Trying to mirror Culver's bored tone, I replied, "Return fire." Then to Peterson, I radioed, "Keep moving forward. We have to get to the bridge."

Culver swung right and chopped loose a couple of bursts from his M240 Golf machine gun. Meanwhile, the drivers maintained their speed and we soon pulled clear of the insurgent kill zone. Culver's weapon went silent. Everyone's eyes scanned for targets.

A rocket propelled grenade suddenly whooshed past our column, exploding on the south side of Diamond. A second later, another one shot past. Cat-quick on their weapons, my gunners tracked and killed two insurgents in the front yard of a house on the north side of Diamond.

A minute later, we reached the intersection with Route Emerald, the north–south road that would take us to the bridge. Beyond Sergeant Peterson's Humvee, I could see a black sedan with orange stripes. It was heading north, windows rolled down. Muzzle flashes erupted from the car. Peterson's voice came over the radio, "Contact, direct front."

DeLatorre got his .50 cal on the target just as Peterson's driver began the right turn onto Emerald. It was a Death Race 3000 moment: The sedan's occupants spraying us with AK fire while DeLatorre unleashed his Ma Deuce. In such fights, nothing is as fearsome as an M2 machine gun. One hit with it will cause a human being to explode.

Its bullets will penetrate cars, walls, even light armor. The sedan never had a chance.

DeLatorre raked his target. The sedan, riddled with fist-sized holes, drifted to a halt, smoke coiling up from its shattered engine. Culver added a final burst. As we went by it, I saw the driver hanging half-in, half-out of the car, his door partway open. He wore a headdress and civilian clothes, now stained red from multiple hits. The gunman riding shotgun had tried to get away. He managed to jump out and take a step or two before DeLatorre's fifty cut him down.

"Keep going," I radioed to Peterson. We sped north, blowing through town as fast as the tanks could go. Muzzle flashes flared all around us. A heavy machine gun opened up, and I saw tracer bullets zip between my rig and Peterson's. Culver and DeLatorre swiveled back and forth, hammering targets with their heavy guns. Fortunately, none of my Humvees had taken a serious hit.

Seven hundred meters from the bridge now. We were a little bubble of Americans surrounded by the enemy.

The Euphrates came into sight. The Ramana Bridge's metal latticework laid over rust-colored pontoons appeared over the riverbank. We'd made it.

Now what?

Off to the left of Route Emerald, we found some high ground. We got behind a weed-strewn knoll and deployed in a line. The tanks rumbled into position, their crews spoiling to get into the fight.

The enemy came to us. Realizing what we were doing, small groups of men began maneuvering toward us on the north bank of the Euphrates. To the south and east, we could see others flowing around buildings and terrain features. Dimly, I wondered if we'd formed the anvil as the battalion wanted, or if we'd just set the stage for a last stand.

The sun rose over the Ramana Bridge. Heavy machine gun fire laced the grassy knoll. My gunners picked out targets and went to work. The tankers begged to get into the fight, but I initially held them back. Using their gigantic main guns can inflict tremendous collateral damage, which frequently resulted in official investigations. When a white truck came into view on the north bank of the river and dashed from one machine gun position to another in order to resupply the gunners, the tankers finally had a legitimate target. One of the M1 Abrams uncorked a main gun round. The huge shell obliterated the truck. No more resupply for the machine guns, at least for the moment. The fact that these Muj had tried to do this while under fire indicated a level of organization and sophistication that was usually beyond your average collection of gunmen.

As the firefight continued, I could not have been more proud of my Marines. They executed their tasks in stellar fashion, calmly assessing targets and coordinating their fire to conserve ammunition. As I watched them, I realized how lucky I was to lead such men into battle. They were a product of the Corps and its training system, and here in the thick of the fight, I could see that system totally vindicated.

We started taking heavy fire from a position to the south that we nicknamed "the shark fin." Corporal Delatorre suppressed the area with his machine gun, but we needed more firepower to put an end to this threat. When we saw two insurgents dive behind a dump truck, one of the tanks put a main gun round right through the big vehicle. The direct hit blew both insurgents into a concrete wall and splattered them as if they'd just jumped off a skyscraper.

Twenty minutes later, mortars began to fall on our position. As we fought back, I made sure that our vehicles moved from one spot to another so the mortar crews could not zero in on us. From a wadi that ran perpendicular to Route Emerald, several insurgents began lobbing rocket propelled grenades (RPGs) at us. We were too far away to get hit with direct fire, so they used them as shoulder-mounted artillery. The rockets sizzled overhead, most of them falling long behind us on the riverbank.

At the same time, we started taking RPG fire from dug in positions on the other side of the Euphrates. The rockets exploded all around us. Then another heavy machine gun let loose, this one sited on the north bank as well. We were caught in a 180 degree crossfire.

From my window, I could see Corporal DeLatorre and Bravo One. They were taking the brunt of the fire, and DeLatorre briefly dipped out of the turret as bullets bounced off the Humvee's armored skin. Then I saw his hand pop up above the blast shield, holding a video camera. It takes a rare kind of cool to do something like that.

In combat, an infantry platoon's first task is to achieve fire superiority over the enemy. To do this requires pouring it on the insurgents until they are forced to either disengage or go to ground. Once they're either driven off or pinned in place, you've gained command of the fight and can dictate what happens next.

Even with the tanks, we didn't have the firepower to gain control of this battle. There were too many insurgents shooting at us from too many places. We needed some help.

War Pig One had cleared the bog at last, but they were still several hours out. I checked my watch: 0645. We'd been in place at the bridge for only about an hour.

The mortar barrage intensified. As near as we could tell, the tubes were emplaced on the north side of the river, but we couldn't see them. We tried to get some counter-battery fire called on them to no avail.

We shifted positions again to keep the mortarmen guessing. At the same time, a fresh team of RPG-carrying insurgents slipped into the wadi to our south to rain more explosives down on us.

I reached for the radio's handset and began calling in airstrikes. Within minutes, sleek Huey Cobra gunships thundered onto the scene to deliver deadly accurate Hellfire missiles into the targets we identified from them.

To the east, the regiment's main hammer was hung up on the river. The Army engineer unit tasked with building the bridge across the Euphrates began to take mortar fire from Ubaydi. Lima 3/25 Marines and Kilo Company assaulted into the town, but progress was slow. The engineers initially estimated it would take them twelve hours to complete the bridge. Now, with the delays the mortaring caused, it looked like it would be almost a day before the main effort could get across the river.

The Cobras kept the enemy from getting any closer to us. Our tankers and their enormous guns made short work of those foolish enough to expose themselves. Still, we didn't have control of the fight. There were simply too many concealed insurgents using the urban terrain to the south to their advantage. Unless we had positive identification of their location, we could not open fire on them. It was all we could do to hang on.

When I started at the Academy, Navy football was in the middle of a rebuilding and transition period. Originally recruited to play quarterback, I ended up contributing at linebacker. The friendships I began on the team led to lifelong relationships I cherish to this day.

My mother and me at the Academy on I-Day, another turning point in the lives of all the young men and women who come to Annapolis. This was taken shortly before we were sworn in.

My sister, Allison, myself, and my mother during my going-away party shortly before I deployed to Iraq in 2005.

During spring break of our senior year, a bunch of us flew to Acapulco, Mexico, to celebrate the last stretch of our time at the Academy. Left to right: Myself, Hank Russel, Bryce McDonald, Joey Faye, and Joey Owmby.

Graduation day from the Academy. From left to right: Joey Faye, Justin Simmons, myself, and Garret Cox right after we threw our covers in the air to make it official. It was the most important day of our young lives.

On May 8, 2005, Corporal Richard Mcelhinny selflessly exposed himself to incoming fire while suppressing enemy machine gun positions as we struggled to rescue wounded Marines trapped inside a devastated M1 Abrams main battle tank. Mcelhinny received a Bronze Star with Valor device for his actions that day.

Sergeant Cherry and me moments before we departed Camp al Qaim on a mounted patrol.

Staff Sergeant Robertson (at left) served as our platoon sergeant during our first deployment to Iraq. He was one of the finest NCOs I've ever worked with, and together we made an excellent team. Staff Sergeant Francis, at right, came to us from Recruiting Command and missed the entire pre-deployment work-up. Nevertheless, he shined as our Alpha Section leader.

During our first tour in Anbar Province, my platoon escorted a busload of Iraqi Army recruits from their villages to our base, where they stayed for three days before heading off to boot camp. These men elected to stay behind in their villages and spend those three days with their families. Insurgents kidnapped them, tortured and killed them, then dumped their bodies in a busy intersection to intimidate the locals. That was the type of enemy we faced.

During Operation Matador, my platoon took every kind of direct and indirect fire the insurgents possessed. Here, one of our Humvees took a sniper shot, which was so well placed it would have probably killed my driver had we lacked bulletproof glass.

Corporal Robert Gass cleans his night-vision goggles while atop his Humvee. He served as Alpha 1's gunner during Operation Matador. Grievously wounded in the head, then shot in the arm during a suicide car bomb attack, Gass' only concern was for his fellow Marines. After leaving us, we underwent multiple surgeries and endured a difficult recovery. He is one of the most courageous men I've ever known.

Sergeant Trevor Wargo and me at Camp al Qaim. Sergeant Wargo and I met at the MACE, where he was a mixed martial arts instructor. We served together through two deployments in Iraq. He later served as an instructor with Marine Special Operations.

Operation Matador,
8 May–19 May 2005

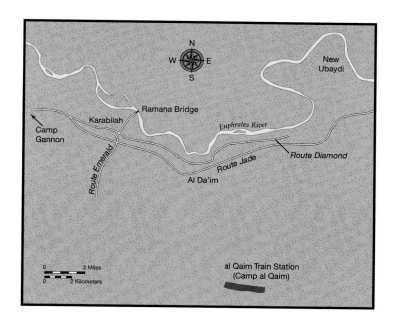

New Ubaydi

Ramana Bridge

Karabilah

Camp Gannon

Route Emerald

Euphrates River

Route Jade

Route Diamond

Al Da'im

0   2 Miles
0   2 Kilometers

al Qaim Train Station
(Camp al Qaim)

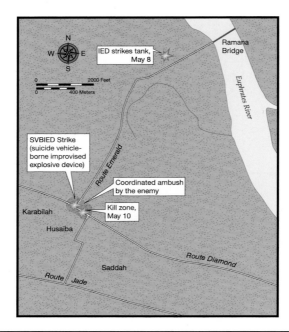

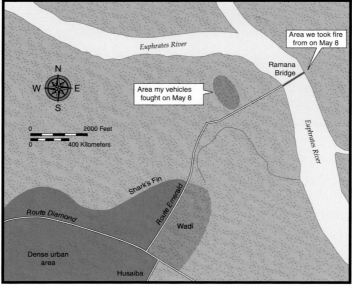

For five hours the see-saw battle raged. Finally, at 1000, War Pig One arrived with ten Humvees. They fought their way to us, and under a constant crossfire, we executed a relief in place. As they took over our knoll to the west of Route Emerald, we shifted east of the road to a small ridge. Suddenly, a huge explosion drowned out all other battle sounds. The ground rolled and shook, as if a fault line had suddenly collapsed beneath us. Ahead, a maelstrom of sand, dirt, smoke, and flames boiled skyward.

Before I could even ask, Sergeant Peterson's voice came over the radio, "Mortar hit one of the tanks."

My column braked to a stop. The explosion morphed into a small dirty brown mushroom cloud over Staff Sergeant Plumkey's M1. No way a mortar did that. This had to have been a massive IED.

Luke Miller called over to me, "I have no comm with them."

I radioed for a MEDEVAC chopper, only to hear that Lima 3/25 had taken heavy casualties in New Ubaydi, and the birds were busy getting the wounded out of the city. Luckily for us, a nearby Huey UH-1 pilot heard my call for help. He told us he was coming in

"Okay, boys, increase your rate of fire to protect the bird!" I called to my platoon. Everyone laid on their triggers to suppress the enemy to our north. We didn't want to see the chopper get hit, too.

Ignoring the incoming fire, he swung over the battlefield and deftly touched down right between the tanks. Almost immediately, Plumkey blew his hatch and pulled himself out along with his driver. Despite a badly wounded leg, he limped to the chopper and flung himself aboard. Seconds after the tank's driver jumped on, the chopper dusted off bound for al Qaim.

With more wounded still in the tank, we'd need another helicopter. I called back to Al Qaim. "Anchorman, this is War Pig Two Actual, we need another MEDEVAC."

Again. None were available. Instead, the same Huey pilot promised to come back and get the tank's remaining crewmen.

We needed to find out their situation. Since Plumkey bailed out of the tank, we hadn't seen any other movement.

My platoon sergeant, Staff Sergeant Robertson, and I dismounted and sprinted forward toward Miller's tank. Robertson reached the tank first and used it to shield himself from enemy fire. After seeing the explosion and Marines moving in the open, the enemy concentrated their fire on the downed tank. Machine gun fire laced the area, and RPG's exploded around us.

I took a deep breath and ran for the burning Abrams. I took only a few steps before I saw Robertson frantically waving me back. Just then, a line of bullets stitched across the sand about ten feet ahead of me. I executed my best football shuttle run and dashed back for cover. Bravo Three laid down suppressing fire, which allowed me to get across the open space on my second attempt.

When I reached Robertson, he shouted, "We've still got two wounded in there!"

We had to get the men out quickly. I climbed onto the tank, Miller following a short time later. The incoming fire was heavy and more than once we had to duck behind the turret.

Below us, Corporal Richard Mcelhinny dismounted from one of my Humvee's and scaled the wrecked M1 to join us. Terribly exposed to the incoming fire, he charged the M240 Golf mounted on the turret and swung it around to hammer the north bank.

Through the turret hatch, I could see Lance Corporal Johnathon Lowe, covered in blood. The IED had paralyzed him from the waist down. Now, struggling to remain conscious, he sat awaiting help. I dove headfirst into the turret, grabbed him, and began to pull. Blood coated the tank's interior. It looked like a crime scene from a slasher film.

I couldn't get Lowe to move more than a few inches. Goddamn! *Why's this kid so heavy?*

I pulled him again, bracing myself with my lower half of my body still outside the turret hatch. No progress.

Another burst of machine gun fire raked the tank. Mcelhinny laid on his trigger to try and suppress the enemy gunner.

That's when I noticed Lowe's microphone cord. He was still plugged in, and the cord was wrapping around his ankle, preventing me from getting him out. Quickly, I reached for my knife and cut him loose.

The Huey returned. The pilot swept over the battlefield, turned and touched down right between the two tanks again.

Sergeant Miller and I pulled Lowe clear. Robertson helped get him off the tank, then Miller carried him to the waiting chopper. A moment later, the two NCOs got the final crewman out and loaded aboard the Huey. Miraculously, the chopper didn't take any serious hits, despite selflessly landing in the middle of a firefight twice.

As the Huey departed, I called in two more airstrikes to try and suppress the fire coming at us from the north bank. The Cobras made strafing and rocket attacks, and for a moment, the incoming fire slackened.

Battalion called up. They needed us back at al Qaim. I looked out across the battlefield to the south. Insurgents still lurked in the wadi. Others used buildings for cover. To get back home, we'd have to drive through that cordon of bad guys.

Miller approached me. "Sir, War Pig One has no tank support. I want to stay out here with him."

"Okay, Sergeant. No problem." Lieutenant Leahy, War Pig One's commander, would need the awesome firepower of the remaining M1.

"Well, we do have a problem, sir," Miller offered, "We're getting low on fuel."

"We'll take care of that, okay? We'll get you some gas."

"Roger that, sir. Good luck."

I moved back to my Humvee and climbed inside. Over the radio, I briefed Sergeant Peterson on what we had to do. Peterson was a stellar Marine. He'd done a hitch before 9-11 in an artillery outfit. After the towers fell, he joined back up and volunteered for the infantry. I saw in him a steady presence and excellent leadership skills. His men loved him. I selected him to be the Bravo Section leader for those reasons, even though he didn't hold the rank for the job. So far today, he'd shown me I'd made the right call. Though naturally loud and charismatic, once the fighting started he'd acted like Peyton Manning running a two minute drill: calm and cool, eyes open and utterly professional.

We'd need all that and more now. There was only one way in to the bridge, which meant there was only one way out of this shooting gallery. The enemy would be waiting.

"Let's go. Sergeant Pete. Oscar Mike."

CHAPTER THIRTEEN

Hard Road South

We mounted up and rolled south in column formation for the Emerald–Diamond intersection. At the moment, the incoming fire from the south had died away. It was an eerie calm, for just minutes ago, the enemy had been using this very terrain as firing positions against us. But like so many other times in Iraq, the insurgents had simply melted away.

Not that we relaxed. My gunners remained extra alert, my drivers stayed ready to ease off the gas and give them a better gunnery platform if necessary. For a brief time, we left Emerald and cut across the desert in hopes of avoiding another ambush. We couldn't go far like that though. The fact was, the Emerald–Diamond and Emerald–Jade intersections were our only options to get home. The enemy knew this, but they didn't know which of the two we'd use. Not that it mattered much, the two intersections were only a long block away from each other.

We ran out of flat, hard desert and turned back onto Emerald. No contact. Everything was spooky quiet; not a soul moved in the street or peered out from behind shuttered windows.

We approached the Emerald–Diamond intersection. Up ahead, beyond Bravo One, I saw something in the street.

"Two vehicle roadblock," Sergeant Pete reported in a clipped, preternaturally calm voice. Sure enough, somebody had parked two sedans nose-to-nose across Emerald in the block that separated the two key intersections.

Sergeant Pete's rig hooked hard left and swung onto Diamond. We followed in Bravo Two, but as we blew through the intersection, a thought occurred to me.

We're being channeled into something.

The world seemed to explode around us. Rockets flashed past. Behind me, Bravo Three took an RPG hit right on the front windshield. Machine gun fire laced across our Humvees. The gunners called out targets and hammered away in every direction.

Ahead, I saw a group of fighters, all wearing black bulletproof vests, flow out of a yard and into the street, AKs blazing. From mere feet away, they shot up our rigs, aiming for my gunners. Our weapons unleashed their full fury and I saw four of these men get chopped down. Still others swarmed onto the street.

"Blow through it!" I called into the radio.

Peterson's driver hit the gas. We struggled to keep up. Meanwhile, DeLatorre tried to clear the path ahead for us. He walked his .50 cal back and forth between the road and the buildings on either side. I watched his .50 tear through a gaggle of black-vested bad guys as they fired at us from the front yard of a roadside house. Even as they were still going down, he shifted fire and let fly with another measured burst that wiped out several more firing at us from an open doorway. He was amazing.

Another RPG sizzled past. Something exploded behind us. More of these heavily armored insurgents boiled into the street. They seemed absolutely fearless as they stood in the open to deliver full auto fire from their AKs.

The incoming became too intense even for DeLatorre. He ducked down into Pete's Humvee, momentarily leaving his .50 cal as a tempest of lead swirled around his turret.

As we sped down Diamond, I got a point-blank view of our enemy. Fortunately, it was through bulletproof glass. Some of these fighters had actually stepped into the road and were mere feet from my side of Bravo Two. Not only did they wear black, bulletproof vests with tactical gear dangling from them, but they also wore black masks—like you see in those old photos of the Black September terrorists who killed the Israeli athletes in Munich during the '72 Olympics. They looked sinister and wielded their weapons with much more professionalism than the other insurgents we'd seen. These men had training, discipline, and courage to spare.

I prayed we didn't lose a rig. If one of those RPGs scored a mobility kill, we'd be in dire trouble. There were too many insurgents for our gunners to hold off for very long, especially with the volume of incoming small arms fire we were taking.

A heartbeat later, we emerged from the other side of the kill zone. The fire slackened, then fell away completely. DeLatorre returned to his bullet-scarred turret. I ordered a right turn. We dashed south, crossed Jade, and found ourselves on Route Silver in full midmorning traffic. Iraqi drivers have no boundaries, and trying to clear a path through them is sort of like playing a real-time version of Spy Hunter. We were fully engaged in this frustration when a sedan sped around a corner and drove at us through the path we'd cleared through the congestion.

The sedan sped up, driving right at us. My rear gunner tried to wave him away, but the man behind the wheel ignored him.

Shit, could be a car bomb!

One of my rigs swept to the side and slowed down. As the sedan closed, the gunner opened fire, his M240 Golf shredding the vehicle's left side. The driver died, hands on the wheel, his midsection torn apart by NATO standard 7.62 rounds.

Was he a hostile suicide bomber? Or was he just a terrified Iraqi civilian who'd lost control of himself and blindly sped into our column? Given what happened to us later, I've long since concluded he was the former. Since we'd been ordered home, we could not stop to assess it.

When we pulled into al Qaim a few minutes later, every one of Bravo Section's Humvees looked like it had just come off the set of an Oliver Stone movie. Bullets had pitted their armored hides, and desert dust coated vehicles and gunners alike.

One look at Bravo Three convinced me that we'd run into a very unusual group of insurgents. The rig's splintered windshield held several steel flechettes still embedded in the glass. I'd never heard of any Muj cell using these anti-personnel weapons before. The wicked spikes would have torn apart my crew had the glass not been bulletproof.

I hurried into the battalion's combat operations center (COC) to report what we'd just been through. The moment I mentioned the ambush we'd encountered on Route Diamond, ears perked up. Later in the day, an intelligence team from regiment came down to examine our vehicles, paying close attention to the steel flechettes embedded in Bravo Three. After giving them a detailed brief, the intel types told me that we'd indeed encountered a very select group of insurgents.

Black vests and black masks, excellent discipline, and first rate weapons were all characteristics of Musab al Zarqawi's personal security detail. Zarqawi was the head of al Qaeda in Iraq and had long been reputed to be hiding somewhere here along the Syrian border after narrowly escaping from Coalition authorities in Mosul the previous fall. At the time, killing Zarqawi was a higher priority than finding Osama bin Laden, as he was the driving force between the growing civil war between Iraqi Shia and Sunni factions. Using Sunni suicide bombers, his minions had unleashed a wave of violence against Shia across Iraq. They were blowing up marketplaces, banks, Shia mosques, and gathering places. With the Coalition unable to stem these attacks, the Shia had taken to forming their own vigilante militias, some of which had turned into vengeance squads that preyed on Sunni civilians with equal barbarity.

Zarqawi had crafted a war plan against the U.S. borne on the bodies of countless innocents, and the bloodletting his cells were causing put in peril our entire mission in Iraq.

Our regimental intel section believed we had encountered his bodyguards. And killed not a few of them, too. Later, after Matador, several media outlets reported that Zarqawi had been wounded during Matador. His bodyguards had stuffed him in a car and raced him to a hospital in Ramadi. There, he was treated and released. As he was leaving the hospital, the doctor who patched him up recognized him. His guards threatened to kill him if he said anything, but word of his visit got into the press anyway.

I'll never know if we had anything to do with it, but I'd sure like to believe that we ran straight into his headquarters on Diamond, and one of my sharp-eyed gunners winged the son of a bitch. During the long and sleepless nights Matador would cause me in the years to come, that thought brings a grim smile to my face.

CHAPTER FOURTEEN

Midnight Run

Day Two, Operation Matador, May 9, 2005

My Marines were flat-out studs. Throughout the afternoon of the 8th, they swapped stories of the morning's fighting as they labored over our battered Humvees. War Pig One was still up at the bridge, clinging to its narrow blocking position with the help of a whole lot of air support. Nobody had any illusions that we wouldn't be sent up there again in short order to help out Lieutenant Leahy. They were so dedicated and sharp that I didn't even have to tell them. They broke down their weapons and cleaned them thoroughly. The brass that littered the inside of every Humvee was carefully swept out. My men checked the engines and tires, replaced air filters, and made sure all the fluids reservoirs were full. Then they loaded the crew served weapons with fresh ammo belts.

Meanwhile, the offensive continued throughout the day. The fighting raged in Ubaydi as the Marines from Lima 3/25 and our own Kilo Company battled building to building. By nightfall, about a third of the town had been cleared. To the southwest, the engineers labored to finish the bridge over the Euphrates under trying conditions. So far, we hadn't been able to develop our drive on the north bank of the river, so Leahy's force was on the far left on its own without anyone sweeping toward it yet. His platoon and Miller's remaining tank endured murderous incoming fire all day long. Now, as darkness fell, the COC received word that his men were running low on ammo and the vehicles were quickly draining their last fuel reserves. Miller's tank was particularly low on gas.

To hang onto that blocking position, they'd need to be resupplied soon. The battalion staff considered bringing in fuel and ammo via helicopter but discarded the idea. The potential landing zones were too hot and the weather had started to turn bad. The job fell to us again.

During the mission briefing, my Marines were given two hours to get out to the Ramana bridgehead, transfer the ammo and fuel from a tanker truck and a seven ton to Leahy's exhausted command, then get back to al Qaim. No doubt there'd be another mission waiting for us when we got back.

To pull this off, we'd need to be flawless. I wasn't worried about my Marines, but when I met the motor transport guys driving the tanker and the seven ton, I grew worried. They didn't have night vision and didn't seem prepared for the tough night ahead. Our job would be to protect these rigs at all costs. Without fuel and ammo, Leahy would be in serious trouble, and we'd probably have to abandon—at least temporarily—the blocking position.

Just before we rolled out, my Alpha Section arrived back at al Qaim after a very dull day covering the jump-off point for the assault force tasked with crossing the Euphrates. They'd encountered no opposition, and my Bravo Section Marines quickly busted out the stories of our busy day, much to the jealousy of the rest of the platoon. Alpha Section was full of aggressive, angry Marines who wanted nothing more than to get into the fight. They lobbied to go out on this run, but I vetoed the idea. Sergeant Pete's men knew the terrain now, and we'd need that experience to shepherd the two trucks to the bridge. I told my Alpha Section they'd have plenty of opportunities in the days to come. But I knew as we left the wire, they remained on base, frustrated and anxious.

This time, we chose to make the run up to the bridge via Route Jade instead of Diamond. In the darkness, we moved fast, our headlights blacked out. If we encountered any opposition, we'd blow through it, all guns blazing.

We reached Jade and swung left, gunners scanning, drivers doing a phenomenal job negotiating the roads with their night vision goggles. The buildings on either side of the road looked deserted. No lights issued from the cracks in their shuttered windows. No forms stood in doorways or lurked in alleys. The ghost town atmosphere made us all even more alert. The locals always knew when a fight would break out, and they'd go to ground to protect their loved ones as best they could from the crossfire sure to come.

Surprisingly, we reached Emerald without a single contact. Sergeant Pete's rig hung a right and headed up the hardball for the bridge. The first thing we noticed was the absence of the roadblock we'd encountered earlier in the day. The insurgents had removed the cars blocking the street between Jade and Diamond, giving us an unobstructed shot straight up to Leahy.

Just before we reached the bridge, battalion called us and cut our mission time from two hours to forty minutes. We'd have to sprint to meet that time hack, and I grumbled at the mid-mission change of orders. Later, I found out it was due to the ability of our command to schedule air support for our mission. Lieutenants see only a small portion of the picture. This incident reinforced that with me.

When we rolled into Leahy's perimeter, the men sprang out of their rigs to work furiously on transferring the ammo to War Pig One's Humvees. Leahy came up to me, his face streaked with grime, eyes full of exhaustion and the strain of command. He and his men had endured continuous attacks since they'd relieved us. "Brian," he said to me, "look, when you get back to al Qaim, tell them I need more firepower. We're hanging on, but we're facing serious opposition here."

I didn't envy his position. After this crazy day, he and his Marines would have to fight through the night without relief, though Leahy did bring up two additional gun trucks to provide more firepower. It was clear his Marines were doing an incredible job and had thoroughly punished the enemy. But the fact was, they were heavily outnumbered and up against well-trained enemy fighters who had proven elusive and hard to identify until after they started shooting. I promised Lieutenant Leahy I'd pass along his concerns to battalion, though I doubted he'd get any more assets, since we were already spread so thin.

Sixty minutes later, our Marines passed the last box of ammo over to Leahy's Humvees. The tanker truck finished refueling all his vehicles plus Lieutenant Miller's remaining M1. It was a remarkable feat, done in combat under sporadic fire and in complete darkness. I could not have been more proud of my men.

Time to head back for al Qaim. Now, under normal conditions, it is an exceptionally bad idea to use the same route twice. Generally, the insurgents will try to plant roadside bombs or establish an ambush point once they see the road the Americans have selected to use. This time, after the multiple running firefights we had on Diamond, I thought it a very bad idea to use that road on our way out. Should we run into those black-vested bodyguards again, our soft-skinned tanker and the seven ton would be in serious danger with some very inexperienced Marines at the wheel.

The only other option was a return down Emerald and a left turn on Jade. So be it. We loaded up and rolled for home.

Seconds after we swung onto Jade, the enemy ambushed us. The black night erupted in laser-like tracer rounds that zipped around our vehicles. Some ricocheted off our armored Humvees and sped off into the night in crazy directions. All the fire came from the north at fairly long range, which made me conclude the enemy had been waiting for us on Diamond, then hastily shifted positions when we blew by that intersection again. An RPG flared in the distance. The rocket arced over our convoy to explode among the houses to our south. Another followed.

"The road's obstructed!" called Sergeant Pete from the lead rig. Down Route Jade, the enemy had used earth moving equipment to build a dirt-and-tire serpentine that led up to a makeshift checkpoint. We'd seen it for the first time a few days before Matador began, and Cobras were sent out to shoot up the insurgents manning it. Now, it formed the far eastern end of the kill zone we found ourselves driving through.

"Get around it," I called back to Sergeant Pete.

Two more RPGs flashed through the velvet night. Again, the Muj had lobbed them at us from long range, and their aim sucked. The rockets sailed overhead and exploded hundreds of meters on the other side of the road.

Corporal Forrest, who manned the Mark 19 automatic grenade launcher we'd temporarily mounted on one of the Seven ton trucks, caught sight of an insurgent as he briefly exposed himself to launch an RPG at us. Cat-quick, he swung his turret and trained his weapon. A pull on the trigger let fly a stream of 40mm grenades. He corrected his aim and got on target until one shell nailed the insurgent dead in the chest and blew him to bloody fragments.

The RPG fire suddenly grew more intense and accurate. One rocket exploded near the berm, only a few dozen meters away from us. Another one skipped across the road and blew up between my rig and the tanker truck, which still had plenty of fuel in it.

One lucky shot, and we'd all be bathed in fuel. The thought of that caused me to make up my mind.

The near miss spooked the tanker driver. He suddenly swerved hard left and bolted down a side street by himself—and directly into the enemy positions. Staff Sergeant Robertson saw this and erupted over the radio, telling the crew to get back on Jade. When that didn't have any effect, Robertson called over to me, "I got these knuckleheads."

His Humvee brought up the rear, and he swung out of line to go nurse the terrified motor T guys back onto the right route.

We were almost to the Muj checkpoint. I keyed the handset and called up to Sergeant Pete, "Cut through the desert, we'll get clear of this and wait for Robertson and the tanker!"

Ahead of me, Bravo One's driver took my order to heart. He hung a sharp right that sent the Humvee skidding down a steep embankment. Toward the bottom, the rig high centered and slid to a stop. Sergeant Pete's driver hit the gas. The back wheels spun and kicked up a plume of sand and dirt. The vehicle was stuck fast.

These are moments when decisive action is needed. A leader cannot hesitate, especially when his Marines are taking fire. Mentally, I ran through our options. We could all hit the brakes and cover Bravo One until Pete's Marines could get unstuck. Our collective firepower could hold the enemy at bay. But that would expose the tanker and the seven ton to the incoming fire, and if one of those went down, we'd have our hands full trying to effect CASEVAC and a vehicle recovery

I called over to Staff Sergeant Robertson and told him to take the rest of the rigs and escort the soft skinned vehicles to a rally point out in the desert. Meanwhile, my Humvee would cover Sergeant Pete's and help him get unstuck.

Once again, my Marines impressed the hell out of me with their steely calm under fire. We pulled up alongside Pete's rig in time to see him complete an ass chewing on his driver. We hooked up to his Humveee and pulled it clear. Minutes later, we all linked back up and sped back to al Qaim without taking any casualties or serious hits. As we rumbled through the front gate, I realized my boys had been up for almost twenty-four straight hours. Now, as the adrenaline drained away, all of us were overcome with profound exhaustion. Nonetheless, our work wasn't done. The vehicles had to be maintained, weapons had to be cleaned, and I had to debrief the battalion staff.

Toward dawn, our heads finally hit our pillows. For

the first time, we slept the sleep of combat veterans.

CHAPTER FIFTEEN

Slow Motion Nightmare

"Goddamn it Lamson!" I shouted as I approached my Alpha Section's rigs. The men were readying for the mission ahead, and as usual, my platoon rebel Lance Corporal Jeff Lamson had his cover pushed back on his head, which made him look like a Hollywood Marine—cool but unprofessional. This was a discipline issue, and I'd already flamed him for it many times.

He gave me a *you caught me sir* sort of grin and straightened his cover. Not good enough, "Lamson, if I catch you again, I'll stick it up your ass! Are we clear?"

"Yes, sir." He said, grin vanishing. He was an Indianan with a slight Midwestern accent who loved basketball as much as I loved football.

When I took over War Pig Two before we left the States, the platoon was known for its rebelliousness. Lamson was usually out in front in this respect, and he drove me crazy for a while with his *fuck-fuck* games. I still hadn't managed to get him to cut his hair, which he kept longer than any other Marine in the company.

Discipline had been an issue with the platoon when I took over. As part of my plan to fix that, I was a stickler when it came to our uniforms and how we presented ourselves. Lamson always pushed the envelope and tested the boundaries. He also had a quick wit and was a total smart ass. He could totally disarm a person with his rapier tongue. At the same time, I'd come across him several times embroiled in profound intellectual discussions. While he seemed to revel in being a thorn in my side at times, I couldn't help but like the kid. At times, he'd crack my composure with one of his snarky comments, and I'd end up busting out laughing with everyone else.

Tonight, Lamson would be the lead driver for our column. It would be a difficult mission, I had no illusions about that, and everyone would need to bring their best. Fortunately, as much as Lamson liked to play fast and loose with some of the regs, he was a stellar combat Marine. He knew every weapon system thoroughly, had learned how to use demo charges, and could maneuver a Humvee like Dale Earnhardt Jr. I'd long since come to count on him to perform.

"Okay, guys. Gather 'round," I said. Alpha Section soon surrounded me, and I began to brief them on the mission.

I had a different relationship with Alpha than I did with my Bravo Section. Alpha Section didn't gel like Bravo did under Sergeant Pete. I watched the dynamic, and a month into taking over the platoon, I made a change at section leader. I gave Staff Sergeant Francis the job.

Francis had been a gamble. He'd come to the platoon from Recruiting Command and missed the entire pre-deployment training package. He hadn't done anything tactical for three and a half years. He was also older than most of the other NCOs. At first, he struggled in his new role. But as he sharpened his skills and came up his learning curve, I could see he was going to make an excellent section leader.

"We're going back to the bridge tonight," I started. Alpha had sat out the last couple of fights. They were fresh and eager to get into the fray. Right now, Bravo Section had all the bragging rights, and that was driving Francis' men nuts. When I broke the news, I saw no fear in anyone's eyes, just anticipation and excitement.

Be careful what you wish for, I thought.

Next to Lamson stood Corporals Goldsmith and Gass. Robert Gass was the .50 cal gunner on Francis' rig, Alpha One. He had the same job DeLatorre had for my Bravo Section. He was a good kid, a South Carolinian who embodied a profound sense of duty and professionalism. I knew I'd be able to count on him when things got hairy that night. Gass was a badass who frequently challenged me to grappling matches in front of the entire platoon. He lost each time, but he fought to the end with such fury that everyone respected him—especially me.

Goldsmith was one of Francis' dismounts in Alpha One. He was another one of my characters. Due to his age, everyone called him "Old Goldie." He was kind of clumsy on his feet, though in a straight line I'd discovered he could sprint like the wind once he got a head of steam up. Recently, we'd caught him running an underground massage operation on al Qaim. He'd been a masseuse and was trying to make a little money on the side. He got busted on that one. Truth was, I always considered Goldsmith as weird as a three-headed cat, but he was my cat so I loved him.

I began to outline the mission. Battalion wanted us to go back to the bridge and execute a relief in place with War Pig One. Leahy's guys needed a break, and we were going to take over for a little while, then come back to al Qaim to function as the quick response force (QRF) again. At the same time, the M1 Abrams that had been knocked out on Matador's first day had to be retrieved and carried back to al Qaim with Leahy's men. Well, recovering a massive armored vehicle is not something that can be done with your average AAA tow truck. In fact, it takes a specialized tracked vehicle, the massive and ungainly Mike 88. Weighing in at seventy tons—ten more than an M1 Abrams—these enormous beasts are among the largest tracks in the U.S. military arsenal. They're also the slowest, a point that greatly concerned me on this day. Listed as having a max speed of about twenty-five miles an hour, in operational conditions they were lucky to make six to ten.

Over the past two days, the speed and maneuverability of our Humvees kept us alive. We could hit fifty miles an hour on straight stretches of road when needed, making us very hard to hit with RPGs. Tonight, we'd lose that precious asset. We'd be rolling into hostile territory at a crawl.

To pull this off, we needed more firepower. Since Miller's remaining tank was still supporting Leahy at the bridge, battalion arranged for us to get another section from Camp Gannon, a small firebase to the west of al Qaim that was named after my former company commander at the Academy. Major Gannon was an amazing man and a tremendous leader who had been killed on a previous deployment to al Qaim.

With the tanks coming from the west and my group coming from the east, we planned to rendezvous in the desert, then push on to the bridge with the tanks providing heavy firepower for us.

As we planned this mission out, we faced the same dilemma getting to the bridge as with our previous runs. There was simply no way we could avoid the Emerald–Diamond intersection. That stretch of road formed a bottleneck, and the enemy had already exploited it.

This time, instead of heading west on Jade to Emerald, or picking Diamond again, we decided to loop south of the towns on both roads and cross open desert to Emerald. We'd make a right turn onto the hardball road and get to the bridge as quickly as possible. We'd still have to drive through the Jade–Emerald and Diamond–Emerald intersections. There just wasn't any way to avoid that.

I concluded the brief by telling my Marines we'd be rolling by 2300—Alpha's four vehicles plus an Explosive Ordnance Detail Humvee to help us locate and defuse any bombs we found up around the bridge. Hopefully, they would help us avoid another nightmare like we experienced on Matador's first day. As exhausted as Bravo Section was by this point, I still had to press them into action. To support us, I'd given Staff Sergeant Robertson orders to swan south of the built-up areas and seize a hill to the south of the Jade–Emerald Intersection. There, they were to report any insurgent activity they saw. Also, since communication with al Qaim was tenuous at best once we hit Emerald, I wanted Bravo on some high ground so they could relay requests and updates back to battalion for me.

Okay, time to go. We loaded up and staged our vehicles at the front gate. Bravo headed out and took up positions on Hill 214. On the way, they encountered no opposition. Now it was our turn. Engines revved, drivers threw their rigs in gear, and we rumbled out the gate and into the Iraqi night.

We moved swiftly off road to the rendezvous point. Right on time, the two tanks from Camp Gannon appeared. We parked, and I jumped out to brief the tankers. The section leader turned out to be a master sergeant who'd been in armored units longer than I'd been alive. As we talked, I breathed a sigh of relief. It is always dicey working with a unit for the first time—doubly so if you don't have a chance to rehearse or conduct a more thorough brief. We didn't have time for either tonight. I sketched the plan, the master sergeant asked a few questions, and that was it. Time to go do it.

I took one last look around. My vehicle commanders had clustered around the master sergeant and me, looking on eagerly. I wanted them to have no illusions about what we faced.

"Look, every time we've been up to the bridge, we've been hit. In ten minutes, we're going to be in a fight. I want all of you to be prepared."

Nods all around. We mounted up and headed for Emerald, using our night vision goggles to see our way forward in the blackness.

We reached Emerald without incident. Alpha One led the way and made the right turn onto the hardball. In the process, we picked up a little speed. On the asphalt, the behemoth Mike 88 could almost hit ten miles an hour.

Emerald was the dividing line between Saddah on our right, and Karabilah on our left. We steamed north like a World War II northern Atlantic convoy, my fast escorts chained to the vital but ponderous auxiliary, while our gunners searched for signs of ambush. It seemed to take forever to reach the intersection with Route

Jade. The buildings on either side of the road looked empty again. Shuttered windows. No lights. No sign of movement or human existence. We rolled through a ghost town.

Ahead, Alpha One could see the next intersection. We'd hit Diamond in just a few minutes. Emerald actually bent around to the left, merging with Diamond for a few hundred meters before winding north again. This meant we'd have to hang a left, then a right to stay on Emerald.

Right then, a massive volley of rocket propelled grenades shot out of the night from Karabilah on our left side. Before my gunners could even return fire, they rippled off another volley. The air around us filled with zipping, sizzling RPGs. They began exploding between us and against the buildings on our right side.

Triggers down. My gunners squeezed off short, accurate bursts. The tanks opened fire with main gun rounds. Entire buildings erupted in fountains of dust and debris. More RPGs streaked through the column. I wanted to tell our drivers to punch it and blow through the kill zone but couldn't do that without leaving the Mike 88 behind, and that was not an option.

Barely managing ten miles an hour, we were caught in a slow motion nightmare. Insurgents appeared on rooftops all along our west flank, popping off full auto bursts with AKs or letting fly with an RPG.

Right away, it was clear this was a far more coordinated attack than we'd faced in the past. While their fellow jihadists fired at us from elevated positions, others used windows, alleys, and walls for concealment. We caught fleeting glimpses of them as they swung out to hammer at us as we rolled past their positions. In a flash, they'd be gone, ducking and moving to another spot.

Our lead tank uncorked a main gun round into a building at our ten o'clock. It exploded with such violence that debris rained down on us and sent a whirlwind of dust and smoke across the road ahead that played havoc with our night vision goggles. Soon, the entire area was sheathed in smoke and flames and concrete dust. We could barely see three or four feet beyond our rigs.

We drove deeper into the swirling clouds, the tanks relying on their thermal imaging systems to pick their targets. My gunners were virtually blind, though. Every few seconds, we'd see a flare through the smoke and another rocket would arrow past us.

A heavy machine gun raked the convoy. Soon more opened up until our vehicles were flayed with ricocheting 7.62 rounds. My gunners stayed on their weapons and fired back as best they could. My gunner, a character named Lance Corporal Jacobs, unleashed a stream of profanity every time he pulled the trigger. "Fuck you, motherfuckers! Get some!" As I listened to him, I recalled reading some combat memoirs where the writers described men shitting their pants in fear in the middle of combat. Not my Marines. They were hungry to fight the enemy.

Alpha One reached the Diamond intersection and veered left. We followed. Something exploded right in front of us. A moment later, Sergeant Francis came over the radio, "We just took an RPG to our rear!"

Lance Corporal Lamson goosed the throttle and their Humvee vanished into the cloud of debris. In the chaos, they missed the right turn needed to take us north on Emerald again. They plunged ahead, going due west on Diamond—right into the middle of the insurgent ambush line.

"Alpha One! You've missed the turn," I radioed to Francis.

Shit. Now what?

Throughout our training, we learned never to hesitate to make a decision. If you lingered over options, you stood the chance of letting events overcome you, and that's when bad things happened. You ran the risk of letting the enemy seize the initiative. You ended up playing catch-up instead of being able to think ahead to plan your next move.

Make a move. What are we going to do?

We couldn't leave Alpha One by themselves, unsupported in this chaos. I radioed the other drivers and told them to stay together. We'd go catch up to Sergeant Francis.

With dreadful slowness, we crept past the right turn and pushed west on Diamond after Alpha One. For a second, the smoke cleared and I saw them fifty meters up the road, waiting for us. Gass was on his .50, suppressing targets. All of us were taking hits from those damned machine guns.

We'd have to turn around on Diamond, double back through the kill zone and hit the turn north on Emerald. I looked out to our left and saw nothing but muzzle flashes. The rooftops crawled with enemy fighters.

"Okay, Alpha One, when we reach you, turn around and we'll follow. Take it slow. I don't want to lose anyone else."

"Roger, sir."

One of the tanks blasted another building into heaps of broken concrete, kicking up another cloud of smoke and dust. It swirled over our rigs, obscuring our night vision almost completely.

Another volley of rockets rippled through us. We had to have been hard to see. The rockets were not nearly as accurate this time.

Finally, we reached Francis' waiting rig. Lamson pulled a U-turn, crossed the road, and moved back toward the rear of the convoy in the eastbound lane.

They ran head-on into a vehicle that barreled out of the smoke between two buildings and careened straight for the rear of the column. Francis' rig stood in the way. Gass tried to get his .50 on target, but he simply had no time.

The ground suddenly convulsed as if a fault line had given way. An unendurable roar—like the sound of a dozen freight trains speeding through the night—blasted our ears. A split-second later, a concussion wave rocked our vehicles. Night became day as hellish orange glow swelled behind us. The sound never seemed to end. It roared on and on until it seemed our skulls would split or our eardrums would burst.

The orange glow dimmed. A roiling cloud of smoke and debris mushroomed out through the back of the column. Chunks of metal, bits of concrete swept across our rigs.

"Alpha One? What happened?" I heard myself say into the radio's handset.

No answer. Was I deafened by whatever just hit us, or were they not responding? I wasn't sure. The massive explosion played havoc with my senses.

"Alpha One?"

No response.

Lieutenant Leahy's voice squawked over the radio, "That was the largest explosion I've ever heard. What happened?"

He was at least two or three kilometers away.

"Alpha One?"

Nothing.

Holy shit. I just got five Marines killed.

I reached for the handset and called over to Bravo Section. "Get a MEDEVAC bird here as quick as you can. We'll meet it at the LZ by the bridge."

I heard Sergeant Robertson acknowledge the order. Then, without thinking, I flung open my armored door and sprinted into the night.

CHAPTER SIXTEEN

A Night of Heroes

The dust choked and clogged my lungs. My throat burned, eyes watered. My legs seemed to work on their own accord, pumping furiously while my hands gripped my M4. Dimly, I could hear my gunners pouring fire back at the insurgents. I ran on, bullets cracking overhead, the din of battle drowning out even the sound of my own rasping breath.

One thought dominated all else: *Get to my Marines.* The thought of them dead or in distress filled me with dread and spurred me forward through the firefight.

Hunks of blackened metal smoldered in the street. One of the tanks fired another main gun round. The ground shook again, and a fresh wave of debris poured across the battlefield.

I passed our last rig and kept running until a shape materialized out of the gloom. It had once been a Humvee, but its entire front had been demolished.

Alpha One.

Oh no. No.

The front passenger side door creaked open in slow motion. I moved around the wreck, hoping to find someone alive.

A boot, burned black hit the ground next to the passenger side. With my eyes, I followed it up past shredded pants and a tattered shirtsleeve. A hand, blackened and smeared with blood, grasped the armored door. Slowly, Sergeant Francis pulled himself and Corporal Goldsmith from the remains of his Humvee. As he did, he turned to see me running for him.

The whole right side of his face looked like melted wax, burned and torn and covered in blood.

"Francis! Francis!" I screamed. I was never so happy to see him.

He flashed a weary grin just as I reached him. "We took a good hit, but we're okay. I think we'll all make it, sir."

"What happened?" I asked. His smile made me marvel at his toughness.

"VBIED," Francis replied, meaning a suicide car bomber.

Francis got Goldie clear of the Humvee's wreckage. He'd also been burned, and had started convulsing violently. We tried to assist him, but he couldn't speak. He'd gone into shock, and I was worried that he might be bleeding internally.

Just then, Lamson appeared on the turret. He'd climbed out of the driver's side and scaled the shattered Humvee, ignoring the heavy machine gun fire that laced the area with tracers. He reached down into the turret, grabbed Gass and heaved him upward.

Gass's head appeared over the turret ring. For a second, I couldn't register what I was seeing. His helmet looked wrong. Then it dawned on me. A seven-inch triangular shaped hunk of shrapnel had gone right through his Kevlar helmet. Its tip was embedded in his brain.

A fresh burst of gunfire sparked off the Humvee. Lamson heaved and pulled until he had Gass's torso clear of the turret. One more effort, and Gass's legs slipped free. But the enemy had the range now. They poured fire on the rig, and Gass jerked violently as a bullet struck him in the elbow.

Seconds later, Lamson dragged him down off the rig to the comparative safety of the driver's side.

Flames boiled up over the demolished engine compartment. Lamson grabbed a fire extinguisher and exposed himself to the incoming fire to douse the growing flames.

With the Humvee destroyed, we had to get the wounded to safety and cover the men while getting them out. I ran back to the last vehicle in the column, grabbed their radio and ordered the tanks to provide front and rear security.

"Kill any vehicles that come at us, clear? Nobody comes close."

"Roger, sir!" called the master sergeant in charge of the Abrams section. His tracks took up position. Another vehicle made a run at us. The tanks blew it to pieces. They were doing a tremendous job.

"Okay, get the wounded to the Mike 88," I ordered.

Lamson half carried, half dragged Gass to the Mike 88, where a corpsman began to work on him. He ran back to Alpha One for Old Goldie and got him to the Mike 88 as well. Rockets sailed overhead. More machine gun fire ripped the asphalt around us. Lamson seemed utterly fearless.

He dodged and weaved back to Alpha One, and I noticed he'd been wounded in the leg.

"Lamson, get back to the Mike 88."

"I'm good sir, just bruised my leg. I'm staying," he shouted over the din of battle. Without waiting for a reply, he wielded his rifle, took cover behind the wreckage, and began searching for targets.

Francis and Lance Corporal Hauslyak reached the Mike 88. Hauslyak had been wounded in the leg, foot, and ankle with shrapnel and was also suffering from a severe concussion. A quick discussion with the corpsman convinced me we had three urgent surgical cases—Gass, Francis, and Old Goldie. Gass and Francis in particular had lost a lot of blood. The corpsman told me we needed to get them out as fast as we could.

"Sergeant Cherry," I called on the radio. "Bring your vehicle up here and prepare to tow Alpha One."

"On my way, Sir."

We had standing orders to never leave a destroyed or damaged vehicle to the enemy. They could gather intelligence material from the wreck, gather weapons, or even gain propaganda value from them. In 2003 and 2004, the wire services ran photographs of insurgents celebrating around burning American vehicles. It spurred recruiting in Muslim countries and the images were seen globally.

I looked over Alpha One. Figuring out how to tow this wreck was going to take time. Our wounded Marines didn't have time to waste.

Do we leave the rig? Should I call Sergeant Cherry off?

Again, my Marine training kicked in. *In a crisis moment, there are always multiple paths you can choose. Be decisive. Pick one and run with it. Indecision will kill your men.*

Right there in the street, amid the smoke and flames, the churning dust and flying bullets, I forced myself to come up with a plan of action.

We'd split up. I'd take Alpha Three and escort the Mike 88 back through the kill zone and up Emerald to the landing zone behind War Pig One. Leahy's men could cover us while we loaded up the MEDEVAC chopper and got my Marines out of here. Meanwhile, the rest of the column would stay here and protect Sergeant Cherry's men as they hooked up Alpha One and towed it north.

I ran over to Alpha Three, whose vehicle commander was Lance Corporal Miller. "Miller, listen up, Stud. I gotta lead the wounded outta here and I need you to take me."

Miller was a wild one, all balls and steel. I knew if anyone could pull this off, he and his crew could. He looked me in the eye and said, "Fuck it, let's do it, Sir."

We mounted up and Miller's driver, Corporal Hernandez, weaved around Alpha One and waited for the Mike 88 to turn around and join us. A minute later, we could see its hulking shape materialize out of the smoke and pull up behind us.

"Okay, let's go."

We were fifty meters from the intersection with Emerald and the left turn we needed to make to get to the LZ. That fifty meters seemed to take forever to cross, crawling along at ten miles an hour. Behind us, the entire column laid down suppressing fire. My gunners chewed through their ready ammunition supply. The tankers scanned for targets. Fortunately, we didn't take any fire as we pulled clear.

Then we made the left turn.

Rockets exploded on both sides of our rigs. Machine guns lashed the Mike 88. Our max speed nowhere approached the sense of urgency I felt, and the whole scene became almost surreal, like one of those terrible dreams where you're trying to run from some threat but you never get anywhere.

Three hundred meters from Lieutenant Leahy's position now. We inched forward, fretting over every meter. The LZ was right in front of his lines. Another few minutes and we'd be there. Almost . . . almost.

"We're hit!" the Mike 88 called. An RPG had slammed into its armored hide. Seconds later, another hit home. The behemoth made a large slow target, and these jihadists could shoot.

All we could do was keep going. Another volley of rockets exploded around us. More machine gun fire. Lance Corporal Jacobs, our gunner, did his best to shoot back, but there was no way he could achieve fire superiority. We were totally overwhelmed with incoming.

Behind us, another civilian car bolted through the smoke and flames, heading straight for the remains of Alpha One. The tankers hit it on the fly with a spectacular shot that touched off a massive secondary explosion. Once again, the ground quaked and a concussion wave nearly knocked us down.

Jesus Christ, they were throwing everything at us.

We kept crawling forward. Two hundred meters to go.

The back end of our Humvee tilted up. A concussion wave slammed through us as another thunderous roar demolished what was left of our hearing. The rig slewed hard left and fishtailed. Hernandez managed to mitigate the skid and hit the gas at the same time.

"IED!" somebody shouted. We'd just taken a near miss from a roadside bomb. It had exploded behind and to our right with enough force to blow a 14,000-pound armored vehicle off course.

"Keep going!" Miller shouted. His voice sounded like he was calling up to us from the depths of a well.

Another explosion wracked us. This one shook us so hard, I thought my fillings would break loose.

"We're hit! IED," the Mike 88 called.

"Status?" I asked.

"Track's blown, sir! Hull's warped. We're down."

Fuck. The bastards just scored a mobility kill. We were trapped in the kill zone, with no way to get the wounded to the landing zone. There was no room in our Humvee or any of the others back on Route Diamond. We needed help.

I radioed War Pig One. "The Mike 88's down. We need vehicle support to get our wounded out. Can you assist?"

Gunnery Sergeant Harmon's reassuring voice crackled back, "We're already on the way, Lieutenant."

A wave of relief rushed through me. We wouldn't be trapped out here and overrun.

Time to level everything. I keyed my radio handset and called in the Cobra gunships, giving them coordinates on the west side and to our south. The skinny, sinister-looking birds swooped down out of the black night and raked the area with Hellfire missiles and 20mm cannon fire. One of the pilots later told me this was the first time he'd ever seen RPG-carrying insurgents through his night vision. He saw them running on the rooftops and firing into our vehicles.

Not for long. The gunships obliterated the neighborhood. The fighting raged on. We hung on and waited for help.

It was not long in coming. Gunny Harmon raced down Emerald and hove into view aboard a 998 Humvee—one of the high back variants with makeshift armor around the back bed. These things were terribly vulnerable to enemy fire, but Harmon never hesitated. His driver pulled up right alongside the Mike 88, and they dismounted in the middle of the firefight to offload our wounded. Gunny Harmon was nothing short of a warrior that day, and his rescue of us was one of many instances that underscored his courage and selflessness.

The Cobras made another strafing pass. A Hellfire rocked the buildings. Meanwhile, the tanks rounded the corner, main guns adding to the terrible carnage. By the time the rest of the column reached us, the firing had died away at last.

Gunny Harmon and his vehicles sped north to get our wounded to the landing zone. Without any way to tow the M88, we left it for the time being, though we could see it the entire time and made sure no insurgents got close to it. Sergeant Cherry, dragging Alpha One behind his Humvee, wound around the wreck as the rest of the column came north, the two tanks suppressing anything that moved. Cherry had done an outstanding job in a very tough situation. How he found a way to tow that rig still baffles me, but that's a Marine for you.

Finally, we staggered into War Pig One's perimeter. I told Miller to get over to the LZ so I could check on our wounded Marines. When we got there, I found Gass waiting quietly for the chopper to show up. He was sitting down with his back against Harmon's 998, smoking a cigarette. The wicked chunk of shrapnel still stuck out of his head and helmet. Blood had caked around the wound and dried in slicks down both sides of his face.

He looked the picture of despair.

"Gass, how you doing?" I asked him.

He looked up at me with haunted eyes. "I can't believe I let 'em hit us, sir."

His words staggered me.

"I should have taken it out. This is all my fault."

"Gass, listen to me," I said sternly, trying my best to not look at the jagged piece of metal embedded in his skull, "this is NOT your fault. You did everything right. You got me?"

He just stared vacantly into the night. Blood still streamed from his head wound, and he was clearly concussed. Nevertheless, he didn't give a thought of himself, only his duty to his fellow Marines.

"Gass. This isn't your fucking fault."

He nodded slowly, but his eyes refused to agree.

I looked down at this despondent Marine who gave no thought to himself or his condition. All he cared about was his job and the men he was sworn to protect. I knew right then that I would never find myself in more selfless company.

Our unit, 3/2 Marines, is known as the Betio Bastards. In 1943, the battalion took part in Operation Galvanic, the invasion of Tarawa. Betio Island was the main target of the landing force, and the Marines faced an entrenched enemy with pre-registered fields of fire on the beaches. The first assault waves were nearly wiped out by machine gun and mortar fire as they waded through the lagoon onto the narrow beach. It took seventy-six hours to clear the island—which was barely two thousand yards long and a few score wide. Over three thousand Marines and sailors died or fell wounded during what became the most ferocious close quarter battle ever fought by the U.S. Marine Corps.

That was the legacy of my unit—a legacy of determination, heroism, and stoic resolve in the face of unimaginable adversity. On May 10, 2008, my Marines proved they were cut from the same cloth.

CHAPTER SEVENTEEN

Siege at Ramana Bridge

In the distance, we could see the Cobras hosing the west side of Emerald even as my men consolidated behind War Pig One. By the time they finished their strafing runs, a lull descended on the battlefield. The insurgents who hit us were either dead or had beat feet to avoid the marauding Cobras.

The lull gave us a chance to get the Mike 88 and the down Abrams out of the bridge perimeter. Sergeant Miller's remaining tank hooked up to the wrecked M1. As he did that, the rest of my column rolled into the perimeter. We'd have to use one of the remaining tanks to drag the Mike 88 back to al Qaim.

I went to go talk to the M88 crew, who had come north aboard Gunny Harmon's rigs.

"Guys, we're going to get you out of here," I told them. "We'll use one of the tanks to tow your track back to al Qaim. Sergeant Miller's going to pull the downed Abrams out. We'll leave my Alpha One here for now."

"Roger, sir."

I turned to go coordinate this with Master Sergeant Martin. Before I could walk away, though, the M88's vehicle commander called to me in a butter-smooth Southern accent, "Hey, sir . . . "

I swung around to face him. He looked weary and tense—about the way I felt. Apparently, he saw it in my face as well. "Tough town tonight, sir."

"Yes."

"You can't put that on yourself."

How could I not?

"Thank you, Master Sergeant."

We moved swiftly under the watchful eyes of the Cobras lurking nearby. Within a few minutes, we had two M1s hooked up to the wrecked tracks, ready to make the run south. They had plenty of firepower to deal with any threat, but we took no chances. I watched them rumble south down Emerald to disappear into the smoke still boiling up over the battlefield. The Cobras escorted them back to al Qaim. Just having the birds overhead acted as deterrent. Besides, the enemy had had enough for one night. The tracks made it back to base without incident.

The town we'd fought our way through—Karabilah was its name—had been devastated by the fighting. I later learned that just prior to Matador, the foreign fighters moved into the area and angered the local smugglers. Karabilah, like most of these border villages, had been controlled by smuggler militias for years—even before we invaded in 2003. The foreign fighters were seen as inter-lopers, and a battle between the groups broke out. The locals lost, and the foreigners quickly implanted a reign of terror to establish control over the area. That's when the checkpoints were set up and people began to disappear into the hellish torture chambers that we subsequently found that summer during another offensive.

Not that any of this mattered on the night of May 10. We'd been hit hard by a well-coordinated and disciplined enemy. Getting the two downed tracks out of the area required giving up two-thirds of our tank support, leaving us with my three vehicles, the EOD rig, and War Pig One's ten Humvees.

With the recovery operation complete, Lieutenant Leahy and I met to come up with a game plan for our situation. There'd be no relief in place—I simply didn't have the strength to hold the position without War Pig One. Leahy and his men would have to stay out a little longer. They were really the unsung heroes of this operation.

We deployed in a long line facing south. War Pig One pushed out to the west a little bit, and my men established positions east of Emerald. Before we risked any more vehicles, though, we sent the EOD team to search the area thoroughly. We'd hunker down and hold the bridge until battalion relieved us.

The rest of 3/2 had crossed the river on the pontoon bridge finally erected by the Army engineers. Those men pulled off a near-miracle constructing that thing while under fire. When it was finished, our Marines pulled out of New Ubaydi—though much of it still had not been cleared—and swept north expecting heavy resistance.

The enemy had vanished. The battalion moved west along the opposite bank of the Euphrates, detaining a lot of suspects but making virtually no contact. Hopefully, we'd be able to establish a link across the Ramana Bridge with them in the days to come.

We settled down and rotated some of our Marines to have them try to get some sleep. Come dawn, we had no doubt the insurgents would return.

And they did. With the first streaks of daylight, mortar shells rained down on us. We shifted our vehicles constantly to avoid getting hit, but even so the insurgents came very close several times. As the morning wore on, small teams of fighters carrying AKs and RPGs used the terrain to the south to infiltrate around us. We fought back with our heavy weapons and called in a few airstrikes as well. Fortunately, Lieutenant Leahy had a very experienced JTAC major with him. A JTAC—short for Joint Terminal Attack Controller—specializes in calling in air and artillery strikes. He became our fist of God. Whenever we could identify an insurgent position that we couldn't knock out with our own weapons, the major brought the heavy stuff raining down on their heads. Without him and all the firepower he controlled, we'd have been in serious trouble.

The day wore on and the sporadic attacks increased. We fought back, our lone remaining tank providing heavy support with its main gun, while my men dismounted on occasion to unleash a Javelin guided anti-armor missile on a target. A Javelin is a devilish weapon. Seconds before it impacts on whatever it's been aimed at, it suddenly veers straight up for several hundred feet before arcing downward to slam into the target's roof. Designed to knock out armored vehicles by hitting them in their most vulnerable spot—their thin-skinned decks—the Javelin also functions as an excellent weapon in urban fights. Taking fire from a rooftop that can't be suppressed with a .50 cal? Let fly a Javelin and it'll smoke everyone on that building. They're simply devastating.

Late that morning, we caught sight of a group of males ducking into a gas station's garage near the intersection with Route Diamond. Minutes later, they dashed out, armed with RPGs and rifles. They ducked around some nearby buildings and disappeared. Then rockets exploded around our rigs.

Not long after, another group of men slipped into the garage to reappear heavily armed and gunning for a fight. They laid down fire and lobbed more RPGs at us. It didn't take a NASA scientist to figure out the insurgents had squirreled away a weapons cache at the local gas and gulp.

I wanted to end this bullshit. I called up Master Sergeant Carroccia and asked him to blast the garage with his 120mm gun. His crew acquired the target and let fly with one of its forty-one-pound shells. Direct hit. Smoke boiled out of the gas station, and we could see one wall had a huge hole blown into it.

Later that afternoon, the insurgents returned and stocked up again. Somehow, we'd missed the cache. This time, I called my Javelin team, who scored another direct hit on the garage. A few more tank rounds and I figured we'd taken care of that enemy resupply point.

Across the river, the drive west continued. Lima 3/25, the reservists from Ohio, had taken heavy casualties during the fighting in Ubaydi. Now, as they swept along the Euphrates, we could hear them closing on the north end of the Ramana Bridge.

That's when an Amtrac, a lightly armored amphibious vehicle, First Platoon, 3/25 struck a land mine only a few hundred meters from our position. We heard the explosion, saw the smoke and flames rising behind us, and then heard the cries for help over the radio.

We couldn't go to their aid. The bridge had not yet been cleared, and we were almost certain it had been mined by the enemy. Besides, we couldn't leave our blocking position without exposing Lieutenant Leahy's left flank.

The track burned as 3/25's fellow Marines and my friend and mentor, Lieutenant Diana from our weapons company, frantically tried to free the men trapped inside.

Inside Alpha Three, I could see the color drain from my men's faces. They looked absolutely stricken. Then the track's ready ammunition began cooking off. With each detonation, I could see my men flinch. I ordered everyone to face south. I didn't want my men to see what was unfolding. Hearing over the radio was bad enough.

Five Marines died inside the track. Everyone else inside suffered wounds of varying degrees. The driver was pulled from the wreckage, his face bloody and missing teeth. The explosion had slammed his head against the vehicle's front console. Another Marine emerged with his uniform on fire. Quick-thinking men nearby got him on the ground and put the flames out with a fire extinguisher.

Of all my experiences in combat, this is the one that haunts me the most. The feeling of complete impotence in the face of such profound tragedy scarred us all that day.

After the Lima 3/25 track was destroyed, the insurgents seemed to melt away from us. A short lull developed in the afternoon. We moved our rigs around anyway and kept alert for mortar fire. The enemy mortar men impressed all of us with their accuracy. They came within thirty meters of my rig at one point after only a few ranging shots. They also moved around a lot, which made trying to knock them out very difficult. By the time we established the point of origin of the last incoming volley, they had already slipped away.

It made me wonder if their tubes were fixed in concealed locations—like spider holes—and the crews simply circulated around between them. They were that elusive.

After evening prayer, we got hit again. Having prayed to Allah, the insurgents grabbed their weapons and threw the works at us again—machine gun fire, rockets, and mortars. Once again, we saw groups of them infiltrate into the garage, stock up with weapons and ammo, and then dash out into Karabilah to use the buildings as cover for their next assault on us.

Frustrated, we poured more fire on the gas station, which by now looked like little more than a pile of rubble. Somehow, we never generated that exceedingly satisfying secondary explosion that would have signaled the end to that weapon's cache. Perhaps, it had been hidden underground, which is how it survived our onslaught.

As night fell, our men were exhausted. Leahy's Marines in particular had seen three straight days of action with little relief. My Alpha Section had spent most of the day mounted up in the cramped confines of our vehicles. We'd started to run low on fuel and water. And by dinner, we'd finished off the last of the food we'd brought with us. The truth was when we left al Qaim the night before, we did not anticipate staying out long. We figured we'd relieve Leahy and hold the ground until battalion could send up another force, allowing us to return to our QRF role.

Well, we just didn't have the assets available and we had to stay.

Fortunately, Lima 3/25 and Kilo Company had swept the north bank of the river and we now could get resupplied from the far side of the Euphrates. Neither Lieutenant Leahy nor I relished the thought of sending the motor transport guys up the gantlet of Route Emerald again.

After sunset, we sent the EOD team over to the bridge to make sure it wasn't mined with IEDs. We also needed to make sure the bridge could handle one of our enormous seven ton trucks. Using the darkness to cloak their movement, the bomb disposal troops crept up to the bridge and quickly discovered the south side was riddled with IEDs. Carefully, they disarmed them and backed off to our position. Without their efforts, the seven ton probably would have been destroyed, and the bridge may have been critically damaged as well.

Instead, the resupply went smoothly. We stocked up on water and MREs, and stuffed our Humvees with boxes of ammunition. We'd burned through almost half our load for the crew served weapons during the battle in Karabilah the night before, and by the evening of the 11th, things were getting pretty tight. The fresh belts and drums of 40mm grenades were much appreciated.

Still, the last three days had taken their toll on all of us. My platoon, or units attached to it, had taken nine wounded in action in the course of our many firefights. I was grateful it wasn't any worse. Without the swift action of our helicopter pilots, I have no doubt we would have lost several Marines to their wounds. Now, as we faced another night in the desert with the enemy moving around us, I wondered how much more my men could take.

We slept in short spurts—fifteen or twenty minutes at a time at the most. Through the night, I moved among my rigs, talking to my men and doing my best to reassure them. They looked grim and exhausted. Beneath their weariness, I also detected rock-solid resolve. After what happened to our brothers in 3/25, they wanted blood.

Every now and then, Lieutenant Diana would call over to me and check on how things were going. When I had first arrived in the battalion, I came under a fair amount of scrutiny. Usually, the weapon's company platoons are given to first lieutenants who have much more experience than a green second lieutenant. I'd been assigned the slot and had to learn as I went. Gabe saw something in me and reached out. He gave me leadership advice, and he helped me with training plans and how to deal with personnel issues. He was always working to better himself as a leader and as an officer. I took a cue from that and did the same. In the end, much of the success I had with my platoon was a direct result of his friendship. For the rest of the time we were out at the bridge, Gabe made a point of touching base with me a couple of times a day. Hearing his voice over the radio that night did wonders for my morale.

The next morning, we saw another gaggle of unarmed men dash into the garage on the corner of Emerald and Diamond. From somewhere in the rubble, they found more rockets and rifles. Enough was enough. If main gun rounds from our tank couldn't get the job done, airstrikes could.

We called in the Cobras, who made a strafing run on the building. Even that didn't get the job done. More insurgents came and went, and the volume of fire aimed at us increased as the morning continued.

I went over to confer with our JTAC major. "Look, sir," I told him, "We've tried everything to destroy that cache. Nothing's worked. They're still using it as a resupply point, and I'm fuckin' tired of getting shot at."

"What do you have in mind, Lieutenant?" he asked me.

"Let's put a JDAM on it." A JDAM is a satellite-guided bomb carried by our jet fighter-bombers. They are the most accurate air-delivered ordnance ever devised. They're also extremely powerful and can do tremendous damage if used on the right targets.

The right target here being that goddamned gas station.

"Roger that," the major said to me.

We called in an F-18. It swooped overhead and dropped a 500-pound JDAM. The bomb nailed the gas station and the entire facility disintegrated in flames. When the smoke cleared, there was nothing left but a blackened crater and some debris. Finally.

When battalion passed the word of what we'd done up to regiment, I received an angry call over the radio. "You'd better be able to answer some pointed questions about that 500 pounder," one of our staff officers informed me.

The comment enraged me. Why was I being second-guessed on something like that? From the sound of it, somebody up the chain of command thought that I had done something wrong by employing such a destructive weapon. True, we tried to minimize the damage we inflicted on the local towns whenever possible, but right now Karabilah was overrun with enemy fighters who were trying to kill my men. I would have used anything at my disposal to wipe them out.

The major overheard the conversation and drove his Humvee over to see me. We both dismounted and he said to me, "Don't worry about that shit. I've got your back."

I breathed a sigh of relief.

Despite regiment's suspicions that we'd employed too much force, the sight of the garage getting wiped out cheered the men up. But we still faced incoming mortar fire that made movement outside our Humvees very risky. As a precaution, we stayed inside them for hours at a time, our laboring air conditioners unable to counter the desert heat. By late afternoon, we felt like sardines in a furnace.

After evening prayer, they hit us again with mortars and rockets. Occasional bursts of AK or machine gun fire kicked up sand around our vehicles, but it wasn't particularly accurate. We called in more fire support missions and airstrikes. The Cobras became our constant companions, unleashing Hellfire missiles and long bursts of 20mm cannon fire into the wadi to our south that had become a veritable insurgent highway to our positions.

The next morning, May 13, the enemy employed a new method of attack. Mortars had rained down on us in periodic volleys, which forced us to keep moving our vehicles. A few RPGs had been lobbed at us from long range to no effect. The occasional rifle or machine gun fire we took had been inaccurate and the least of our worries.

That was until a bullet nearly killed my gunner, Cpl. Josh Langsdon. It bounced off the armored shield protecting him in the turret. Another few inches and it would have hit him in the head. A few minutes passed, and another well-placed shot struck our remaining tank. It bounced off the turret near the commander's hatch, narrowly missing Master Sergeant Carroccia.

Sniper!

We shuffled positions again while searching for the shooter. The day wore on and he took periodic shots at us. He was an accomplished sniper. By now, we'd been living for days out of our rigs, bailing out only to go to the bathroom. The mortars made that dangerous enough, but with a sniper out there, just taking a whizz could prove fatal.

At last, Langsdon caught sight of the sniper on top of a nearby roof in Karabilah. I ordered my gunners to concentrate their fire and just inundate the target area with lead. On command, everyone opened up and shredded the building's entire front façade. The sniper either died in the maelstrom of lead or broke contact and fled. I didn't really care which. All I cared about was the well-being of my Marines. Life had become an exercise in survival and protection.

On May 14, Operation Matador came to an end. After the fighting in Ubaydi, our regimental combat team didn't encounter much heavy resistance once across the Euphrates. The sweep yielded thirty-nine detainees, and Regimental Intel estimated it killed some 125 insurgents, mostly in Ubaydi.

We had no idea how many foreign fighters met Allah at our hands. We had no time to count or conduct any sort of battle damage assessment. Whatever the number, the strength and frequency of their attacks against us decreased by the morning of the 14th. We'd certainly thinned their ranks out.

Problem was, we could not hold the ground. With the battalion spread all over the area, we had no choice but to leave Saddah and Karabilah to the foreign fighters once Operation Matador came to a conclusion.

We headed to Camp Gannon, our remote outpost to the west. Lieutenant Leahy and I packed up and pulled out, towing Alpha One's remains with us. After spending the afternoon at Gannon, we slipped back home to al Qaim in time for dinner. Behind us, the insurgents collected and buried their dead.

We'd be back for them in July in what became known as Operation Spear. It would be three months before we had the strength to clear the towns on the south bank of the Euphrates. Until that time, the reign of terror these "holy warriors" inflicted on the Iraqi population knew no boundaries.

Matador was at best a mixed success. Kilo Company fought alongside Lima 3/25 through the entire operation, suffering one Marine killed in action. Lima Company paid the heaviest price. Between the house-to-house fighting in Ubaydi and the Amtrac that was destroyed on the 11th, the reservists suffered nine killed and twenty-one wounded in action. Their suffering continued later that summer, when another Amtrac hit an IED and fourteen more men from the company died in the blast and fire. When we saw the company's surviving members toward the end of the deployment, they looked like zombies.

When I returned to the battalion COC that night of the 14th, I fully expected to be grilled by one of the JAG lawyers from regiment. Why had I dropped that bomb? What was the target? How did I know there were no civilians in the area? I could see the whole line of questioning—I had dealt with a JAG witch hunt already once before that nearly derailed my military career before it began. I didn't trust them, and I was furious to think that some pencil pusher sitting safe in an FOB would have the audacity to question the decisions made by an officer in the middle of battle. I had absolutely no doubt using that JDAM was the right call. It was the only thing we had at our disposal capable of destroying that weapons cache.

Not that I wasn't doubting some of my other decisions. During lulls in the fighting, my brain immediately clicked back to those violent, chaotic minutes on Emerald and Diamond during the ambush on May 10. The Academy trained us to be decisive and make snap decisions. As officers, it was our responsibility to be able to process massive amounts of information rapidly and come up with a course of action.

I did that. But had I made the right calls? The situation haunted me. Should I have waited until Sergeant Cherry had hooked up Alpha One? We could have all gone north together at that point. Would those four or five minutes made the difference between life and death for our wounded suffering silently in the Mike 88?

I expected to be hammered with some very direct questions on my conduct during the ambush. The loss of so many Marines under my command had eaten away at me, almost to the point where I suffered a crisis in confidence. Nine men in a week of combat. What had I done wrong? What lessons could I learn? My mind obsessed over those questions.

Inside the COC, I braced for the shit storm. Captain Ford Phillips, my company commander, spotted me as I came through the door. He swiftly took me aside. *Here it comes*, I thought.

"Brian, excellent job. You did everything right out there. Thank you."

My jaw almost fell open. Those were the last words I had expected to hear. I greatly admired Captain Phillips and had long since learned he always meant what he said. His words were never designed to make somebody feel better. They were designed to make a man a better officer and Marine. Always.

His words eased the pain of the last seven days but did not erase the guilt that I felt. To this day, I question the decisions I made that night. That is the onus of command: you always bear the responsibility for those under you. When they suffer wounds or are killed by the enemy, it is impossible for an officer not to second-guess himself and own part of their suffering or deaths. As leaders, we understand control. That is where we operate. Having it is a comfort.

But combat and the enemy strips that away at times. Once the bullets fly and the violent chaos of a firefight reigns, control becomes an illusion. A platoon commander cannot determine which enemy bullets will strike what vehicles. He cannot select the moment when an insurgent triggers an IED. He cannot dictate who survives and who doesn't. All he can do is fight back and try to demolish the chaos with enough firepower that the enemy dies or runs away. Almost everything else is beyond a leader's control.

Those limits of leadership were never drilled into us at the Academy. When I experienced it for the first time during Operation Matador, I came gradually to understand on an intellectual level. But in my heart, I still wonder if I could have done something else that might have saved my Marines from harm. I still spend sleepless nights replaying every moment in my head, hoping men like Robert Gass and Jonathan Lowe can forgive me.

Later, to my utter astonishment, I received the Silver Star for Operation Matador. This was the third-highest award for courage under fire after the Medal of Honor and Navy Cross. I had no idea my chain of command put me in for the award. I'd been busy writing my men up for awards of their own—Lamson and Mcelhinny both earned richly deserved Bronze Stars for their bravery in battle. I took tremendous pride in their awards, but mine left me full of guilt. I did not deserve such an honor. My platoon did. This was their award, not mine.

I wore it only for them and the opportunity to tell their story. During those seven days in May, my Betio Bastards wrote a new page in the Corps' long legacy of valor.

PART IV

Reinvention

CHAPTER EIGHTEEN

The Fifth Stage

Las Vegas, August 2008

I feel Teressa's arms around me, warm and strong. She's a bright and vital spirit with plenty of Pennsylvania ruggedness girding her heart. I fell for her the first time we met, though I didn't let on just how hard until much later.

Still, this is not an easy moment for me, and it's not the man I need to be for my family. A slip, a moment of weakness, that's what this is. A few years ago, I probably would not have forgiven myself for it. But marriage and maturity has shown me there's more to being a man than suppressing emotions and playing the role of the tough stoic.

She holds me against her, our cheeks touching as she whispers a few words of comfort to me. At once, I need to hear them and need to be strong enough to not ever have them tumble into my ear again. The moment is at once disorienting, humiliating, and consoling.

Teressa's always been a fighter; tough and independent, she put herself through college by working three

179

jobs in Philly and Scranton on top of being a part of the Philadelphia Eagles cheerleading squad. I've never seen her ask for anything. In the five years we've known each other, I doubt I've seen her cry more than four times. When times get rugged, she handles it. When I was in Iraq for my second deployment, there were times I'd get angry. She didn't seem to need me, or even miss me. There I was, thousands of miles away, feeling like half my heart had been torn away. During our occasional phone calls, I never heard her sob. I never heard her complain. Such deployments do one of two things to a young couple: they either destroy the relationship or cement it. We were lucky. The quiet loyalty we shared fused us together.

I turn my head to kiss Teressa on her cheek. Her lips find me instead. For an instant, I feel the intensity of our connection. Profound. Life affirming, like nothing else I've ever known. Its power has been our greatest strength, one that has held us together despite distance, combat, and plenty of uncertainty.

She stands up and takes my hands. "We're going to be late."

I slip off the bed to splash some water on my face. The weekend has seen my emotions roller coaster to every extreme. Now, after a sleepless night, I'm just drained. When I return from the bathroom, I've composed myself again.

I finish packing up. The last item to go into my bag is the WEC light heavyweight belt. Though Cantwell is the champ now, the belt each previous winner earned in the cage becomes a lifelong symbol of that achievement. All the former champs keep theirs, and per WEC regulations, we bring it back for title fights.

Carefully, I tuck it away and zip up my bag. We take one last look around to make sure we didn't leave anything behind, then we're out the door for the airport. In the cab, I sit in silence. Okay, the truth is, I'm brooding. The morning after, and I'm still going through the classic five stages of grief. Well, I've hit four of them so far anyway. Denial: yeah, did that last night while I walked into the arena. Bargaining: did plenty of that during the fight. Anger: oh yeah, let's just call that one self-loathing for now. Depression: this morning was a new low, that's for sure.

What about acceptance? Not there yet. Not by a long shot. The morning's reminder of why and for whom I fight managed to underscore the other stages and take me further away from any sign of getting over this quickly.

I look out the window as we drive down the Vegas strip. Things are pretty quiet this Sunday morning, but the strip's always a spectacle. Right now, I want it to be a distraction, but my brain refuses to shut down. I find myself going through the fight again, second-guessing everything I did. I have no doubt my mind will torture me for a long time to come, just like it has over the decisions I made during the May 10 firefight in Karabilah.

Yeah. There's a pattern there. As I realize it, I can't help but think about my Marines again. How many were watching last night? I flashed back to Gass, sitting there at the LZ with that triangular chunk of shrapnel embedded in his head. Did he watch last night? The thought sent a wave of shame through me again.

Gass came home to face multiple brain surgeries. He'll have a U-shaped scar on the side of his head for the rest of his life from them. By the time the surgeons were done, he had lost the ability to speak. He went through intensive speech therapy and had to relearn the art of communication. He never gave up and now lives on his own in South

Carolina. Last time we talked, he told me he was going back to school.

And then there was Staff Sergeant Francis. A lot of guys with his wounds would have ended up taking a medical discharge, but not this die-hard leatherneck. He got as far as Germany, stayed there for a few weeks at the hospital in Landstuhl, then hopped a flight back to Iraq. I remember seeing him carrying his gear from the flight line one afternoon about six weeks after Matador.

"Hey, sir! I'm back," he called to me.

I wanted to give him a hug. So did his Marines. Alpha Section's morale soared after he returned.

What a tough old salt. He ended up in the battalion COC during our second deployment, so we served two tours together.

Lamson—my rebel. Did he watch me lose from his house in Indiana? He's out now, married with kids and going to college. He does a lot of public speaking these days and has become a role model in his town. Staff Sergeant Robertson came home to his three kids, picked up a promotion to gunny, and became a drill instructor. He'll be a sergeant major for sure someday. He was one of the best platoon sergeants I've ever known, a true leader under fire and always an outstanding Marine.

The cab reaches the airport and pulls up to the curb at the departures area. Teressa and I climb out. I grab our stuff from the trunk and we head off to check in at the counter. Teressa's been wonderful through all this. She knows I've got to sort through all these emotions myself. She isn't pushing me to share my feelings. Nor is she trying to drag me out of my mood. She's just letting me be, and that's exactly what I need right now.

In the terminal, I'm recognized by a few fans. They offer words of encouragement. One thanks me for my service. Another asks for a photo of the two of us, which I oblige. Some fighters see these moments as intrusions or annoyances. I don't. They remind me that there are those out there who get my message, who understand what I'm trying to do with my fighting career. I'm grateful for them and their interest in what I've got to say. They remind me that I am doing some good after all, no matter what the comments are on the internet.

We make it through security and find seats at our gate. As I sit down, I realize how sore I am. Cantwell really put the hurt on me last night.

Another fan approaches. I thank him for his interest, sign an autograph, and chat with him for a few minutes. He thanks me for what we did over in Iraq. We shake hands and as he walks away, I can't help but feel a little better.

I may have lost last night, but the message about my Marines still will reach people. The humiliation I'd been feeling since I picked myself off the mat eased up—just a bit. There will be a chance for vengeance. The thought of a rematch makes me smile.

We got a rematch against those insurgents around Karabala right after Matador. In June, our scout sniper platoon commander, Lieutenant Habenicht, received permission to insert two of his teams into a house south of Route Jade. The plan called for my platoon to drop them off in the desert and then position ourselves on a hill nearby. After taking a look at the terrain, we found a perfect spot to conceal our Humvees and serve as a quick response force should the sniper teams get into more than they could handle.

We pulled this off one night in June. A few kilometers from the objective house, we dropped Lieutenant Habenicht's snipers off in the desert. They continued on by foot as we headed for our hilltop. All was going very well until the COC called up and told us to freeze in place. A regimental-level raid force was about to blow through our area, and their mission took priority over ours. The snipers piled into the nearest house and settled down to wait.

Dawn arrived, and we were all disappointed and a little angry our mission had been derailed. The snipers couldn't move forward to the objective now that the sun had come up. They were stuck in place. As it turned out, that was a good thing. A few hours later, a sedan drove up and parked near Habenicht's men. Five insurgents jumped out, popped open the trunk, and started passing AK-47s out. We couldn't believe it. With no regard to security, they set up a target range and calmly practiced their marksmanship. They adjusted their sights, checked their targets, and burned through a fair amount of ammo, all the while clueless to the watchful eyes of our snipers.

When they packed up and climbed back into the sedan, they drove right past Habenicht's men. The snipers used a couple of M249 SAW light machine guns, leaned out of one window, and raked the car until all five insurgents had been killed. We found RPGs and a bunch of AK-47s in the trunk when my platoon arrived to set up a security cordon around the sniper teams.

Not long after that, Lieutenant Habenicht came up with an even better scheme. This time, he took a forward air controller (FAC) out with four sniper teams, and we dropped them in the desert in the dead of night again.

They reached the objective house from the first mission and had a great view of "Muj Alley," which ran north–south into Jade. Come dawn, a number of foreign fighters showed up in the alley and moved around from building to building. The snipers watched them as the FAC called in an air strike. The first bomb took the Muj totally by surprise. The survivors fled the street and poured into a nearby building. Our FAC called that one in and blew it up. "Oh fuck!" The FAC called over the radio, "That was awesome. I just saw body parts flyin'!"

More Muj flowed into the alley, looking for the source of the explosions. The FAC dropped another bomb on them. The enemy had no idea where Habenicht's men were, and they milled around in confusion as the FAC rained death on them. He dropped seven JDAM satellite-guided bombs on the alley or nearby buildings and killed a host of insurgents before they finally detected the sniper teams. Mortar fire fell around the house, and a few RPGs sizzled from the alley.

Finally, after a rocket slammed into the house and a mortar round landed in its yard, Lieutenant Habenicht called for help. We sped down the hill to go extract them. Originally, the snipers had planned for us to pick them up about 200 meters from their house. But with mortars raining down, we decided to go all the way to them. We roared up the street, and the platoon screeched to a halt next to the objective house just as a mortar exploded only a few feet away. When the first snipers came outside, the look of relief on their faces was well worth the danger we faced by getting in close. They piled on and we bugged out for home with another one in the win column. Behind us, the Muj mortar teams demolished the objective house. We'd gotten there just in time.

Those were good days. We almost certainly killed some of the same bad guys who had lit us up during Matador, so our platoon felt like we'd helped exact some revenge for Gass and the others. It isn't every day in an insurgency when you score such clear-cut victories.

Later, after we got home, I wanted to do something for my platoon, to show them how much they meant to me.

The thought of having what they endured fade into anonymity just was not acceptable. The least I could do was tell their story and show all who'd listen the caliber of men I served with in Iraq.

I can still do that. Hell, I can still do that even if I'm not fighting anymore. The WEC just gives me a broader audience to reach.

Over the loudspeaker, we hear the boarding call for our flight. Teressa and I line up and make our way to the back of the plane. We share a few words, but my wife understands I'll need space for a while yet.

Matador was just the first chunk of my first tour. We had months of combat left ahead of us when we finished that operation in May. And that was just the first tour. The second one was far worse.

Just after we deployed again in 2006, I was pulled from Weapons Company to become the executive officer for India Company, 3/2 Marines. It happened so fast that I didn't have time to get to know my new Marines before we ended up in country again. We deployed to Anbar Province to an FOB near Habbaniyah. Soon our company was broken up and sent to four different patrol bases. I moved around between the various bases but never had the chance to get to know the men as well as I wanted to. We hit the ground running, and we kept the operational tempo going at a furious pace.

If anything, Anbar had gotten worse in the year since we'd been gone. The battalion started taking casualties almost from the first week we returned. The enemy had adapted and grown even more cunning. Not only did we face ambushes and roadside bombs, but now snipers became a daily menace. Some of these killers copied the tactics used by John Malvo and John Allen Muhammad when they terrorized the D.C. area with their attacks in 2002. They cut firing positions out of the trunks of inconspicuous cars, then parked them near our bases. The sniper need to lie in the trunk, peering through a narrow slit hacked through the car's sheet metal, until a Marine presented himself as a target. He'd take the shot, and his driver would throw the sedan in gear and merge into the local traffic stream to disappear. Other times, they used elevated positions, keeping at least one terrain feature between us and them. This way, they could make good their escape without having to worry about us counterattacking their positions.

My company lost four Marines killed. Lance Corporal Don "Champ" Champlin was our first. He was killed by a roadside bomb on the main road running through our area. That was at the end of August 2006. A month later, on the 24th, our company commander sent a platoon out after an insurgent who'd fired a rocket into one of our patrol bases. They'd gone out without a special device that blocked incoming cell phone signals and prevented insurgents from remotely detonating IEDs.

Sure enough, the platoon got hit with a bomb. It blew Lance Corporal Rene Martinez seventy meters into the air. He died instantly.

That one really hurt. I'd been on the base at the time. I took great pride in going out on patrols, not to ride herd on the platoon commanders, but to be there as an additional asset and to share the risks with my Marines. This time, I'd been tied up and couldn't get out with the men. When I heard what was happening, I grabbed a Humvee and raced to the scene. We carried Rene back to the morgue. Inside, I stood next to him, held his hand, and said my goodbyes. I will carry the guilt of that day for the rest of my life. I should have been out there with that platoon.

I turn to look at my wife. She knows how tough that second tour was for all of us. She was a rock for me. I can't even imagine what it would have been like without her rock-solid support.

Our flight attendants go through the safety brief I've seen a million times. Are there *really* people so clueless that they can't figure out a seatbelt buckle? The attendant demonstrates how to open one and close it. I see a few people in the cabin had forgotten to buckle up, and now they're scrambling to do so. A few others realize their seats aren't in the fully upright position. A flurry of last minute adjustments takes place.

A few minutes later, we're airborne and climbing for our cruising altitude. It is going to be a long flight, this one. My mind wanders back to that second tour.

We kept taking casualties that fall. Even units just passing through our area got hit. One EOD rig got hit with a roadside bomb. Though the blast didn't destroy the armored Humvee, it set off a couple of phosphorus-based incendiary grenades the EOD team had left on the floor of their rig. Before we could even get to them, the white-hot chemical fire had melted them where they sat. The sight was indescribable.

After that scene, morale in the company plummeted. The men questioned the mission. What was the point?

We were getting shot at almost every day. Going into Habbaniyah to patrol was a daily nightmare of snipers, bombs, and ambushes. Half the time we couldn't even fire back. The rules of engagement were so strict that if there were civilians in the area, we could not engage the enemy. Since there were almost *always* civilians in the area, our Marines had to show incredible restraint even as they watched their brothers die.

Mike Brown was our next casualty. He'd been up in one of the guard towers, pulling security on base behind an M240 Golf machine gun. It was a scorching hot day, and the towers, which were buttressed with sandbags and covered with camouflage netting, became furnaces in the afternoon heat. Mike had been on duty for almost three hours, languishing behind his gun in the stale air. Finally, unable to take it any more, he leaned forward just a bit to catch some fresh air from the firing port.

A sniper had patiently waited for him to do just that. When Mike leaned forward, he exposed himself for just a split second. Five hundred meters away, the sniper took the shot. We raced up there to help him as soon as we heard the report, but nothing could save him. The sniper hit him in the temple and killed him instantly.

Aboard our flight, the fasten seatbelt sign was turned off and people began moving around the cabin. A line developed for the bathrooms a few rows behind us. A flight attendant came by and took our drink order. I stared out the window, my thoughts lost in the clouds.

October 2006 had been a hellish month. The battalion lost a lot of men killed and wounded. I remember one mission we'd been sent out to deliver space heaters to the local civilians in Habbaniyah. Winter was coming up, and the temperatures would soon drop into the forties or below at night.

The streets were too dangerous for us to simply walk down and knock on doors. The snipers would have just clobbered us. We dashed from house to house under the cover of smoke grenades, moving as fast as we could and getting indoors whenever possible. It took five hours to finish a patrol that covered only a few city blocks.

Two days after Christmas, we lost Lance Corporal William "Willy" Koprince to yet another IED. The Marine contact team assigned to notify Willy's family couldn't find them at first. His folks had recently moved from Lenoir City to Oak Ridge, Tennessee, and the Corps hadn't received their new address yet. When the contact team finally found them, Willy's family was at a restaurant having breakfast together.

Willy was twenty-four. He had already been over once and had hoped to go to college once he finished his enlistment.

We took other casualties as well. A recon platoon was attached to us for only a few days to give us additional strength. One of their Marines got killed on their first patrol into Habbaniyah. The platoon got pulled out right after that.

Earlier, we had lost one of our best Iraqi interpreters. We called him Bill, and he worked with us despite threats against himself and his family. When he was hit by shrapnel from another IED, our corpsman worked furiously to try and save him. When I reached him, the corpsman was giving him CPR. His body had been so badly torn that with each compression, I could see his internal organs. There was no hope, but we tried everything to save him.

We lost our civil affairs officer in a terrible way. He'd just joined the unit and was doing a tremendous job reaching out to the local population. Another IED blew off his jaw. A corpsman managed to reopen an airway in his neck and save his life. He had three kids and came home to face years of plastic surgery to reconstruct his face.

Winston Churchill was right. When you're going through hell, you just have to put your head down and keep going. That second deployment became a test of endurance and sanity. Coming home in 2007 didn't end the struggle, either. It just changed form.

After I fought Cantwell the first time, I was given command of Headquarters Company, 8th Marines. This turned out to be the East Coast dumping ground for all non-deployable Marines. Some were medically or mentally unfit to go overseas. Others had legal action pending against them. There were shirkers and cowards, druggies and sex offenders. Some of the worst men in the Corps ended up in my unit. I had to search the barracks with NCIS officers almost every week to look for dope.

The day I took command, one of the men died in a motorcycle crash. Not long after, one of my India Company Marines committed suicide. He'd been out with us on that second tour. When he got home, he discovered his wife had been cheating on him. If that wasn't enough of a blow, he never got over the things he'd seen.

We'd all seen.

Third Battalion, 2nd Marines came home in 2007 after suffering fifteen killed in action. It could have been far worse for all of us if we hadn't seen any progress in Habbaniyah. Then all those questions we had over the mission and its value would have returned home to torment us for years to come. In fact, we did see progress, and that made things a little easier to accept.

When we first arrived and began patrolling Habbaniyah, the civilians would not even speak to us. The local sheiks, when approached, would deny there was any insurgent presence in the city. The mosques served as resupply points for the Muj, and we always seemed to take fire from them as well. Once, my company commander went to speak to one of the sheiks in an effort to establish some rapport. I listened to him as he passionately explained to us that there was "no violence in Habbaniyah!" Not ten seconds after our interpreter translated this, we came under heavy fire. The sheik dove for cover as the rest of us tried to find and neutralize the threat.

Through the fall, we worked hard to build trust. Much as we hated the rules of engagement, they did help. Time and again, I'd see our Marines take extreme care not to hurt civilians caught in the middle of an engagement. By December 2006, the locals started passing intelligence to us. Eventually, the sheiks gave us lists of names of insurgents. Average civilians, fed up with the fighting, took to dropping tips to us when we made our daily rounds. Other times, they'd creep up to our gates at night to pass along information.

By the time we left, Habbaniyah had grown calm. We no longer needed smoke screens to patrol the city's streets, and the locals were free from the terror and oppression the enemy fighters always seemed to inflict on their host population.

Our drinks arrive. Beside me, Teressa reads a magazine and waits for the in flight movie to begin.

My Marines gave everything to our cause in Iraq. They left nothing on the table and served as a constant source of inspiration for me. Last night, those watching saw me fail. They won't see me quit. But where do I go from here?

I take a long pull from my drink, then stare back out the window. Where else but at forty thousand feet can one find perspective? Maybe what I need to do is break down everything that happened before the fight and scrutinize the details. Once I do that, perhaps I'll see the bigger picture in a different light. Or, maybe that's just an excuse for obsessive self-doubt. Hell, I don't know. I just know I can't quit.

Somewhere over the Midwest, a thought occurs to me. During that marathon of shit our second tour became, nobody quit. Not a Marine in our company stood up and said, "I've had enough. Send me home, lock me up if you have to, but I'm not going out again."

Instead, we studied our enemy's new tactics. We developed our own counters. We worked in subtle ways to win over the civilians so the insurgents couldn't hide among them. We adapted to overcome the adversity we faced. Did it work all the time? No. We failed, but we learned from our mistakes and had the discipline and flexibility to change.

I hadn't adapted as a fighter. As I moved up from amateur fighting to the pros, I trained the same way with my Marine friends. As I found success in the WEC, none of that changed. I never had a coach, just peer mentors who gave me pointers and tips. Since leaving the Corps, I had been training at multiple gyms with multiple coaches. I realize now that was a scattershot approach. It left me more confused and unfocused than anything else.

I brawled my way to the top. No finesse, just brute force. Now, I'm at a level where brute force is not enough. Cantwell drove that home last night. I can't be one-dimensional anymore. It is time to take a page from that second deployment and change up my tactics and techniques.

To do that means I've got to put in the effort to learn the nuances of the sport. Everyone says I've got natural talent. The caveat that inevitably follows is that my talent is raw and needs to be developed. Perhaps Cantwell did expose me last night, but that doesn't have to be the end of it.

Four hours later, as we touch down in Atlanta, I've come to accept that I cannot continue in the WEC in the same manner that got me to this level. I am going to have to make serious changes in my life. I don't know what those changes are yet. That'll have to wait until I have a chance to thoroughly dissect everything that happened in my last training camp and during the fight. I'll pinpoint the mistakes, correct them, and move forward. When I do return to the cage, I will make my Marines proud and tell their stories to anyone who'll listen. That is the least I can do after what they gave of themselves in Iraq.

CHAPTER NINETEEN

Invitation to Albuquerque

Okay, easier said than done. The week after I returned from Atlanta, I felt drawn to the internet again. At night after work, I sat and read post after post on the MMA boards. From that moment of hope and expectation for the future I felt as we returned home, my mood plummeted into depression again. Rory Singer tried to console me and has reminded me repeatedly that every fighter goes through this. Perfection is unobtainable. You're going to stumble. The trick is using the stumble as a growth experience.

All that week, I read what people said about me. One anonymous poster who claimed to have been at the Academy called me a dick on the forums. Others had other poetic ways to voice their opinions:

I hate ALL people who brag or constantly have to drop the fact they are either a current solder in the armed forces or a former solder. The first time they showed

WEC on Versus & they profiled Brian Stann, I hated him after he finished what he had to say. That's like me bragging I knocked out Quinton Jackson come to find out I did but it was some kid who's name happens to be QJ. If Brian Stann had a public e-mail address, I would tell him to get a life! I would be more impressed if he won a gold medal at the olympics in judo or wrestling, or if he played pro ball, or if he was a former D-1 college athlete, or if he's banging some hot piece of ass, LOL!

After a few nights of torturing myself with this sort of stuff, I realized that it was not helping me grow from this experience. I shut off the laptop and resolved to never look at the MMA boards again.

How to grow from this loss? That is what occupies my thoughts now. To answer it, I've replayed every decision and action I made during the summer. I've come to several conclusions. First: my training camp was a mess. I had too many people coaching me at too many gyms. The unease I felt on fight night can be traced directly back to that.

I have to start taking this more seriously. I need to find a single coach who can take me to a new level as a fighter. The competition is too good, too well trained and developed for me to continue working as I have these past years.

In all my seven pro fights, I always charge head-on into my opponent. When in doubt, I charge in and just bang away toe-to-toe. Cantwell expected and used it against me. He maneuvered where I just bull-rushed. Every future opponent I face will watch the tape of this fight and know what to expect of me. Problem is, I lack the training to do anything else right now. Already, there's been talk within the WEC of a rematch between Cantwell and me. For me to win back the belt, I can't be a one-dimensional fighter anymore.

Later in the month, I attend a WEC event in Atlanta. During the weigh-in, Greg Jackson approaches me.

"Brian, I want to tell you that I appreciate your service."

"Thank you," I reply, trying to keep the awe out of my voice. Greg Jackson is a legend in our sport. He's the man who has helped redefine mixed martial arts. Where others copy and synthesize, Greg innovates. His team down in New Mexico has become the single most successful outfit in the UFC today.

"Brian, listen," he continues. "If you're looking for a coach, I'd love to work with you. I think we'd be a good match."

I want to blurt out, "You're freakin' kidding me!" Instead, I attempt to maintain my composure as I thank him for his offer. What an opportunity this would be if it works out.

"Look, tell you what. Come on down to Albuquerque for a week and see what you think. You can meet the other fighters and coaches and get an idea of how we work."

A week later, I step off the plane in New Mexico, eager to see Greg Jackson's setup.

Over the years, I've found that a gym reflects the character of its owner and coaches. Some are flashy, with new equipment and lots of style. Some are run down dumps that symbolize a lack of effort on both a financial and personal level. Some are meathead factories that cater to the self-involved. Those are the ones with mirrors everywhere so those working out can gaze upon their bodies as they sweat through their routines.

Greg's gym is located in one of those "at risk" neighborhoods politicians like to bring up during campaign season. Empty warehouses, vacant buildings are scattered through each block surrounding it. Greg's building looks adequately maintained from the outside but far from perfect. Above the front door, somebody has painted a serpent and a tiger. The tiger represents striking and power. The serpent represents grappling. They are the twin disciplines of this gym. I later learn they also symbolize the strengths of Greg Jackson and his partner, Coach Mike Winklejohn.

I walk through the front door into the gym's main lobby. It is small and cluttered. A desk dominates the room. The walls are covered with photographs of the team's fighters, newspaper clippings about Greg and Mike, and stories about their gym.

I study the fighters. There are some great ones, starting with both Greg and Mike. Greg comes from a long line of wrestlers, and the back wall of the lobby is covered with photos of his dad, grandfather, uncle, and brother during their heydays in that sport. In the 1980s, Greg studied a variety of martial arts and began to combine different aspects with wrestling techniques. What emerged was a hybrid system of submission and grappling that Greg further developed in the mid-'90s when he began studying kickboxing under Mike Winkeljohn, as well as Brazilian jujitsu.

From adapting different techniques from the martial arts disciplines he studied, Greg went another step further: he began to craft his own brand and style. Using his knowledge and experience, he created moves, developed new techniques, submission holds, and tactics. This gym was the nexus of all that creative energy. It helped launch his fighters to ten world championship titles and earned his team the highest winning percentage in professional MMA competition.

Mike Winkeljohn had become Greg's partner in the gym the year before in 2007. Mike has been kickboxing for twenty-seven years, holds three world titles and retired with a record of 25–7–3. Now, he coaches some of the greatest athletes in the sport, including Holly Holm, the best female boxer in the world. Coach Winklejohn is known as one of the toughest men in martial arts. His ability to push through barriers of fatigue and exhaustion are legendary within our sport. When you train with him, you train for technique and toughness. Like Greg Jackson, he is an innovator and constantly comes up with unorthodox striking techniques and unusual game plans, both of which have been critical to the success of the entire team.

When these two legends came together, they created a chemistry that has left almost every other MMA team behind. The lobby wall speaks volumes about that. Photos of Keith Jardine, Rashad Evans, kickboxing star Duane Ludwig, Georges St. Pierre, Nate Marquardt, and Joey Villasenor cover the entire left side of the room.

These men are at the top of our profession. Keith Jardine is 14–4 as a pro. In May, he lost to Wanderlei Silva. Now, he's in camp preparing for an October fight against Brandon Vera. Keith ranks as one of the top ten fighters in his UFC weight class, and his future looks very bright.

Rashad Evans is another star. Earlier this month, he knocked out Chuck Liddell with a ferocious overhand right that left the legend unconscious on the mat for several minutes. Evans is now in training for a December match against Forrest Griffin for the light heavyweight title.

He and Keith Jardine starred in the Spike TV series *The Ultimate Fighter*. During the tenure of the show, Rashad beat Keith in a decision. After the series, they both joined forces with Greg and Mike. I've heard that they are close friends now and have refused to fight against each other again in the UFC.

As I stare at this wall of superlative athletes, Greg Jackson enters the lobby to welcome me. We shake hands, and he takes me back into the gym for a tour of the facility.

Our first stop takes us into the office area where the team can gather and study fight film. The place is a cluttered mess. Nothing fancy here. Just a group space with some flat screen TVs and a couple of computers. The furniture looks like it got dragged over here from a government surplus auction. There are cardboard boxes scattered around with stuff stacked on top of them.

We pass Greg's desk. It is piled with folders and paperwork. A *Star Wars* light saber rests on the desk. Hanging on the wall next to his desk are images of Abe Lincoln, George Washington, Genghis Kahn, and interestingly enough, Ernest Shackleton, the famous British Antarctic explorer.

The moment I stepped into this room, I knew this was the gym for me. Nothing pretentious here at all. Nothing's for show, what's here is functional and no resources are expended on presentation. The fact that Greg counts two of our greatest presidents among his heroes—as evidenced by the wall—cements my respect and admiration for him. He's not only a great coach and martial arts genius, he's also an American patriot.

Through another door, we step into the public section of the gym. A group of kids are working out on a mat together. Nearby, the exercise machines are utilitarian, old-school cycles. Nothing fancy, just stuff that gets the job done well. Next to those are sets of free weights. A shelf full of trophies runs high along one wall. An octagon dominates the main room, which is stocked with pads, mats, and climbing ropes. Here, the walls are white painted cinderblock.

As I stand there with Greg, looking around, I feel totally at home. It even smells right—the kind of old school sweat palace that back in the day could have produced the likes of Joe Louis. For an instant, I recall the rancid old gym I trained in back at Camp Lejeune between my Iraq deployments. The mats were moldy and vile. The place smelled of Vietnam-Era, Baby-Boomer sweat mingled with mildew and rot. It was a place only the most committed would use. Nothing cozy or comfortable: a place to work your ass off and nothing more.

This gym is the same kind of place.

"Let me show you the dorm area," Greg explains. He takes me back into the office area and points to a set of stairs. "Go pick a bunk and drop your gear off. Get changed, and let's get to work."

I head upstairs. The dorm reminds me of a Marine enlisted barracks—Spartan and functional without distractions or creature comforts. This is a place where only the dedicated come to live.

I find a bunk, get changed, and meet Greg downstairs. One by one, he introduces me to the team. Keith is focused and quiet. He doesn't say much after our handshake. Rashad cracks a few jokes and seems more light-hearted than Keith. Underneath that façade, he's scoping me out with silent intensity. As the new guy, I figured I'd be under a microscope, but this is pretty hard core.

Joey Villasenor volunteers to be my first sparring partner. Greg turns us over to one of the gym's other coaches, Chris Luttrell. He's an Albuquerque police officer who's also on their SWAT team. After we're introduced, listening to him convinces me that his depth of knowledge and tactical acumen is nothing short of remarkable.

After warming up, I climb into the octagon with Joey V. Joey's waiting for me, leaning against the cage, cracking jokes with Chris. He seems very easy going, relaxed, and friendly. He smiles at me. "You ready?" he asks casually.

I nod.

"Five minutes," Chris tells us.

We step forward and get it on. I'm ready to be assessed and evaluated, perhaps critiqued a little after each round. Joey bounces forth, his feet beating the mat like a hummingbird's heart. His speed and movement totally catch me off guard. The next thing I know, he's hammered my face with crushing strikes. Even with headgear on, the ferocity of his attack leaves me dizzy.

Holy shit. What was that? I thought we were sparring, not playing Rock 'em Sock 'em Robots!

He backs away, I move straight at him. Suddenly, he lunges forward as if on springs and hits me again with a fierce combination. I uncork everything I have, and for a few seconds, we batter each other with everything we've got.

What the hell?

He rocks me on my heels. My head swims, I try to move and avoid his follow up, but he's too fast and too agile. The next thing I know, he's taken me down and tapped me out.

We stand back up. He comes at me again. I give him everything I've got, pounding away on his head and upper body. It feels like I'm beating my fists on concrete. He's that rugged and tough. Here for the first time, I can see the effect of Coach Winklejohn's training for toughness.

We break contact and circle each other. Fuck it. If this guy wants to go full speed, then we'll go full speed. I wade in after him, landing blows that seem to have no effect. He slips aside and lashes out with a couple of devastating combinations.

He takes me down again. By now, my heart's pounding, we're both bathed in sweat. Grappling Joey V is like grappling a fucking grizzly bear. He pins me in place with another submission hold. I tap out.

Shit.

Back up on our feet now, I'm determined to give a better accounting for myself. I throw myself at him, head-on, fists flailing. I nail him with my trademark right cross and I see it rocks him. At last. I try to close and capitalize, but he's so light on his feet that he darts out of harm's way, delivering several counter-blows as he does.

Jesus. Joey's speed and agility are beyond anything I've ever faced. He hammers and dodges, using the entire octagon to pick and chose his moments to attack.

When the round ends, I stagger back to my corner, bells ringing in my ear. Joey leans against the cage wall, breathing hard.

"Jesus Christ!" Chris Luttrell shouts, "Are you two mad at each other?"

Joey shakes his head. "No. I just wanted to make sure Brian respects me."

My jaw drops. "Well, you've got nothing to fuckin' worry about there."

He cracks a grin. "Let's go again."

My head's still ringing, but I head back into the fray. In seconds, Joey's got me on the mat again and taps me out.

I have a lot to learn. Tons. But if these guys allow me to join their team, I know this is the place where my education will commence.

Later that afternoon, Rashad climbs into the cage to take a turn sparring with me. He is chiseled and lean, with bulging leg muscles and a stare like Mike Singletary's during his heyday with the Bears.

The round begins, and I drive forward. He nearly levels me with his first punch. I've never seen such explosiveness. One minute, he's coiled up and moving fast. The next, he unleashes a wrecking ball. Before I even have a chance to react, he punishes me with a flurry, then suddenly backs away, feet dancing, head bobbing and weaving.

His speed is incredible. I strike at him. He slips away and I try to follow him. I land a few blows. He's heavy on top, like a slab of armor plating has been fused into his upper body. Hitting him in the chest, stomach, and head is like beating on the side of one of the Humvees we used in Iraq.

When the round ends, he has thoroughly beaten me down. In the past, when I've experienced this with a superior sparring partner, most of them have simply walked away with an *I just kicked your ass, deal with it* sort of attitude.

Rashad does something different. As I'm leaning against the cage, trying to unscramble my brain, he comes over to give me some pointers and tactical suggestions. The gesture solidifies my opinion of him. He is a phenomenal athlete. More important, he's a first rate human being as well.

At the end of the day, Keith Jardine comes over to spar with me. By this time, the Brian Stann beat down fest has left me absolutely smoked. My head's full of cobwebs, every muscle aches. Keith has been working out on the periphery of the cage all afternoon with what can only be described as relentless fury. Between sparring rounds, I've been able to watch him. He pushes himself further and harder than anyone I've ever seen. I almost wonder if he hates his body. The abuse he puts himself through astonishes me.

I stand in my corner, watching Keith limber up to take his shot at me. I've got to wake myself up. I bounce on the balls of my feet and punch my own face. That gets the adrenaline flowing, at least for the moment. I'm as ready as I'll ever be.

When the round starts, Keith flies at me with eyes of cold fury, as if he just found me in bed with his mother.

Oh my God. He's going to rip my fucking head off.

A freight train slammed into me. Then another. Keith backed away, looking for an angle as I reel from his blasts. He comes at me again and I bash him in the face and jaw with two quick jabs. I've put all my power behind both, but he doesn't even slow. He ducks low and seizes my body, flinging me to the mat. Take-down.

Shit.

Back up again, we're circling and sizing each other up. He slides left and strikes hard. The blow feels like it loosened teeth. I close and hammer him high and low. I feel his knee drive into me. We keep going, striking, kicking, pummeling with reckless abandon. This is a man who relishes a test of heart. He holds nothing back and clearly expects his sparring partners to do the same. He takes me down again, and we grapple until he taps me out.

Twice. He's taken me down twice. I've got to do better. We get back up and go at it again. Five minutes later, we're still pounding each other with ruthless blows. Kicking, kneeing, punching, we ignore the bell and keep at it. Finally, Chris shouts at us. We bump gloves, then go hang on the ropes to get our wind back. As we do, I catch what looks like a hint of respect in Keith's eyes.

As we lean on the ropes, Keith gives me some tactical advice on how to get back up after somebody's taken me down. I ask a few questions. Before long, we're deep into a discussion on sweeps and submissions. Just like with Rashad, this impresses the hell out of me. Keith doesn't need to take the time to mentor somebody like me, especially a guy who isn't even a member of the team yet. Still, he talks shop passionately, and I can see this role as in-cage coach is a satisfying one for him.

We finish up for the day and Chris comes over to me. "So, how'd you think it went?"

"Indoctrination through pain," I say. We both grin.

Mike Winkeljohn approaches us. He's been watching me most of the afternoon. "Look, Brian," he begins. "You have speed and agility, but you don't use your feet. We can teach you that."

"We need to develop our fighting rhythm," Chris adds.

"We'll teach you how to move side to side, and cut angles," Mike says. "And we'll work on your grappling. That's what we'll start with."

They're speaking as if I've already been accepted. This encourages me. I've tried to keep my mouth shut all day and earn everyone's respect. I took this discussion as a very good sign.

Joey V comes over. "Brian, after dinner, let's work on your ground game."

"Thank you, Joey," I say, surprised that he'd volunteer to stay late to help me out.

Late that night, I drag myself upstairs and collapse into my bunk. After an afternoon and evening of facing some of the elite fighters in the UFC, I sleep more soundly than any time since Iraq. My body shuts down and my brain goes comatose until seven the next morning. No second-guessing myself tonight. Gone are the incessant doubts over decisions I've made in the cage and in combat that keep me awake until the sun comes up. In their place is blissful blackness, born of a profound exhaustion the depths of which I have never known.

The next morning, when I come downstairs, I find Keith Jardine already in the gym. He seems totally oblivious to everyone around him. He paces and shadow boxes, his face set with an expression of absolute focus.

"At the start of each day, Keith runs through everything he wants to accomplish in his head. Everything. He's the most detail-oriented fighter I've ever seen," Chris tells me.

Joey arrives and gives me a warm smile. "How ya doin', Brian?"

I lie and tell him, "I'm good!" Truth is, I'm still feeling the effects of the previous day's sparring.

He nods and laughs. "Yeah, you mesh. You'll do fine here."

Though I've barely been here a day, it is clear that Joey and Keith are the team's sheriffs. What they say goes. To be brought into the team requires both their approval.

I begin to warm up with some pad work. Keith comes over and regards me for a moment, his face expressionless. Finally, in a soft voice that seems totally out of place coming from the guy who was a raging beast in the cage yesterday, he says, "Yeah. You fit in." Without letting me say a word in response, he walks away to begin his morning workout. Right then, all the aches and pains inflicted on me the day before vanish.

I couldn't wait to get back into the cage and start my new education.

I look around the gym to watch and get an idea of how it operates. Rashad and Keith are discussing submission techniques in one corner. Joey V is about to do some sparring with me and he's getting his gloves taped. Chris and Greg and Mike are circulating among the other fighters doing their thing. The morning is all business; everyone is focused and busy preparing or learning something new. There's an electricity about the place based on common purpose and likeminded intensity. In this moment, I knew I'd found a home.

Five years ago, a place like this became my refuge during one of the worst times in my life. I escaped from public ridicule and humiliation into the depths of the martial arts culture within the Marine Corps. As the months unfolded, and my career hung in the balance of an upcoming court martial, MMA became my lifeline. Now, as I look around Greg and Mike's gym, it feels like the same sanctuary that at once saved me and set me down the path of a professional fighter. I walk to the pads to begin my warm-up routine. I lash out at the pads, feeling the satisfying impact with each blow. Yet the exercise doesn't occupy my brain. Instead, my thoughts drift to that dark time in my life, and the memories fill me with cold fury.

CHAPTER TWENTY

The Scarlet Letter

Camp Barrett, Quantico, Virginia,
November 2003

It was a night for celebration. Over the years, I'd been
pretty uptight at times. I didn't usually cut loose and
rarely got drunk. During the spring, as we closed in on
our graduation date, I made the mistake of getting a little
loose on a Saturday night. We took a cab back to a friend's
house outside the Academy, but once there I was asked to
give someone a ride back on campus. Even though several
hours had passed since my last drink, I never should have
done this. Once on campus, I got nailed by the shore
patrol for a DUI. This showed me that even letting your
guard down once can lead to disaster. Six months later,
freshly graduated from the Academy the previous June, I
should have remembered that lesson.

Fresh out of Annapolis, we Marine second lieutenants have to attend something called the Basic School.
Twenty-six weeks long and composed of both classroom
work and field tactical exercises, the Basic School molds us

into the officers the Corps wants us to become. At the end of the program, we are all given our Military Occupation Specialty (MOS). This can range from aviator to infantry; it doesn't matter what your specialty ends up being, every Marine officer has the same foundational underpinnings and knowledge, thanks to the Basic School.

On this particular Friday in November, we completed a twelve mile hike in full battle rattle and returned back to our company area to discover the school had posted our MOS designations. This was a huge moment for all of us, as whatever the Corps gave us would make an otherwise uncertain future come into better focus at last.

Nominally, we all get to select our top three choices. How much that gets weighed against the immediate needs of the Corps is anyone's guess, but if pressed, I'd say not much. Your MOS becomes something of a crap shoot, and we'd been anticipating this day for weeks.

J. P. Blecksmith and I stood side-by-side that afternoon to discover we both got our first choice: infantry. We whooped and hollered and slapped backs. Then we decided to go celebrate that weekend.

Since graduation, I'd rented a townhouse in Annapolis. On weekends when we had liberty, we'd head up from Virginia to hang out with all our buddies like Travis Manion who were underclassmen and still at the Academy. My place became the crash pad, and at times we'd have a dozen or more Midshipmen and second lieutenants snoozing away on couches, futons, beds, and floors come Sunday mornings.

On this evening, we teamed up with a group of friends from another Basic School company and piled into our cars and drove north for the Maryland line. When we got to Annapolis, we pub crawled through downtown. I made sure to go light on the alcohol, and through the entire night I had four drinks, never even getting buzzed. The memory of my one slip the previous spring kept me from crossing that line.

There was a female second lieutenant from the other company, a friend of a friend, who I began talking with that night. Second Lieutenant "J" and I hit it off right away. I'd been single for quite awhile and having some female company felt wonderful, especially since we were all in such high spirits after getting our MOS assignments.

Late that night, we took cabs back to my townhouse. A DUI can do tremendous damage to an officer's career. Even though I wasn't drunk, I had been drinking and I refused to take any risk at all on this front. So, I caught a ride with the rest of the group. At the townhouse, we all settled down for the night. Just before I shut off my light, Second Lieutenant "J" knocked on my door.

"Can I sleep in here?" she asked.

"Okay," I said, opening the door to let her inside. "I'll take the floor. You can have the futon."

That didn't last. We ended up kissing on the futon. At first, it was tender and passionate. I felt a growing connection to her. About ten minutes later, she pulled her lips away from me and looked distressed.

"What's wrong?" I asked.

"I can't do this," she said, averting her eyes.

"Why?" I asked, sitting up.

"Can't . . . do . . . this . . . " she said again, offering no explanation.

I stood up, helped her to her feet, and walked her to the door. I gave her a hug and said I understood, though I had no idea what was going on.

A moment later, she left. I later found out she spent the night in another room with an officer from her platoon.

Her sudden attitude change made me wonder if she had a boyfriend.

The next morning, we all gathered in the main room to eat breakfast and watch football. We hung out. Lieutenant "J" was friendly to me. Everyone was talking and laughing about the craziness of the previous night. There were twelve of us all together that spent the night in the townhouse.

That Monday, after we got back to Camp Barrett, I discovered two SPCs waiting for me in the barracks. One was my own platoon commander. The other was Lieutenant J's. I didn't think anything of this at first, assuming that they had a PT or training issue to discuss with me.

I said, "Good morning, gentlemen." My SPC, Captain Cook, who'd been my mentor throughout that fall, replied "Stann drop your gear off and meet me in five." I was ranked first in the platoon, second in the entire class, and much of the credit for that went to his guidance and advice to me.

Once we were in his office, he asked, "Lieutenant Stann, did you get into any trouble this weekend?"

"No." The question caught me off guard. *What the hell?*

"You sure?"

"Yes."

"That's not what we've heard," Cook said, his voice flat.

"What have you heard?" I asked warily.

"There've been some accusations that you sexually assaulted a fellow officer."

"What?" I was floored.

"Brian, calm down and tell us what happened."

"There's got to be some sort of mix-up," I mused.

For a second, I couldn't even speak. Such an accusation could destroy my career and take away my life. Then discipline conquered emotion, and I related everything that happened over the weekend with Lieutenant J, but Captain Cook cut me off.

"We have to go see the company commander, Major Nicewarner," Captain Cook said quietly.

In a daze, I walked over to his office, was asked for my side of the story, and was told that I needed to talk to JAG (Judge Advocate General's office—the Marine Corps' legal system). Major Nicewarner told me that what Lieutenant J was saying was vastly different.

I returned to my Basic platoon to languish in a classroom for the rest of the morning, my mind crawling over what just took place. When the lecture ended, I approached Captain Cook and said, "Sir, no matter what, I'm not lying down. I'm fighting this."

He looked at me, mouth tight, eyes hard. "Good. I believe you, Brian."

His words were a huge relief. Until he added, "But her SPC doesn't. It is going to get ugly."

That afternoon, while attending another class with my platoon, I was called into the major's office. "You're out of the company," he announced when I appeared before him. "We're putting you in Mike Company until this is resolved."

"I can't graduate with my platoon?" I asked.

No response. Mike Company was a holding unit, the place where injured officers or ones with legal issues were sent until their situations are resolved. This was like being thrown into a holding cell at the local jail. It effectively put my career on hold pending whatever followed the accusations.

By the time I reported to Mike Company late that afternoon, the story was all over the school. Rumors were flying, and I was at the center of all of them. The Mike Company commander ordered me to report to formation twice a day. Other than that, I was confined to barracks with no duties.

I called the JAG office, and a lawyer was assigned to me. "Don't talk to the criminal investigators," he told me. "They'll use anything you say against you. Don't say a word."

The next morning, the investigation team paid me a visit. They obviously assumed I was guilty and treated me as such. I listened to my JAG lawyer and barely said a word. Before they left, they handed me a letter that ordered me not to speak with anyone who was in the townhouse with us that night. Since those ten other people were all my closest friends, the gag order effectively severed me from my support network.

I sat in the barracks and stared at the ceiling, a prisoner of the deepest despair I'd ever known. With nothing to do, I dwelled on my predicament. Getting accused of sexual misconduct in the Corps is like a teacher being accused of child abuse. It doesn't matter if you're innocent or not, the very allegations become a scarlet letter. There's no escaping that and the destruction the stigma does to a man's reputation. No escape.

Why was she doing this to me? I asked myself this question a thousand times during those first days as I sat in an empty barracks. I replayed the night over and over. How could someone turn a make-out session into sexual assault? I was devastated; my friends could not believe this was happening.

I stood up and walked to the door with her. She never acted threatened by me at all. If anything, she looked guilty, not fearful, when she left. There must have been something more going on than I realized. I wanted to hear her side of the story, to understand what was going on.

I phoned my mother to tell her what had happened. I held nothing back. As I explained, I could hear her crying on the other end of the phone. She had always been there to guide and support me through every moment of adversity in my life. Though twenty-three years old now and on my own, I needed her love and trust more than ever.

When I finished, she said to me, "Brian, fight this."

"I know, Mom. I am."

"No," she said, her voice full of the strength I had lost since they'd thrown me into this empty barracks. "You need to fight it. No matter how long it takes, you fight this."

She was right, and I needed to hear that. Trouble was, I was entering a war whose rules I didn't know.

That following Friday, the entire school was called to formation. I stood apart from my former classmates and peers in my original company, feeling completely left behind. The base commander, Brigadier General James Laster, stepped in front of the formation and delivered a liberty brief. These are usually short speeches before the weekend that remind everyone to conduct themselves well when they're out on the town.

Laster's speech was all about me. "We had two lieutenants last week who acted like they were in a frat house, not like they were Marine officers. It was behavior that was foolish and extremely immature that could permanently damage a career."

My cheeks burned with shame. I'd just been made an example of in front of the entire school. Those who hadn't heard the story soon would. And if anyone had doubts as to my guilt or innocence, General Laster's comments pretty much took care of that.

After the formation broke up, many of the captains who served as instructors at TBS glowered at me. I handled it the only way I knew how—by looking them directly in the eye. Most would avert their gaze, uttering comments under their breath as they passed me. I would not walk around in shame, the only thing I did wrong was let the wrong girl in my room.

Every day, I sat in the barracks alone, praying that this whole mess would be resolved. Several times, the investigators called me over to the NCIS office. They would make me wait for sometimes two or three hours before calling me into an office and asking me a few follow up questions. They ordered me not to speak to anyone in my Basic School class, which completed my on-base isolation.

The days became longer and longer after that. I had hoped the whole thing could be straightened out by Thanksgiving, but the holiday came and went with the wheels of Marine Corps justice moving like molasses. I went home for that weekend. Even though I was surrounded by family, I remained locked inside my own head, slipping further into depression.

My godfather, my Uncle Robert, offered to help me with my legal defense. He was a civilian attorney in Maryland, but he knew lawyers who had worked on such military cases in the past. He set me up with one and even helped pay for his services. In our family, when somebody's threatened, we all circle the wagons. Frankly, without their support, I'm not sure how I would have made it through this ordeal.

When I came back after the holiday, the investigators started to throw offers at me. Cop to a lesser infraction

Rodney Wallace Fight: After over a year of training at Greg Jackson's gym, Brian came out and showed considerable depth and talent in this fight, which seesawed back and forth from a stand-up striking match to a battle on the ground. Brian started the fight with a leg kick that Wallace caught and used to take him down to the mat. That set the tone for the fight right away. Wallace kept getting Brian down, but Brian would get back up and deliver devastating punches or kicks. The fight lasted three rounds and ended with both fighters raining blows and attempting takedowns. Brian really shined with his countertactics to Wallace's takedown attempts. Wallace was never able to make Brian submit, and Brian was able to land more blows.

Brian won in a unanimous decision: 30-27, 29-28, 29-28 *Courtesy UFC*

Steve Cantwell Fight III: The final rematch in September 2009 proved
to be a chess match instead of a street brawl like the pair's other two
fights. Brian, using the techniques and tactics he'd learned at Greg
Jackson's gym, out-thought and out-fought Cantwell, who grew
impatient and frustrated by the end of Round 1. Brian relied on
movement, agility, and quick striking attacks to score points and evade
Cantwell's counterblows.

The fight lasted three rounds and ended with a victory for Brian.
Unanimous decision: 30-27, 30-27, 29-28. *Courtesy UFC*

Doug Marshall Fight: This was Brian's title fight for the WEC Light Heavyweight belt. When the bell rang, both fighters came out with furious intensity and aggression. They stood toe-to-toe and banged away at each other, trading vicious blows. There was no pacing, no trying to establish a rhythm in this one. It was a stand-up street fight from start to finish.

At the climax of the action, Marshall and Brian were exchanging rapid-fire flurries of left-right combinations when Brian surprised Marshall with a left uppercut that caught him on the jawline.

He went down on his back, and Brian knocked him out with a couple of final jabs. *Courtesy UFC*

and I'd get non-judicial punishment. They made it sound like at most, it would be a slap on the wrist.

I refused. I had gone over that night again and again in my head for weeks now, and I knew that I had done absolutely nothing wrong. I could opt out, take the hit, and move forward, or I could stand my ground and defend my innocence. I chose the latter and demanded a court martial.

My JAG attorney told me this was my best move. I knew in my heart that a court would not find me guilty, but if I copped a plea, everyone would think I was guilty and I'd never escape the stigma of these charges.

Not that any of this helped. December in Virginia is wet and cold. The barracks I lived in were dreary and lonely. Several times, the thought of suicide crossed my mind. Then I'd think that if I took the coward's way out and killed myself, "J" would win. Whatever her lies were would be enshrined as my legacy. That was not going to happen.

One day, I got a phone call from Travis Manion. Travis was finishing his senior year at the Academy. He hadn't stayed at the townhouse that night in November, so I was under no restrictions and could speak freely to him. Hearing his voice was like having a lifeline thrown my way.

"Brian, we're hearing all sorts of shit here. What the hell is going on?" he asked, the concern in his voice evident.

I told him the whole story. When I finished, he let out a long breath and said, "Jesus Christ, Brother. I can't believe this is happening to you."

"Neither can I. Thanks, Trav."

"Look, I'll get down there as soon as I can, okay?"

"That'd be great, Trav."

After that, he called me three or four times a week. We rarely talked about the case after our first conversation, because there was no point.

He'd been having a rough year himself. He'd looked forward all summer to the upcoming wrestling season, only to suffer a shoulder injury. It essentially ended his athletic career at the Academy. It just about broke his heart. Our conversations ended up lifting both of our spirits.

Christmas came and went with no resolution, and no court martial date assigned. The investigators badgered me repeatedly to take non-judicial punishment. I refused every time. I stopped going out in public. Walking around the base had become an ordeal, and I grew tired of the questions and snarky remarks. I spent weeks with nothing to do, living a hermit's existence in the barracks.

In January, my JAG attorney contacted me. A court martial date had finally been set. I breathed a sigh of relief. Finally, I could defend myself. I couldn't wait to get on the stand.

"When is it?" I asked.

"August."

"You've got to be kidding me," I groaned. I would have to live in this state of career suspended animation for another eight months? J. P. Blecksmith and the other members of my Basic School company had already graduated. J. P. had been assigned to a platoon in 3rd Battalion, 5th Marines. They were working up for an Iraq deployment and would be in country probably before my court martial.

My friends were going off to war. I was sitting on the bench doing nothing. I couldn't believe this was happening to me. My anger at this situation swelled into full fury toward J and what she was putting me through.

Through January, my legal team went to work on my behalf. Bit by bit, the information they collected started to put the pieces in place. My JAG attorney discovered that J had made these accusations before, and they'd been equally unfounded. Apparently, she had threatened to call her Congressman if an investigation wasn't undertaken against me.

My Academy friends had gone to work finding out what they could. One weekend two of them called and dropped a bombshell on me.

"She's engaged to another Marine officer. He's overseas."

"What?" I erupted. "She wasn't wearing a ring!"

But it all made sense now. Her interest in me while we were out on the town, her arrival at my door, followed by her sudden reluctance to continue—it was all motivated by guilt. She had felt guilty for what she'd been doing, which is why she asked to stop. Then, knowing that there were ten other Marines in the house who would probably talk about her whereabouts that night, she concocted some cover story to keep her fiancé from being furious with her.

She was destroying my life to cover her ass. That realization made me thirst for my day in court.

CHAPTER TWENTY-ONE

One Mind: Any
Weapon

In early February, the Mike Company commander told me to report to Lieutenant Colonel Joseph Shusko. The colonel needed some work done, and he'd asked Mike Company to provide him with an officer for the job.

Finally I had something to do again. Lieutenant Colonel Shusko was well known on Quantico as the commander of the Marine Corps' Martial Arts Center for Excellence, or MACE.

The MACE program had been established in 2001 to revolutionize how hand-to-hand and close range combat was taught to Marines. But from the outset, it was also designed to develop leadership techniques, teach morals and values, and instill the warrior ethos into every Marine who went through the program. The program was open to non-combat Marines and navy personnel, who were encouraged to take the courses offered to hone their offensive, fighting spirit. In the nearly three years since its establishment, the MACE program had been a tremendous success. As a result, satellite schools had been set up on bases all over the U.S., though the main facility remained at Quantico.

As part of the Basic School program, every officer had to go through the MACE tan belt program, which takes about twenty-eight hours of instruction to achieve. I'd received my tan belt the previous year with my Basic School platoon and had loved the program.

I stepped into LTC Shusko's office. "Let's take a walk and I'll show you what I want done," he told me after I introduced myself.

I followed him to a beautiful new building that was under construction. He explained that this would be the MACE's new 1.8 million dollar facility and that it was to be dedicated to the Marine Raider battalions that served during World War II. The Raiders had been the first of the Corps' special forces units and had earned a tremendous reputation during the Pacific War. The Raider battalions still rank among the most highly decorated units in the Corps' history. Of the six thousand men who served in them, almost a thousand were killed in action during the war.

Colonel Shusko explained that he wanted to honor the Raiders with a display of photographs and artifacts. He needed an officer to shepherd this to completion in time for the August dedication of the facility.

The assignment excited me, and he could clearly see that. I'd never spent three months doing nothing before. I was ready to go postal. The assignment made me feel like an officer again.

As we walked back to his office, he asked me, "Lieutenant, why are you in Mike Company?"

Joseph Shusko has Marine DNA embedded in his core. He and his six brothers all joined the Corps. Among other things, he had served as one of the helicopter pilots assigned to fly for President Reagan aboard Marine One. He had served in the Gulf War and had been the commander of the Basic School until taking over the MACE recently.

He was a man in his early fifties who still ran three miles in under eighteen minutes. Time after time, he was seen on the obstacle course going through it with his Marine students. Other times, he'd go out on nine mile runs in full battle rattle. He also had a reputation for being a direct straight-shooter who was a passionate Marine and completely intolerant of bullshit or red tape.

I wasn't going to deny my situation or mitigate it to him, even if it meant getting pulled from this project. As directly as I could, I told him I faced charges of sexual misconduct and was awaiting my court martial.

He stopped in mid-stride, turned, and bored his eyes into mine. "Did you do it, Lieutenant Stann?"

I didn't even hesitate, "No, sir. Absolutely not."

He studied me for a long moment. Then he nodded curtly. "Okay then."

After all the aspersions cast my way since November, the rumors and the assault on my character, Lieutenant Colonel Shusko took me at my word as an officer and a Marine. Right then, I would have driven through brick walls for him.

In the days that followed, I worked with the Marine Corps Raiders Museum in Richmond to find artifacts and photographs for the Raider display. My work usually wrapped up by late morning or early afternoon, and I'd find myself at loose ends again. The thought of returning to the exile of the barracks would dim my mood. I started to find excuses to stay at the MACE.

I started working out there every morning and afternoon. The physical exercise offered release from the stress of my legal and professional predicament. The more I worked out, the better I felt. The better I felt, the more I wanted to work out. I became a gym rat, and the MACE became my escape.

All my time in the MACE drew the attention of several instructors. One, Gunnery Sergeant Marlow, took an interest in me. He struck up a conversation, then began giving me pointers on my workouts. Since I had virtually nothing else to do, I asked if I could start attending other classes at the MACE. Gunny Marlow told me I could sit in on any course I wanted. Colonel Shusko agreed.

Within weeks, the MACE dominated my life. It became my sanctuary. Every morning, I'd head over to it for a workout, sometimes arriving before 0530. Master Gunnery Sergent Ricardo Sanders, Gunny Marlow, Sergeant Richmond, Sergent Wargo, and Gunny Collette would usually be there training as well, and they gradually took me under their wing and started teaching me mixed martial arts techniques.

In the mornings, I'd work on the Raider memorial. I spent the afternoons and evenings attending classes at the MACE or doing more training. I returned to the Siberia of my barracks only when I absolutely had to in order to get a few hours of sleep.

As my relationship with these three staff NCOs developed, they began mentoring me on leadership skills as well as martial arts techniques. It was from them I learned the dos and don'ts of commanding an infantry platoon. They gave me the NCO's perspective, and I valued everything they shared with me.

At the same time, I began attending Gunny Marlow's Bible study group. With my career in limbo, I began searching out other support systems, and it was during this period of my life I first started to invest energy in my spiritual life.

Gunny Collette became almost a big brother to me. He'd just bought a house and had an extra bedroom, which he offered to me on the weekends. I'd leave Quantico and all the tension over my legal situation behind on those precious days and spend the time fishing with Gunny Collette and his son. Other times, we'd just hang out and watch football.

As close as we became, we never crossed the line and became *too* familiar. We never referred to each other by our first names. They called me "Sir"; I called them "Gunny." Nevertheless, in me I think they found a young officer in need of help. They saw my work ethic, they grew to know my character, and they sympathized with the position Lieutenant J's charges had left me in.

And they went to bat for me more than once. The MACE program includes a belt system that starts with tan and works up to a black belt (instructor trainer qualified). Each belt requires a certain amount of time and training, along with written essays and classroom work on character and leadership. Every hour of training is designed to foster the development of one of three elements in each student: the physical, the mental, and the Marine's character.

The program was designed to prepare Marines for combat in all three of these aspects. On the physical side, the training included hand-to-hand combat techniques as well as the use of bayonets, knives, and weapons of opportunity. The MACE's motto, "One Mind: Any Weapon," conveys that sense of opportunism in desperate close quarters situations, as well as the intent to inculcate every student with a rugged warrior spirit.

To develop a student's mental strength, the MACE syllabus includes a variety of simulations and exercises intended to recreate some of the stress and tension of combat. In one drill, our class gathered in a windowless room that included different types of exercise equipment that ranged from stationary bikes to weights. The class was broken into twelve stations. Some students mounted the stationary bikes. Others stood by the weights. Others were told they would be grappling with some of the instructor-trainers. At one station, the students had to stand at attention with a pair of M16s outstretched in the form of a cross.

The drill forced each station to maintain a certain level of physical performance. We were only allowed to rotate when our leader attained that level at his current station. That put tremendous pressure on our class leadership, since every station was an exercise in physical endurance or punishment. Once the drill began, the instructors shut off the overhead lights and blasted us with sounds of combat. Gunfire echoed through the room, followed by screaming babies. The room filled with smoke, and the instructors flicked on strobe lights that thoroughly disoriented us. We took turns leading the class until everyone experienced the stress of being responsible for everyone else's misery. It was an incredibly effective way to teach the mind to function despite an exhausted body.

In our classroom work, we had to write papers on Marines of character who preceded us. Some of us wrote about Medal of Honor recipients. We also received an assignment to deliver an oral report on a martial society. In learning about history, the MACE courses intended us to use the past as a guide for our own careers.

To develop our character, our instructors gave us lectures on alcohol awareness, courage under fire, and facing tests of our values with moral bravery.

I graduated from tan belt to gray, then to green belt instructor before I reported to MACE. Colonel Shusko, who had been watching me and my passion for the program, decided to see how I would do as an instructor. In practice, if not via administrative transfer, he essentially pulled me from Mike Company and made me a part of the MACE's staff.

The Marine with the scarlet letter now was giving lectures to officers and NCOs from around the Corps on values and character. For me, this new job proved supremely redemptive. I put everything I had into it, embracing the program wholesale and doing my best to impart its lessons to my students. When word got around the Basic School about what I was doing, Lieutenant Colonel Shusko went to bat for me and crushed any opposition before it developed. In short, he gave me a chance to earn my reputation back.

My first class included a number of senior officers and NCOs, including Brigadier General Huwk. During one grappling exercise, I accidentally broke one of General Huwk's ribs. Injuries during the tan belt courses were not that uncommon. Fortunately, General Huwk bore no ill will. Later, when he took command of my division, he pinned my Silver Star on my chest and made a joke about the injury.

One afternoon that spring of 2004, Sergeant Ricardo Sanders, Gunny Marlow, and Gunny Collette suggested I try my hand at some of the amateur martial arts competitions in the area. I loved the idea. The daily workouts and training had restored my sense of identity as a young warrior. The thought of testing these newly developed skills in one-on-one combat excited me. I went into training.

I told Travis what I was doing, and he came down on weekends from the Academy to work with me on my ground game. Travis' wrestling career had ended on a sour note. Not only did he ruin his shoulder with the injury he sustained, but for whatever reason a lot of his teammates turned against him. He felt betrayed by that. His trips down to see me became his escape from that ugly social situation.

I had a key to the MACE facility by then. We'd go inside after hours and work our tails off. Initially, we worked on takedown drills and how to defend against them. I'd never done any wrestling before, and my technique was all based on football tackling. Travis worked with me to break those long-ingrained habits.

Both of us were hyper-competitive. As we sparred, we'd both sometimes lose our temper and really go at each other. Many times, Trav would duck low and try for my lead leg. I'd pummel him. He'd back off, then come again at me with lightning quickness and knock me flat on my back. Then he'd show me how he did it.

The fact was, I brought almost no skill set to the table when it came to my ground game. Most of the MACE program focuses on striking and weapons. There is some grappling work, but it forms only a portion of the curriculum. Travis pushed me hard and took great pride in my development. At the same time, his sense of humor and confidence made these hours in the dojo a lot of fun. He possessed a self-disparaging sense of humor that he never failed to use as we rolled around and beat the hell out of each other on the mats.

My first fight was something called the Combat Sports Challenge in Fredericksburg, Virginia. Several of the other MACE NCOs joined in to help me prepare for it during the week. In the very early mornings, Sanders worked with me on the basics of kickboxing and striking. Gunny Marlow and Gunny Collette would work with me during the days and frequently in the evenings as well. Often, I stayed and worked out until ten or eleven every night. When I did, chances were good one of them would stay with me to help me train.

Finally, the day of my first fight came. We drove down to the location, finding it to be a run-down warehouse full of about eighty beer swilling, rowdy fans. The floor was concrete and covered with sawdust to soak up the blood, like something straight out of *Fight Club*.

I stepped into the ring and faced my opponent. He was a tall, ruggedly cut dude who had tried to cultivate a Chuck Liddell sort of look. Shaved head, mustache, soul patch, and chin beard. He struck me as sort of a wannabe with that affectation. Whatever. Didn't matter. I just wanted to mix it up.

The bell sounded and we moved at each other. He struck first, trying to get me in a guillotine choke hold. It was tight as hell, and the small crowd could hear me sucking for air. As he squeezed, my airway closed and I could feel myself becoming lightheaded. I struggled to get free, but he held on fast. Eventually his arm grew weary.

Suddenly, something tumbled into place deep inside me. After all I'd been through since November, the idea of losing in front of these screaming drunks became utterly unbearable. A surge of strength born from pent-up fury broke his headlock. As I escaped, he poked me in the eye. Blood started to streak down my face. My vision grew fuzzy, but I didn't care. I walloped him hard with a right cross. The blow sent him stumbling. I charged forward and beat him down with relentless, rabid blows. I split his forehead open. Blood flowed, and he didn't want to continue after the doctor examined him. He threw in the towel. The fight had lasted just two minutes and forty-five seconds.

The crowd, which I later found out was full of veterans, went absolutely wild. Beer was slung into the ring, and both my opponent and I were doused with it. Master Gunny Sanders and Gunny Collett, both of whom cornered for me that day, rushed over to congratulate me. I finally cut loose for just a minute and celebrated the victory, spurred on by the reaction of the crowd. It was a glorious moment, and when we left that dilapidated warehouse, the excitement and natural high I felt stood in stark contrast to the despair that had colored my life for months. By the time I reached my barracks at the end of the event later that night, I knew I would fight again.

CHAPTER TWENTY-TWO

Benchwarmer's Guilt

That June, Trav graduated from the Academy and came down to Quantico to attend the Basic School. With my career still in stasis, I saw a lot of him. We took weekend trips together when we weren't training at the MACE dojo. Other times, we'd go for runs together. Thanks to Trav and Gunnys Marlow, Collette, and Sanders, I entered and won two more amateur fights. Those victories gave me a shot at the Virginia amateur light heavyweight title, which was scheduled for mid-November.

My work at the MACE wrapped up at the beginning of the month with the dedication of Raider Hall. We filled the display area with incredible photos and memorabilia of every Marine Raider battle fought during the Pacific War, then invited some of the remaining veterans of those units to help us dedicate the building. It was a tremendous day and set the stage for what happened in court the following week.

Nine months after the original allegations, I finally had my day in front of a court martial. We planned a straightforward defense: tell the truth and let the case stand on my word and the word of the other people in the townhouse that night. Though we had uncovered damaging information about Lieutenant J, we did not use it or bring it up in the courtroom.

The prosecution's case fell apart with their first witness. Lieutenant J took the stand and for the first time I heard her side of the story. She said that I had pinned her to the futon and would not let her up. She tried to struggle free, but I gripped her arms and kept her immobilized. Though she was probably a hundred pounds lighter and several inches shorter than I, she claimed a sudden burst of energy gave her the strength to throw me off her, and she ran from the room.

In a court martial, the jury is allowed to ask questions of each witness. In my case, the jury included three female Marine officers, all of whom had pointed questions for Lieutenant J. Why hadn't she called for help? With friends—male and female—in the townhouse, help was only a shout away. Lieutenant J had no answer for this. Why had nobody in the townhouse come to her aid if a scuffle really had taken place in the room? Surely, in the thin-walled condo, somebody would have heard something? No answer to that one, either.

What about physical evidence? She had no bruises, no injuries of any sort. She had no answer for that, either.

Her story unraveled from there. Why had she waited two days to report it? Why had she not called the police? Why did she stay the night and hang out with everyone—including me—the next morning if she felt endangered by my actions?

She couldn't answer any of those questions the jurists asked of her. Next, the prosecution called several witnesses who were at the townhouse that night. Instead of buttressing the prosecution, all of their witnesses ended up damaging their case and making ours.

When the time came for us to mount my defense, I took the stand first. I looked every jurist in the eye as I told the story of that night. I was meticulous and thorough. Every detail, every movement and action I recalled and explained as clearly as I could.

When the case went to the jury later that day, it took less than three hours for the verdict to come back. I was found innocent of all charges. The jury's verdict had been unanimous in my favor. At the end of the trial, the judge pointedly remarked, "Good luck to you, Lieutenant Stann." It was the closest the Marine Corps would come to an apology for the nightmare the last nine months had been. That and the looks the jury gave me as we filed out of the courtroom left me feeling that I could survive this, regain my reputation, and carry on with the goals I had within the Corps.

But the experience left deep scars on me. Since that incident, I have been extremely reserved around females. For the rest of my time in the Corps, I never let myself be alone in a room with a female. On base, if I ended up in a room in mixed company, I always opened a door. I would leave a room if a female entered it and nobody else was around.

My personal life evolved in a similar fashion. I had first met Teressa during the holiday break in December 2003. We saw each other in a group environment several times after that. When we started dating, she was puzzled by the lack of goodnight kisses at the end of our evenings together. It wasn't until we had offically became a couple that I broke down and told her the whole story. The pieces finally clicked into place for her. We took things slowly, and I learned through her love to trust again.

Those were issues that would take time for me to sort out. Meanwhile, I finally had my career back. I immediatly went into IOBC and joined a martial arts class. By now, many Academy classmates had already deployed to Iraq. The nine months of limbo cost me dearly on that front. I felt like I'd been left on the bench while my brothers fought on without me. All I wanted to do was finish up my school so I could get out there and be with them.

In September, I returned to Scranton on leave between graduation from TBS and starting Infantry Officers Basic School (IOBC). I was working out in a local gym when my cell phone rang. It was one of those calls.

Ron Winchester, who'd been an upperclassman and member of the football team at the Academy with us, had been killed by a roadside bomb outside of al Qaim. Ronny had been a brawler of an offensive lineman. His senior year, he gave one of the most inspiring locker room speeches I've ever heard: "Hey, I may not be all that good at football, but I know I'm good at one thing, and that's fighting."

When he graduated and joined his battalion, he took that spirit with him. His men loved him. He had just reached Anbar Province and was still doing right-seat, left-seat orientation patrols with the unit his men were supposed to replace when he died.

Feeling numb, I hung up the phone. I tried to continue my workout, but that was a lost cause. I went home and spent the day lost in thought. Gradually, the numbness went away, replaced by grief and benchwarmer's guilt. Ronny was the first friend I'd lost in combat. His death underscored my absolute uselessness to the Corps over the past nine months, which spurred my sense of guilt. I was sitting at home in Scranton. My place was in Anbar Province with the rest of my classmates and brothers.

Late that day, my cell phone rang again. Paul Fisher, another Academy classmate of ours, came across the line. "Brian, Brett Harmon was shot and killed today."

Confused, I replied, "That's not right. Ron Winchester died, Paul."

"No, you don't understand. Brett got shot."

"What are you talking about?"

"Something happened. A fight at the N.C. State football game. He and Joe Clemmey were at a tailgate party. Somebody shot Brett."

For the second time that day, my system went numb from shock. Brett had been on the wrestling team with Travis. They were very close friends, and through Travis I'd gotten to know and like him. He was a talented officer, at once tough and perpetually cheerful. Dimly, as I listened to Paul, I remembered a running joke we all had with Brett. He owned a green Saturn econo box, which earned him a lot of grief since it was a beat up piece of crap. One day, while somebody was giving him a ration of crap for driving such a wimpy car, I took Brett's side. "Screw that, Brett!" I shouted to him, "That's a *manly* Saturn!"

Brett feigned seriousness, "Why thank you, Brian. You're right. It is a *manly* Saturn."

After that, we must have run through that routine a dozen times in response to all the comments made at his car's expense.

That memory pierced the numbness. As I hung up, a double dose of grief set in.

Travis was devastated. He counted Brett among his closest friends, and this was his first personal experience with death. Both of us struggled with it.

Later, I called Joe Clemmey to find out what had happened. Joe and I met in my first Basic School class. He was a wild man, one of those Marines who has a *Break Glass in Case of War* sort of aura about him. Joe was a hurricane of energy, with a magnetic personality that naturally drew people to him. At times, some people found him obnoxious and loud. I found him endearing and tremendous fun off base. He embodied the footloose and furious sort of lifestyle I could never relax enough to experience. Going out on the town with Joe never failed to turn into an epic adventure. He had earned a black belt at the MACE and sparred with me early in my fighting career.

When I got in touch with Joe months later, he could hardly talk about what happened that day. He and Brett were tailgating with friends. A truck sped through the parking lot and nearly hit a little girl. Joe, Brett and Brett's hometown friends went after the truck and confronted the driver. Brett came over to moderate and keep things under control. The conversation ended. Brett and Joe returned to their party. A few hours later, the two guys who'd been in the truck walked up to Brett and shot him at point blank range in the chest. He died in Joe's arms, saying, "I'm good. I'm good." Joe held on to him long after his last breath, holding him in a brother's embrace.

Later that week, we flew out to Bretty's funeral and memorial service. Travis and I sat together on the flight out with the Academy's wrestling coach, Joel Starret. It did not take Joel long to see that both Trav and I were really struggling to get a handle on our grief. We were young and inexperienced with the magnitude of loss we faced.

Joel asked us to use the rest of the flight to write our own eulogies. If this was our funeral, what would we want people to know about us? At first, I recoiled at the idea, but when I saw Travis take it seriously, I started to give it serious thought. How did we want to be remembered? The question cut to the heart of who we wanted to be and the fundamentals of our character.

Joel handed us each a small note card on which to write our answers. I stared at it, unable to craft an answer. Next to me, Travis struggled as well. When he got stuck, he'd get fidgety. He kept glancing back to Joel, who silently encouraged him to keep working through it.

I wrestled over the question as well. I made several false starts, gave up, then tried again. Finally, I wrote a single sentence. When I read it back over, it still didn't feel right. I played with it until we landed.

So did Travis. He spent most of the flight lost in thought, eyes on his blank card. Before we landed, he began to write. Before I could see what he'd put on the paper, he tucked it away.

The next day, we attended the funeral, and it stripped away all the defenses I'd subconsciously tried to build up around the pain. For days, I'd held out hope that there had been some terrible mistake. Brett hadn't died; it was somebody else. The funeral shattered that denial. As the finality of it all set in, so did a profound sense of hopelessness. Why would such a fine man and officer be taken in such wanton fashion? It was a question that had no answer, but one that would linger long after we'd said our final goodbyes to our friend and classmate.

We returned home from the memorial service a few days later, hurting like we'd never experienced before. In the end, we lost ourselves in work and in workouts. During the days, I poured my energy into the IOBC program. Here, we were taught the fundamentals and advanced tactics of leading infantry into battle. It was complex and challenging enough that we could lose ourselves in the field exercises, or the tactical discussions around the sand table in our classroom. At night, to keep our minds busy, Trav and I met at Raider Hall to train for my upcoming fight in November. I beat on those pads with total abandon. With each punch, grief, anger, and guilt spilled out of me. The workouts became cathartic for both of us. By the time we finished up, both of us would be too exhausted to let our minds dwell on what had happened.

My upcoming fight would be for the Virginia amateur light heavyweight belt. Gunny Marlow and Travis would corner me, and we were all confident that I had a legitimate shot. Trav kept me focused on developing my ground game. Gunnys Marlow and Collette worked with me on my movement and striking techniques. Despite their help, my priority remained fixed on the IOC, and we spent most weeks in the field learning how to lead infantry in combat. Truthfully, I had no business taking a fight at this point in my career, but I said yes anyway since it gave me a shot at a title.

On November 11, 2004, Travis and I drove down to Virginia Beach together. It had been two months since Brett and Ronny had died, and we had just begun to move forward from escaping our grief to confronting it and accepting what had happened. It had not been an easy process, and we'd come to realize that the pain would never leave us. But it had become more manageable, and I think we both felt like we'd reached a turning point.

We checked into the hotel and headed up to our room. Trav was anxious and vibrating with so much energy that he couldn't stand still. We dumped our gear in the room, then settled down to wait for Gunny Marlow, who planned to join us that afternoon before the fight began.

Trav bounded around the room, pacing furiously and offering tidbits of advice as they occurred to him. Hypercompetitive, aggressive as hell, Trav loved days like this one. He'd get lost in the build up and keep me ruthlessly focused.

He also had a knack for knowing what lingered in my mind. One look, he could read my mood like nobody else aside from my mom and Teressa. Once he figured out where my head was, he'd go to work to make sure I found the zone needed for the contest ahead. Occasionally, he would almost go too far, being such an intrusive guys at times.

Travis' cell phone rang. He stepped out of the room and into the hallway. As the door closed behind him, I heard the tone of his voice go flat but couldn't catch his words. When he returned a few minutes later, his pre-fight energy had evaporated. I looked up to see him staring morosely out the window, his face betraying a mix of shock and rage.

"What's up, Trav?"

"Nothing."

I stood up and walked over to him. "What was that phone call, Travis?"

He looked at me with pain-filled eyes. A flutter of dread coursed through me.

"Nothing," he repeated, his voice devoid of strength.

"Don't bullshit me, Trav. What the fuck is going on?" I said, trying to control the panic I felt.

"I'll tell you later," he evaded.

"You'll tell me now," I demanded.

He looked away. "After the fight."

"No. Give it to me straight," I demanded. "What is

going on?"

"J. P. Blecksmith was killed in Fallujah last night."

The mention of his name brought back memories of the tall blue-eyed athlete whose competitive fires evoked so much admiration in me.

Then it dawned on me what Travis had just said.

"What?" I asked weakly.

Three of us in one fall?

"He was shot on a rooftop. That's all I know," Travis said. He looked absolutely miserable.

"I shouldn't have told you. I'm so sorry Brian. I should have waited until after the fight."

I sank into a chair. "No. I needed to know."

Trav tried to rally. "Look. Focus on the belt. Okay? Win the fight. Then we'll deal with this, okay? Go out and fucking win."

I nodded vaguely, thinking I had no idea how to compartmentalize like that.

An hour later, we met up with Gunny Marlow after he arrived at the hotel. We found him at the elevators. One glance at me and he knew something was wrong.

"What's the matter?" he asked me.

"My boy J. P. Blecksmith just died in Fallujah."

Gunny Marlow exhaled fiercely. "Oh, fuck."

We walked back to the hotel, Gunny fuming at Travis for having told me the news. It wasn't his fault. I basically forced it out of him.

In the final hours before the fight, Travis grew increasingly angry. J. P.'s death had filled us both with a volatile combination of grief and rage. I swam in and out of those two emotional currents, completely incapable of controlling either.

"You gotta kick his ass," Travis said over and over.

"You cannot lose this fight. You will not lose this fight. You've got the heart." He stormed around the room, face red, eyes hard.

When I stepped into the ring that night, I exploded at my opponent as soon as the bell rang for the first round. My fists became the only outlet for the fury I felt, and I pummelled him wildly. My opponent reeled back. I charged in after him. He landed a solid takedown that sucked all the rage right out of me. A sense of pure hopeless grief remained in its place. I could not get out from under him. In my rage, I tried to take his head off. I faltered, and he seizeed the opportunity and drove me to the mat. Before I could recover, he'd pinned me and the ref had called the fight.

Travis lost it, his grief morphed entirely into anger now. After the fight, we retreated to our hotel room, where we met up with buddies, stationed at Norfolk. While the rest of us sat in communal silent misery, Trav paced around the room. He wanted this fight, *needed* the win as a tiny bright spot in an otherwise dismal time in our lives.

I'd let him down, but that's not how he saw it. By telling me when he did, he blamed himself for getting me out of my zone and wrecking my chances for the win.

I saw all this on his face. Trav and I had spent so much time together since the spring that we could get into each other's heads quite easily.

I wanted to turn to him and tell him that it was just a stupid amateur fight. Given the magnitude of the loss we all faced, it seemed inconsequential to me. We needed to keep perspective.

But Trav would have called bullshit on me. Fuming over the fight was partly transference of the grief we felt about J. P. But the fact was, we were both do-or-die competitors. We made no excuses. We went out and took care of business. That's what motivated us both and helped bond us as friends.

We were also Marines. We drive on no matter what the situation. We execute the mission. We take care of our own.

Competitors and Marines: Those were our two defining features. But right at that moment, being both was utterly devastating.

CHAPTER TWENTY-THREE

The Birthplace of Character

Quantico, Virginia, December 2004

"My head felt like I'd been beaten with a piece of rebar. The previous night, we had thrown caution to the wind. We went over to Georgetown and drank way too much. Now I was paying for it.

"Brian! Brian!"

"Trav—what the hell. Get outta here," I moaned.

"Get up, Brother!" He poked me. I rolled over and buried my head under a pillow. "Trav, I've got a skull-splitting headache. Let me sleep."

"No way. Come on get up. Best cure for a hangover is a workout."

He tore the covers away, and I finally roused myself. Sitting on the side of the bed, I looked up at him. His eyes were red-rimmed and bloodshot.

Travis goaded and prodded until I finally made it outside in running shoes and sweats. Joel Starret joined us a few minutes later.

"You guys ready?"

"No," I said. I took a long pull from a water bottle. I was dead tired and mildly hung over. Trav was in far worse shape. He'd been hydrated entirely by beer. Now his head throbbed so badly that I swear his eyeballs bulged with every pulse.

Trav, our friend Gary Hess, and I had finally had enough of grief and despair in the wake of J. P.'s funeral. We had headed to Georgetown to lose ourselves in the loud music and stiff drinks of the local bar scene. It had worked, too. But we got more than we'd bargained for later in the night.

"Come on, let's go for a run," Joel ordered. He turned and loped away. Trav smiled at me and said, "See ya on the high ground." He dashed off after his former wrestling coach. I groaned and followed, bits and pieces of the night before starting to fall into place within my memory.

Things had been going well until we hit one particularly crowded night club. The dance floor was packed, and as we made our way to the bar, Gary accidentally bumped into a beautiful brunette woman as she danced with her boyfriend.

"Excuse me," he said over the music.

The woman spun around and suddenly shoved Gary so hard he staggered backward at least ten feet. Somehow, he kept his balance and didn't fall over. Seconds later, her boyfriend descended on Gary. Travis and I rushed over to hear him screaming at our friend for touching her.

Gary kept trying to apologize, but the woman and her boyfriend were both so lit they just uncorked on him. As they both screamed at him, Gary started to get angry. "Dude, listen," he told the boyfriend, "you need to control your woman!"

Well, that couldn't have been more offensive, and the girl went berserk. She wound up and drop-kicked Gary right in the balls, who turned surrender white and barely kept his knees from buckling. Then she turned and tried the same trick on Travis. Trav was waiting for her and caught her foot just inches from his crotch. "No way, Darlin', no way!" he said in a mock scolding voice.

I grabbed my two friends and dragged them out of the club. The last thing we needed was trouble. "Look, let's go get a burger or something," I said to them.

Food appealed to us at that moment. Brunette and boyfriend forgotten, we headed around the corner to a Johnny Rogers and found a booth. Unfortunately, the boyfriend had assembled a posse and sortied out of the night club after us. With their girlfriends in tow, they found us at the burger joint and stormed inside. The brunette and a couple other women stood outside watching through the plate glass windows as their men walked up to our table and leaned over us.

Travis and Gary looked up at the boyfriend and his buddies, expressions blank. This was not a good thing. Gary was a former enlisted Marine who served in the artillery. He'd grown up in a rough section of New Orleans and was a veteran of plenty of Big Easy street brawls. At six feet, two twenty, he was leather hard. We currently roomed together as we went through Infantry Officers Basic School, and many times we'd sparred together over at the MACE. He was not a guy to mess with lightly. And when their faces went blank like this, it meant both he and Trav were about to unleash a whole lot of hurt on somebody.

"Hey guys," I said to our visitors. "Look, I know you're trying to impress your girlfriends over there." I nodded to the window. They looked up briefly. The brunette was watching expectantly from the sidewalk, her friends clustered around her.

I continued, "But I gotta give ya fair warning. Unless you guys are packing heat, you are messing with the wrong people."

"So, why don't you turn around and walk back out of here with your dignity intact and go have a good night. Otherwise, it is about to get really ugly."

The boyfriend locked eyes with me. As he studied the intensity behind my words, I saw his bravado slip away, replaced by naked uncertainty. After a long moment, he finally said, "Okay guys, thanks. Have a good night."

He and his posse walked out of the Johnny Rogers without another word. Travis watched them leave and grew agitated. "What the fuck, Brian?" He demanded.

"What?" I said, surprised by his reaction.

"Who the hell gives a guy who wants to beat our asses a goddamned pep talk?"

The three of us busted out laughing. It was the first time since J. P.'s funeral that I'd been able to do that, and it felt utterly cathartic.

Unfortunately, that next morning, I paid a premium for that fleeting lighthearted moment.

"Come on, Brian!" Trav called to me as we jogged after Joel. Sweating profusely, I followed them along a trail and up a steep hill. Two miles later, gasping for breath, our stomachs in knots, we reached the top to find that Joel had pre-positioned some pads for us.

Joel stepped over to us and sniffed the air. "Jeez, you guys smell like a brewery."

For the next hour, we whaled on the pads until our upper bodies ached. Then, we started our run back down the hill.

Curiously, when we finished, both of us did feel better. Four miles and a workout just didn't seem like a conventional hangover cure. But that was Travis, always going through life at full throttle.

After we showered and got cleaned up, we met over at Joel's place to barbeque and shoot the breeze. Somewhere along the way, the conversation drifted from small talk to shop talk.

"Hey Brian, what do you think makes a good leader?" Joel asked me.

"Well, Gunny Marlow once told me, 'a good officer has balls of steel—or at least acts like it.' " We laughed, then I added, "I think a good officer has the ability to find the point of friction and immediately make everyone feel better just because he is there. His men believe in him and know he'll make the right decision regardless of the chaos around them."

He grinned. "Yeah. Presence on the battlefield. That has to be important."

Joel got up to flip the burgers. The smell of meat cooking made my stomach growl. I hadn't eaten anything at all that day, thanks to my hangover. With the alcohol flushed from my system by our four mile fun run, I was ready for some grub.

Travis took a pull from a soda can. "Also, you've got to work harder than anyone else. Set the example with your dedication."

"True. And you've got to be accountable," I added.

"Not just that, the decisions you make have to reinforce your authority," Travis said.

"What do you mean?"

"Being decisive and not hesitating is only part of it. You know? The orders you give have to earn the respect of the men under your command. They need to know that when you make a decision, it is the best one for them and the mission. Once they come to trust your judgment, they'll hang with you when it gets nasty."

"Good point."

Joel returned with a bowl of chips and sat back down. The day was unseasonably warm and clear, with little wind. We sat in sweatshirts and enjoyed the interlude in the otherwise dreary autumn weather.

"Hey Trav, if I forgot to say it the other day—thanks for the sandwich. Your timing couldn't have been better," I told him.

I had just gotten back from an intense field exercise as part of the IOBC syllabus earlier in the week. It had been a grueling one, and we'd been out in the rain and mud for days without sleep, eating nothing but MREs while on the run. I had been cleaning my rifle when Travis bounded in with a foot long sandwich from Subway. He'd loaded it with meat, and every bite was like eating a five star meal after what we'd been doing.

"No worries, Brian. And you thanked me enough that night."

"Thanks for looking out for me."

He looked surprised by that. "What the hell else are friends supposed to do?"

That was Travis: Totally loyal, without concept or understanding of any other way to live life.

We sat in silence, enjoying the afternoon and the intoxicating smells wafting off the grill. Then Travis asked me, "Okay, suppose we do everything right. What about our Marines?"

"What about them?"

"What sort of men do you want with you in battle?"

I'd actually given that a lot of thought recently. "You know, all things considered, I think I want men who've suffered adversity and overcome it."

This surprised both Joel and Travis. Joel asked, "Adversity, why?"

"Think about it. I don't want to go into combat with guys who have had perfect, safe little lives. Those guys are the ones who've never been tested, and you won't know how they'll react when they finally are."

"Good point," Travis mused.

"I heard somebody say at the Academy once that 'Adversity is the birthplace of character.'"

"Well, we've seen our share of that recently," Travis grumbled.

"No doubt," I replied, thinking about J. P., Brett, and Ronny. If that wasn't enough, Travis had just received his MOS. Instead of infantry, the Marine Corps had made him a supply officer. He had taken that bitter pill quietly, but I knew it tore him up. More than anything, he wanted to follow in his father's footsteps. Counting beans and bullets did not factor into that equation.

"Maybe all this shit has a purpose," I said, thinking half-aloud.

Travis got up and checked on the meat. He began tossing the patties onto a plate. Joel and I went over to help.

"Maybe it does, though it isn't always clear what the purpose is," Travis said. "At least, not at first."

"What do you mean?"

"Think about it. It takes time for things to unfold," Joel said as he slipped a burger onto a bun and started garnishing it.

"Yeah," Travis agreed. "Take a look at everything that happened to you, Brian. Without all the shit Lieutenant J put you through, you never would have started fighting. Now, you're involved in something that has made you a better leader."

I hadn't thought about it that way before. I'd been too overwhelmed by it all to have that sort of perspective. I'd still rather have gotten to Iraq with the rest of our classmates. But Travis was right. The entire court martial ordeal turned out to be a gift.

We ate and talked until the shadows grew long late that afternoon. Finally, we said our thanks to Joel and headed home. As we drove back to Quantico, I finally asked Travis a question that had nagged me since our flight to Brett's funeral.

"Trav, what did you write as your eulogy on the plane that day?"

He didn't respond at first. Then, silently, he pulled the note card from his pocket and handed it to me.

Travis Manion was a man unafraid to stand for what was right.

That was one of the last times Travis and I were together. Within a few weeks, the Corps pulled us in different directions. I graduated from IOBC first in my class and was initially assigned to a battalion headed for Okinawa. I wanted to get to Iraq, so I traded slots with another officer and got orders to 3/2 Marines at Camp Lejeune, North Carolina. Travis joined the 1st Reconnaissance Battalion out of Camp Pendleton. The Corps sent us to opposite coasts. Our deployments never coincided, so when I was in Iraq, he was back in the States. He went over after we got back. Still, we kept in touch via e-mail and periodic phone calls. It wasn't the same, though. I missed our workouts and fun runs, and the hours we spent in the dojo pushing each other with our compatible competitive spirits. Most of all, I missed him always having my back.

CHAPTER TWENTY-FOUR

Rumble in the Rose Garden

Travis, Gunny Marlow, and Gunny Collette had planted the idea of trying to turn pro in my head. While deployed to al Qaim in 2005, I thought about it a great deal. After what happened during Matador in May of that year, I used what little down time I had to train as much as I could. It was a tremendous stress reliever, plus I didn't want my MMA skills to atrophy. I'd worked too hard with Travis and the staff NCOs at the MACE for that to happen.

That fall, as our deployment entered its final months, I undertook a search for a promoter willing to sign me. In December 2005, Ryan Schultz, who worked with Sportfight, contacted me. He offered me a spot on the undercard for an upcoming MMA event in Portland, Oregon. The pay was five hundred bucks, and I had to pay for my own flight out. I had two and a half weeks to train.

At the time, 3/2 was back at Lejeune. Travis was stuck in the purgatory of his supply billet in California, so he wasn't around to help me get ready. Joe Clemmey and Gary Hess were both stationed at Lejeune, and they offered to help me. Together, we found an old, beat up gym on base that was seldom used any more. It was in such bad shape that the building was rarely locked up. Inside, we found ancient, mold-filled mats stacked in one corner. We joked that they probably had been used to teach hand-to-hand combat techniques to Vietnam-Era Marines.

We had nothing else, so we dragged them into the middle of the gym and went to work. The mats turned out to be so filthy that we all developed ringworm from them after our first few sessions in our new hideout. We didn't care. We cleaned them up as best we could and returned for more every night. We also sparred together in the early mornings so that we'd book end our work days with training time.

Joe and Gary both proved to be outstanding sparring partners. Good thing, too, as nobody else seemed willing to give up their free time so I could punch them in the face. Big, tough, and a little bit crazy, they loved mixed martial arts. Both were amateur fighters with several victories each under their belts. Joe was the stand up brawler. He flat out loved to scrap and did so with no regard for his personal safety. He just waded in, all guns blazing. Gary, the Marine from the Big Easy who'd been my roommate at IOBC, specialized in grappling. He worked on our ground game. Joe and I worked on our striking. We learned together from each other. No coach, no mentor. We were three eager Marines willing to challenge each other to become better at our sport. We had no idea at the time, but we didn't know shit.

Just before I left for Portland, I had arranged a special surprise for Teressa. Since I'd returned from Iraq, we had grown quite serious, and I'd finally stirred up enough courage to tell her how I felt. She was working three jobs at the time, including bartending at a place in Philly. On the weekends, I'd fly up to see her from North Carolina and sit at the bar while she worked. Saturdays, she had a job back in Scranton. And Sundays were devoted to the Philadelphia Eagles cheerleading squad. Somehow, we always found time to be together, even if it was only for a few hours.

Right before Christmas, I contacted the Eagles' front office and asked if I could propose to Teressa on the field during the final regular season game at Lincoln Financial Field. When I told them I was a Marine and would be heading back to Iraq soon, the Eagles' administrative staff moved mountains to set this up.

On New Year's Day 2006, I stepped onto the field after the Eagles unfortunately lost to the Washington Redskins 31–20. The entire cheerleading team had assembled at the fifty-yard line. Teressa had no idea what was about to happen until she saw me appear before the squad. On one knee, I produced the ring and asked her to spend her life with me. I am, to this day, terribly relieved that she didn't say no. The crowd in the stands gave us a rousing ovation.

The following Friday, I flew out to Portland after a full week of work with 3rd Battalion, 2nd Marines. Frank, my future brother-in-law, offered to pay his own way and corner me. Together, we crossed the country, showed up at the Portland airport late that Friday night, and caught a ride to a fleabag motel. The next morning, I weighed in.

Nobody knew a thing about me. I was a complete unknown on the West Coast and so new to the sport that

I had no reputation or film for my opponent to study. At the same time, I knew very little about the fighter I would face. Aaron Stark was his name. I'd heard that he'd been a Big Ten wrestler in college. He was a member of MENSA and owned a winery. I never saw any fight film or knew anything about his style.

That night, I climbed into the cage in the Rose Garden Arena, the home of the NBA's Portland Trailblazers. The place was packed with jovial, screaming fans. I'd never been in front of a crowd this large before, and I couldn't help but feel a little intimidated by the spectacle. We arrived in Portland so unprepared that I had to borrow tape from another fighter just to get my gloves on. Fortunately, Frank, the lone man in my corner, took good care of me. Having an ally, especially one who would be family someday soon, kept me on an even keel.

The first seconds of the fight went all Aaron's way. He managed to take me down and knock me on my back. Before I could get away, he'd come down on top of me. Fortunately, Travis and Gary had taught me how to deal with this situation. Using my hips, I slid out of his way every time he drew back to beat on my head. Simultaneously, to keep him from delivering the full weight of his punches on me, I grabbed his neck and pulled his head toward my chest. He couldn't posture up to deliver a knockout blow.

I quickly realized that while these two tricks of the trade had saved me from an early defeat, I lacked Aaron's technique and refinement. All I had going for me were heart and mental strength. I refused to give up and kept buying time. Every time Aaron tried to make me submit, I'd do just enough to slip away. Finally, the ref stood us back up.

I was in my element now. I went straight at Aaron and caught him with repeated left-right combinations to his head. He ducked away, came back, and tried to take me down. I darted away and beat on his head again. The fight developed its own cadence: he'd try for the take-down, I'd keep it upright. We battled back and forth, but I could see the blows I landed taking a toll on him.

He came at me again, this time moving like quicksilver to snare my forward leg. As he lifted it off the mat to try and knock me off balance and get me down again, I hopped on my back leg and drilled him square in the face. He released my leg and staggered back. I charged forward to land one final right jab, left hook combo. That did it. He dropped to the mat three minutes and fifteen seconds into the first round. I won by TKO.

Frank jumped into the cage, screaming like a banshee. Before I could react, he swept me up into a fierce embrace and lifted me off my feet. Laughing wildly, I threw my gloves over my head as the crowd cheered for the unknown underdog Marine. That first win was one of the highlights of my life.

Sports Fight liked what they'd seen from me and wanted me back. I had a future as a pro fighter now.

At the end of the night, Ryan Schultz dropped Frank and me off at an all-night restaurant near our motel. We ate a late dinner, talking excitedly, my gear bag under the table between our feet. I called back to Lejeune and told my Marines that I was now 1–0. The company went wild, and I could hear my men shouting and screaming. Their excitement meant the world to me.

Dinner done, I threw my bag over one shoulder and stepped out into the rainy Oregon night. We promptly got lost looking for our motel. Well after midnight, we wandered the empty streets looking for our place. Neither of us minded. It gave us a chance to talk and get to know each other better.

We busted out with another celebration right there in the rain. Frank threw his arm around my shoulder and said, "You know Brian, everyone was wondering, 'Who the hell is that guy?'"

I started laughing. "It seemed that way."

"I'll tell you one thing, though," Frank said through an ear-to-ear grin.

"What's that, Bro?"

"They sure know who you are now!"

CHAPTER TWENTY-FIVE

Triple Six

About a week after my first pro fight, Gary Hess and I crept into the old gym at Camp Lejeune one night after a long day with our companies. We were looking forward to working up a sweat, but as we entered the main part of the gym, we found two other Marines battling on the mold covered mats. Both were muscular and well-conditioned men, and as we watched them spar, we realized that their skills were far more advanced than ours.

It turned out to be one of the best chance encounters of my life. Chris McCort and George Lockhart were both dedicated, professional MMA fighters. Already George had fought four pro fights. Chris had one under his belt. The four of us agreed to train together.

My first night sparring with George and Chris was one of those ass-kicking moments you never forget. Both outweighed me by about twenty pounds. All night long, they punished me until I was sore. I could stay with them and give them a real fight if I stayed up on my feet. But when they took me down, I discovered their ground games were far more advanced than mine.

Perfect. They could help me grow where I was the weakest. And I could help them where I was the strongest. One blade sharpened the other.

Twice a day, we met in that foul old gym and got our sweat on. Occasionally, we'd arrive to discover somebody had locked its doors. No matter, we trained on the grass out front in any weather.

That spring, George went out and won his fifth fight. A short time later, the World Extreme Cagefighting League (WEC) contacted me and offered me a fight in June against Miguel Cosio, another newcomer. My battalion's training cycle included a trip out to Twenty-Nine Palms in Southern California for some final combined arms field exercises before we headed over to Iraq again.

For six weeks, we worked furiously in the Southern California desert. We ran urban combat exercises, we cross-trained on weapons so that every man in the battalion could use any of the weapons we would carry with us into Iraq, and we devoted ourselves to night operations. At the time, I was an acting company commander while functioning as 3/2's fire support coordinator as well. Wearing two hats meant twenty-hour days, which did not allow me much time to train for Cosio.

We finished up in the desert, returned to Lejeune, and began our final preparations for our second combat deployment. A week before my second pro fight, I threw my back out during a personal fitness test each deploying Marine had to take. A doctor prescribed muscle relaxants and Valium for me, but it essentially scuttled any chance I had at training before the fight. Consigned to bed rest, I spent two days flat on my back trying to move as little as possible so my back might heal. On the day Frank and I were supposed to fly to California for the event, I managed to get upright and limp around, but I was not sure I could fight.

Out in California, we had three days to prepare for fight night. I spent two of those resting my back. On day three, I had to work out for the cameras. I took it gently and felt stiff, but by the time the dog and pony show was over, I knew I'd be able to get into the cage.

This time, a whole posse of friends and fellow Marines flew out just to see me fight. Jake Jackson, my childhood friend from Scranton, had joined the Corps recently but somehow found time to get out to California to support me. Bryce McDonald and Joey Fay flew in as well. I had hoped Travis would be able to make it, but his unit had deployed to Iraq. He wished me luck via email and said he wished he could be out with us.

On fight night, I climbed into the cage at the San Manuel Indian Casino in San Bernadino and faced off against Miguel Cosio. When he took off his shirt prior to the first round, I saw that he had 666 tattooed across his back. The sight of that enraged me. As a Marine officer, I had seen true human evil up close in Iraq. We'd witnessed suicide bombers who targeted civilian marketplaces just to score a high body count. We'd encountered murderous insurgent bands that preyed on the innocent. We'd encountered torture chambers and found the bodies of men horribly defiled before they were killed.

And here was my opponent, apparently embracing evil, as evidenced by that tattoo. I couldn't wait for the bell to ring to start the fight. I wanted blood. His blood. There is no redemption in evil, nothing glorious or worthy of admiration. It is vile and repellent. Though I didn't know Miguel, at that moment, I hated his guts.

The round began and I flung myself straight at him in a complete state of rage. Miguel waited to receive my attack, but he didn't move fast enough. I landed two fury-fueled blows and he collapsed to the mat, out cold. Two punches, sixteen seconds. I was 2–0 now.

That night, my friends gathered together for a post-fight party. Teressa had flown out with me. This was her first taste of my fighting career, but it was also her first opportunity to meet my old friends. She got along famously with everyone, which made the weekend even sweeter for me.

As we sat and reminisced at the park that night, I felt so blessed that my MMA career provided this opportunity for us to reunite. These chances were becoming fewer and farther apart as our careers unfolded and sent us to the distant corners of the globe. Bryce, our bruising fullback from Missouri, had just returned from a tour on Okinawa in the western Pacific. His unit was working up for an Iraq deployment to Anbar Province. He'd be overseas in a few months. Joey Fay and Jake were also Iraq-bound. And by summer's end, I'd be gone as well. We had become an American warrior clan. Some of us had wives now. Some, like me, had a fiancée. Our clan had grown and developed, but there were empty places that night.

I couldn't help but think of J. P. Blecksmith and Brett Harmon. Sudden death had taken them from us. We never got to say goodbye—hell we were so young and naïve we didn't think we needed to do that. Instead, we blindly stumbled into the future, not comprehending that death would become a constant specter in our midst.

Our reunion became more poignant as we turned serious and discussed our lost friends. I think all of us realized that this wasn't just a chance to get together and talk about old times. It was a gift, a fluke of circumstance that found us all stateside on the edge of new deployments. Soon we'd be in harm's way again, and we'd grown enough since 2004 to know the odds did not favor all of us coming home. I looked around at my friends, all of us sitting together around the fire, and wondered who of us would be missing the next time my fighting career brought us together again. Maybe it would be me.

No, this wasn't just an opportunity to reconnect. It was our chance to say goodbye.

CHAPTER TWENTY-SIX

Title Shot

When I returned from Iraq in the spring of 2007 I was a changed man. That second deployment wore all of us down, tested our endurance to the limit, and battered our morale. Losing four men from my company made for countless sleepless nights. It also meant more second-guessing, more guilt, more memories I wish I did not have.

If anything, the second deployment made me even more serious and rigid as a human being. I saw how one slip in discipline could cost a family their loved one. I grew hyper-vigilant and more structured, and I rededicated myself each day to keeping my Marines alive as best I could.

Underneath the professional persona—presence, as Travis called it—I felt more emotionally exhausted than at any other time in my life. Spiritual weariness, that's what it was, triggered by the deaths of too may fine young men whom I loved as brothers.

One thing the Academy never taught us was how to shut off that sense of responsibility we accept when we assume leadership roles in combat. It was so ingrained into us by the time we reached our units that I think all of us young officers took it to extremes, at great personal cost.

Combat is so utterly random that only a fool believes it can be controlled. And that is the issue we all faced in Anbar Province. Warriors are purpose-built control freaks. We thrive on order and discipline because we believe both will save lives once the bullets start to fly. It is our way to try to control the uncontrollable.

When that moment comes, every man in our unit can do everything right and still Marines can die. It just happens; that's the randomness of combat. It overrides professionalism. It trumps discipline. It beats personal courage and valor. It is the sudden mortar barrage, the fluke RPG, the IED that, if placed another six inches to the left or right, would have exploded harmlessly and done no damage. It is the bullet fired anonymously by some spraying-and-praying insurgent that somehow hits flesh.

There is no controlling those things. That's just a fact. But in every leader's heart, we still believe we can. That's why, when men die under our command, we blame ourselves and the decisions we made. And as we take ownership for these things, the guilt associated with them eats away at us. Left unchecked, I have seen it destroy families and the careers of fine Marines.

That spring of 2007, I struggled with that issue in the weeks after coming home. Intellectually, I knew I could not have done anything different that might have saved Rene Martinez. My heart refused to believe it. Same thing with Mike Brown and Champlin. My intellectual side and emotional side went to war against each other. My ability to sleep was caught in the middle.

During those long and difficult nights, I would think of my Marines and their actions under fire. Tremendous human beings they were. The thought that they would not be acknowledged or even remembered for what they did in Iraq was just something I could not stomach.

I needed an outlet, some way to focus all these things rolling around inside me.

My MMA career became that outlet. What had started as a means to escape from the charges leveled against me in the Basic School had grown into a second professional career for me. But what did that mean? Was it just some frivolous lark now, some way to keep athletic competition as part of my life?

While still in Iraq on my second deployment, I received an e-mail asking me to call the WEC. One night, I used a satellite phone and had a chat with a WEC official. He told me the league had just merged with Zuffa, the parent company that owns the UFC. After he broke that piece of exciting news, he asked me to take on a young fighter named Steve Cantwell. Steve was being called the "next Chuck Liddell" thanks to his fierce striking ability, movement, and technique. I took the fight, even as I struggled with why I wanted to keep going in the sport.

Yes, fighting was an outlet, a diversion, and a way to feed the competitive heart I possessed. But that wasn't enough. The WEC planned to give a lot of exposure to my fight with Cantwell. The more I thought about it, the more I realized that media attention could be used to celebrate the lives and accomplishments of the Marines I have served with in battle. Those on camera interviews became my penance.

March 24, 2007, I met Cantwell during WEC 26 in Las Vegas. As I walked to the octagon, I did so as an underdog. The pundits had compared our physicality, dissected our striking technique, our ground game, and our quickness. They had studied our fight films, found our supposed weaknesses, and noted our strengths. I admit, they were thorough.

But they couldn't know what was in my heart.

J. P. Blecksmith
Ron Winchester
Brett Harmon
James Brown
Doug Champlin
Rene Martinez
Willy Koprince
Robert Gass
Jonathon Lowe

Their names became my mantra. When the bell finally rang, I felt like a dam exploded inside me. I went straight after Cantwell, nothing fancy. My aggressiveness caught him off guard, as usually the first few moments of a fight are spent sizing up an opponent. He lashed out with one leg, aiming for my sciatic nerve. I evaded the blow and closed the gap between us so he couldn't try to deliver another kick. I jab at him, but he's incredibly elusive. Fast and bird-quick with his movements, he saw my punch coming and had time to react.

I kept coming until we clenched up. Then I landed an uppercut that seemed to rattle him. He backed up as I gave chase. Before he could react, I nailed him with a quick kick to the upper thigh, then followed it up with a left-right combination jab. He tried to get away again, but I stayed on him. I unleashed a right hook that hit him in the back of the jaw. Cantwell sagged to the mat, at best partially conscious. I beat on his head to make sure of the victory until the ref called the fight forty-one seconds into the first round.

Cantwell fans believed the ref called the fight too early and gave me a victory I did not deserve. Almost from the moment we left the octagon, cries arose for a rematch. Sooner or later, we knew we'd face each other again, and I had no doubt that he would be better prepared than he seemed to be that night in 2007.

Beating Steve put me on the fast track for a shot at a title fight. The WEC matchmaker scheduled my next fight for June against Craig Zellner. Craig was another up-and-coming fighter with a 4–1 record. Prior to his MMA career, he played football at the University of New Mexico, tried his hand at a pro boxing career, and even had a few pro wrestling bouts under his belt. At his peak, he weighed in at 260 pounds. The photos I saw of him at that size made him look like a manscaped beast, rippling with muscles. No wonder people called him Big Z. To fight in the light heavyweight division, he had to lean down some, but he was still the largest fighter I had ever been up against.

Watching film of his fights revealed he possessed a first rate ground game. He'd won most of his fights by submission. Submission, hell. He charged in with deceptive speed and flung his opponents around like rag dolls. His superior size and incredible strength gave him a tremendous advantage, and I had no illusions that if he got me on the mat, I'd be in trouble. My ground game remained in its infancy; I simply didn't have the knowledge or technical expertise yet. To win, I'd have to keep the fight upright and beat him with my fists.

Back at Camp Lejeune, George, Gary, and I went to work. Every morning and evening between our duties as Marines, we met up at the ancient gym to spar and train. None of us had a coach, and while in the past I hadn't been troubled by that fact, I was now. Right after coming home from my second deployment, I had flown to Vegas to train for a couple of days at a professional gym run by John Lewis. The experience opened my eyes and forced me to realize that my situation at Lejeune put me at a disadvantage against fighters like Cantwell, whose full-time training was carefully managed by outstanding coaches.

Nevertheless, I felt comfortable working with my fellow Marines. We ruthlessly critiqued each other and developed a free-flowing, open style to our makeshift training camps that helped us grow as fighters. We made sure our skins were thick and our ears were open.

Twice during my training before the Zellner fight, I flew back to Vegas for further work. My wife flew out with me and spent the first day downstairs at the gym getting the fisheye from every young fighter in the place. After that, she retreated to the hotel to wait for me. Meanwhile, Lewis' coaches worked with me on my ground game. We practiced new defenses against takedowns and other counter-wrestling techniques that I'd never used before. Lewis and his coaches also gave me tactical tips and helped me build a game plan for the fight. This was also new to me, as I'd always just entered the cage with one objective: overwhelm my opponent with my heart and firepower. Coach Ron Frazier from the Extreme Couture Gym in Las Vegas opened my eyes to the tactical nuances of the sport and how to train for a specific opponent in order to take advantage of his weaknesses and minimize my own.

In Vegas, I also had the opportunity to meet and spar with the current light heavyweight champ, Forrest Griffin. One afternoon, he stopped by and watched me during a shark tank drill. This involved me going up against a new opponent every minute. As your strength drains away and you get more exhausted, you continually face fresh opponents. The drill was designed to build endurance and get fighters used to functioning despite high exhaustion levels.

The first time I flew out, I forgot my mouth guard. I wasn't about to borrow one from another fighter, so I went into the cage to spar that first day without one. Forrest climbed in with me and we started banging on each other. Sure enough, he popped me right in the mouth with one of his steel-reinforced fists and chipped a tooth. He broke out laughing and said, "Who gives a shit, Brian? Don't you Marines have free health care?"

Those interludes in Vegas gave me plenty of things to work on and think about as the bout loomed closer. I came back to Lejeune with a more focused training plan that Gary and George helped me implement. Meanwhile, the WEC began a public relations push on me and my story as a Marine. They promoted me as the "All American Brian Stann" and landed me spots on national television. Reporters from *USA Today*, the *New York Times*, and other papers came to interview me, and I was booked on radio talk shows, including Howard Stern. I was not comfortable with the media attention. I got the sense I was expected to brag about myself, but that was something I refused to do. Instead, I made sure whatever I discussed during these interviews always came back to the men I served with in the Marine Corps. This was my chance to be out there telling their story, and I was very grateful to have that opportunity.

Craig Zellner and I met in Vegas at WEC 28 *Wrekcage* on June 3, 2007. George Lockhart, my brother-in-law Frank, and Ron Frasier cornered for me. In the final minutes before the fight, Craig arrived in the cage wearing his trademark black skull-and-crossbones trunks. His coaches gathered with him for a final chat. He looked huge, with broad shoulders and long, tree-trunk-thick arms.

The bell rang and the first round began. Right away, Zellner went for the take-down. I evaded and counter-punched. He came at me again, I kneed him in the mouth. Within a few seconds, I could see that I had the advantage as long as I stayed on my feet. Zellner recognized it too and tried everything he could to bring me down. I wouldn't let him. I kept sliding away from his attacks, counter-punching as I eluded him. What developed was an unusual fight for me. Usually I came out and dominated the fight with sheer aggressiveness. Nothing fancy, just plain firepower and heart. Zellner matched my aggressiveness and kept me reacting to him, searching for an opportunity to do some damage.

In the middle of the round, he exposed himself long enough for me to deliver a series of blows to his head. They slowed him down, and I could see in his eyes that I'd rung his bell. I took the offensive and battered him with repeated blows. The fight began to go my way, but his strength kept him in it. He lashed back at me until finally, I landed a bell-ringer that dazed him. He fell on his back and I pounced to finish him off. With three seconds left in the first round, the ref ended the fight as a TKO in my favor.

I won the fight, but more importantly, I learned a lot of lessons from Craig that night. I had been lucky to deliver a couple of good punches that changed the tide of the bout in my favor. Before that happened, I sensed he was not only stronger than I was but better conditioned. His coaching staff ensured that. What we were doing at Lejeune was in some ways counter-productive, and after the fight I reexamined every aspect of our training regimen there. We concluded that we'd been doing too much weight lifting, too much of the wrong sort of conditioning. To get to the next level, we began making changes.

My battalion commander, Colonel Todd Desgrosseilliers, had been a huge supporter of my fighting career. As it became clear I needed more help with my training camps, he introduced me to John Bardis (still a close friend), the leader of the U.S. Olympic wrestling team. He also served on the board of USA Wrestling, the governing body that oversees amateur competitions in the States.

Though he's a CEO of a major corporation, John finds considerable time to devote to charity and helping people. He lives his life in service to others, and I've never met anyone else who has made such a global impact with his actions. It did not take me long to look up to him and seek out his advice. John is a deeply patriotic American and he eagerly helped me out by introducing me to Team Quest out in Portland, Oregon, where I was introduced to a number of UFC fighters including Thierry Sokoudjou. I trained with them whenever I had the chance to fly in. At times, Thierry would fly out to Lejeune to help us.

In early 2008, the league gave me a shot at the title and scheduled a fight with Doug Marshall, the current champ. We were to be the main event for March's WEC 33 *Back to Vegas*. The camp I had for this fight was the most brutal of my career to date. Thierry and the other members of Team Quest completely changed my conditioning program and pushed me further, harder, and faster than I'd ever experienced. Many times, my body rebelled at the abuse, and I'd end up puking on the gym floor.

Over time, the Corps pulled apart my core group of Marine training partners. George and Chris left Camp Lejeune for different assignments. In their place, I found new partners in Richie Ferrel, Jody Carter, Tony Moenich, Aaron Powell, and a U.S. Navy sailor named Mike Brown. I'd also made the decision to leave the service and would soon be departing Lejeune for the civilian world. I loved the Corps and my role in it. I'd been promoted to first lieutenant and was up for my captain bars within the year. Nothing gave me more satisfaction than leading Marines. It defined who I was and how I judged my own self-worth. At the same time, Teressa and I were married now and had a baby on the way. If I stayed in, I almost certainly would have been deployed a third time sometime in 2008. The strain of my second tour in Iraq had been tough enough on Teressa; to go through it again while in her final months of her first pregnancy, then give birth to our child without me just was not an option. I had a family now, and I had to put my wife and child above my passion for the Corps.

My fight with Doug Marshall would be my final while wearing the uniform.

CHAPTER TWENTY-SEVEN

Warrior to Warrior

Las Vegas, March 26, 2008

Doug Marshall burst into the arena, all tempestuous energy and showmanship. His arrival electrified the crowd. He played to them, fists high, strutting and dancing as he made his way to the octagon. His charisma was magnetic, and he fed off the crowd's reaction to him.

I watched him from my corner, Frank and Thierry nearby. I never had the showman's spirit, just the quiet resolve of a warrior representing those I loved. And tonight would be the last time I'd be able to do that as a member of the Corps.

We met at center cage, tapped gloves, and the fight began. Right away, I tried to seize the initiative. I came straight at him, flinging left jabs at him that he deftly avoided. I feinted left twice more, then surprised him with a power kick to his lead leg. Though I delivered a solid strike, he barely even reacted. Doug was a tough SOB, well conditioned with a wiry strength that complemented his speed and explosiveness. He had been in plenty of brawls in and out of the cage. He specialized in Brazilian jujitsu and Muay Thai, and was known for his ability to kick like a mule.

Doug backed away, covering the movement with a jab that I dodged. I stayed on the offensive and followed him. He tried to slow my advance with a kick aimed at my left leg's sciatic nerve. Instead, he hit my kneecap and did no damage. Before he could recover, I waded into striking range and grazed him with a fierce right hook.

So far, I controlled the pace of the fight, but Doug was able to slip away every time I closed with him. Damn. He was so elusive and light on his feet I had a hard time hitting him, even when the opportunity presented itself.

Once again, I went after him. Suddenly, he counter-attacked and swept his leg into my hip. The blow rocked me, but it also caused him to lose his balance. He stumbled backward even as I bull rushed him. Somehow, he escaped, found his footing, and slowed me down with a vicious left jab. Fortunately, I blocked it with my right glove, otherwise that could have done some damage.

Right then, he seized control of the fight. Stepping forward in a counter-attack, he swung twice and forced me to evade. I struck back with a right jab that caught him on the chin. In the past, such a blow would have rocked my opponent. Not Doug. It didn't look like it even fazed him.

We backed away, circling each other now with both respect and an eye for an opportunity. I didn't see one, so I decided to try and force the issue. Nothing fancy, no grand tactics, just another head-on charge led with feints and jabs. He slid left, evaded my attack, and uncoiled a brutal kick to my leg. It momentarily slowed me down. Nevertheless, I had maneuvered him against the cage. I thought I had an opening, but then I made a mistake and left my head unprotected just as I was about to go to work on his midsection.

He saw his chance. With both gloves, he snared the back of my neck with a Thai clench. Trapped in his vice-like grip, I was vulnerable. This was one of Doug's trademark moves. Once pinned in place, he could batter his opponent with his knee-kicks to his thighs and gut. I had practiced countering it with my fellow Marines in the old gym at Camp Lejeune. If I could press my hips against his, he wouldn't have room to use his knees on me. That could buy me enough time to get out of the clench. I had no plans to take this fight to the mat. I wanted to bang.

But I couldn't get against him, and I could not tear away from his bear trap grip on my neck. Doug drove his knee into me. I struck back with half-strength punches, but he nailed me again.

I was in trouble.

I tried once more to press against him, but he was too strong. He kept enough space between us to use his knees again. Finally, I managed to land a right hook on the side of Doug's head. That distracted him long enough for me to get my left arm under his right. I used that leverage to try and break his clench. Instead, it separated our bodies by a few more inches, giving Doug the chance to knee me in the right side.

I had to get free. I swung at him with another right hook. I followed that up right away with a solid body blow that hit him just under his right ribs.

That did it. I broke away from his clench, intending to get some distance between us and then try to regain control of the fight. Doug never gave me the opportunity. Instead, he blasted me with a fusillade of lefts and rights. My head reeled from the repeated impacts until I finally went defensive and covered up. Training had prepared me for this. I know Doug goes for broke at a certain point in every fight. This was that moment. Doug hammered my forearms and gloves, looking for any entrance. He sensed victory was close and threw his full body behind every punch.

I dropped my gloves, exposing my face. Doug reacted swiftly, landing the only solid punch of his barrage. I'd given him this opportunity on purpose. Nobody ever won a fight by going defensive. My only chance at this point was to drive him off with my fists.

I unleashed a counter-offensive, and for ten seconds we stood face to face as warriors, whaling away on each other as if in a back alley brawl, the likes of which I had not seen since those days back in South Scranton when I was a kid.

The crowd gained its feet, sensing the fight had reached a climax. Thousands of voices screamed at us as we traded blow for blow. Then Doug nailed me with a left cross that felt like I'd been struck with a bag of bricks. My head started to ring, and my body grew taut with that weird duality of adrenaline and exhaustion. There was no way I could take much more of this.

I unleashed a spasm of left-right combinations. Fighters usually meter out their energy so they can go the distance and not be worn out by their opponents. That's why pace and rhythm are so important to a fighter. Doug had totally taken away my rhythm. Now, our battle had become a test of resolve. Nobody could continue the frenzied pace of this fight. Somebody was going to get knocked out.

But who would break first?

You gotta have heart for the fight, Bro.

I threw every ounce of energy and strength I had left into this final flurry of punches. I threw him a right cross. He had no counter, but my aim was wild and my glove managed only a glancing blow. A split-second later, I surprised him with a left hook that caught him right on the jawbone. He fell backward and tumbled onto the mat. For an instant, I wasn't sure what had happened. Then I saw him, eyes rolled back, lying in front of me. This was my chance. In a flash, I was on him. Two more hard strikes and I had him. His head flopped onto the mat and his arms went slack. I had knocked him out cold.

I could hear Frank screaming from my corner. The ref ended the fight.

I had done it. A wave of pure exultation crushed my normal reserve. Flush with victory fever, I pounded my chest and bellowed to the crowd. That counter left hook sealed the deal. I was the new WEC light heavyweight champ.

With that realization, my elation evaporated. My arms fell to my sides, and pure emotion sent me to my knees. I covered my face, not wanting the camera to see this reaction.

At one of the many funerals I attended, I heard someone say, "The best way to commemorate our lost brothers is not to grieve but to live and be successful. Live for them and keep their memory alive."

Those words returned to me at this pinnacle moment of my life. My lost brothers were with me in the cage tonight. Their spirit had infused my heart with the strength I needed to win.

I sensed them all by my side as surely as I felt the presence of the ref and Doug himself. And now, gloves over my face, knees on the mat, I silently called out to them.

This one's for you, my brothers.

PART V

Redefinition

CHAPTER TWENTY-EIGHT

Gut Check

UFC 19 Oklahoma City,
Cox Convention Center, September 2009

The locker room buzzes with activity as tonight's fighters prepare with their coaches. I sit in a folding chair listening to Guns N' Roses belt out "Welcome to the Jungle." Tonight, '80s hair metal seems to fit my mood perfectly, and this song was one of the best from that era.

I close my eyes and feel totally relaxed. The music enfolds me and plays to my spirit.

In the jungle
Welcome to the jungle
Watch it bring you to your
shun-n-n-n-n-n,-n-n-n-n-n,n knees, knees
I wanna watch you bleed

I'm last on the undercard tonight, which means I have the longest wait. There are five other bouts before mine. No worries, no need to rush. I stay lost in the music. Motley Crue's "Wild Side" comes up next. I can't help but bounce my head in time with the thundering bass line.

Eyes closed, I feel myself grin. The music is perfect for my mood.

A year and a month ago, I lay on the mat in the Hard Rock Café, a raw fighter who had snatched the belt from Doug Marshall with my fists and heart. I'm not that fighter anymore, but only my coaches and teammates know it.

The past year, my work in New Mexico demolished my old fighting style. Once torn down, Coach Jackson and Coach Winklejohn molded me into an entirely different athlete. Gone are the days of my reckless headlong charges and one-dimensional striking style. My signature had always been the right jab. I was not known for kicking or moving around, or for any tactical flair. Heart and heavy fists—that was me.

A sudden commotion breaks out in the locker room. I open my eyes to see doctors and paramedics pouring through the double doors. Not far away, Phillipe Nover lies on the floor, twitching violently in some sort of seizure.

The place becomes a madhouse. Coaches, players, and hangers-on mill about as the docs and paramedics go to work on Phillipe. A number of UFC officials show up to assess the situation. For a few minutes, total chaos reigns. Then Burt Watson, who functions sort of like the UFC's behind-the-scenes sheriff, storms inside and clears everyone out who doesn't need to be in the locker room.

Phillippe regains consciousness and sits up. He looks shaken but otherwise unharmed. But the UFC is not taking any chances. They scrub his fight and the paramedics take him out on a stretcher.

George Lockhart appears in front of me. He flew out from Quantico earlier in the week to be with me. He's an instructor at the MACE these days and continues to fight professionally when time allows.

"How ya doin', Brian?" he asks. I give him a thumbs up. He grins at me and pats my shoulder, "Stayin' loose?"

"Always."

"This one's all yours."

Having George here this week has been a tremendous boost for me. We've reminisced about all those nights we spent in that sweat-stained gym at Camp Lejeune, teaching ourselves as we prepared for our next fights. He is the reminder of my roots that I've lacked since leaving the Corps in the summer of 2008.

While George is my link to the past, Coach Jackson and Coach Winklejohn represent my present and future. They've flown in to Oklahoma City to be with me tonight. They know the stakes—both professional and personal; they're here to give me the support and in-fight tactical advice I need.

Coach Winklejohn steps up next to George. He leans down and says quietly, "Brian you can fight and hang with anyone in this locker room. You're at the same level now. Don't ever doubt that."

"Thanks, Coach."

He's noticed a sort of inferiority complex in me ever since I began training with Team Jackson in New Mexico. As I have learned the Jackson-Winklejohn system, he's constantly reminded me that I have earned my place in the UFC.

I listen and nod, but I still don't feel that way. After the second Cantwell fight in the summer of '08, the WEC abolished our weight class. A lot of fighters suddenly found their contracts canceled. I was one of the lucky ones the UFC picked up. Now, I am fighting in the elite of the professional mixed martial arts organizations.

Unfortunately, my debut in the spring didn't reward the UFC's faith in me. I was pitted against Krzysztof "The Polish Experiment" Soszynski, a veteran fighter of great reputation. He was 16–8 in professional MMA bouts and had been fighting since I graduated from the Academy.

It was a mismatch from the beginning. Krysztof comes from a wrestling and Brazilian jujitsu background. I had planned to keep the fight upright, but his speed and quickness caught me completely off guard. He took me down in the first round and won with a Kimura submission.

That one still hurts. I had worked all fall and winter to learn Coach Jackson's system only to get my ass kicked on international television. After the fight, the UFC was not happy. I hadn't put on much of a show, and some fighters would have been cut from the league for such a performance. Instead, they gave me one more chance. Tonight, it is gut-check time. I either win or I get sent back down to the minor venues, fighting for beer and pizza money again.

Until I win one, this sense of inferiority is not going to go away. It hasn't actually been a bad thing, though. It has made me work harder and longer than any other time in my career. I've spent months at a time in New Mexico, away from my wife and infant daughter, training for this moment. In the process, I have not only found a place to grow as a fighter, I have found an extended family.

Unlike some MMA outfits, Team Jackson is exactly that: a team. We live, work, and play together in New Mexico. Our wives and kids have grown close. When one member of the team enters camp before a fight, the rest of us take time out of our schedules to fly in and help our teammate prepare. One blade sharpens the other. It is a lot like how we trained at Lejeune in the old gym. We have all vowed never to fight each other. Our job is to make the team better than just one man (or woman), to use our collective skills to make us better than any other organization in mixed martial arts today. I love that culture, and having this extended family in Albuquerque helps ease the loneliness I feel when I'm away from Teressa and my daughter.

The first few times I flew into New Mexico, I stayed above the gym and lived like a Spartan. Then Joey V offered his couch to me. Ever since, I've become a semi-permanent houseguest at his place.

Joey functions as our team's big brother. Since he was a boy, he had held his own family together, so he embraces the role he has with the other fighters. They come to him with their problems or to seek career advice. He makes sure we're all taken care of when we're in Albuquerque.

Since I lost to the "Polish Experiment" in the spring, Joey's made a point of working with me on my ground game at night after dinner for weeks at a time. Doing that solidified our friendship. I'd run through walls for him now.

Though I have to say, there is one down side to crashing at his place. Holly owns two cats. Now, don't get me wrong, I love animals and have a dog. But these scruffy little bastards are about the most annoying and intrusive creatures I've ever encountered. They actually belong to Holly, but Joey is just stupid-crazy for them and calls them his "furry children."

Several times, while they've been gone and I've held down the fort, Joey's furry kids have insisted on climbing all over me, shedding and sticking their butts in my face. I mean, seriously, why do they do that? One of these two little scofflaws is a Siamese that seems fixated on the television in Joey's living room. Whenever he and Holly aren't around, and I'm working on my laptop in front of the tube, the damn Siamese has to get in front of it and block my view. If it isn't doing that, it tries to warm its paws and butt by sitting on my laptop. No wonder the catapult was invented.

In the locker room, I burst out laughing thinking about those two critters. Greg and Mike take this as a good sign. Their prodigy isn't tight tonight. Not by a long shot.

By now, the locker room has returned to normal. The paramedics are gone. The doctors and UFC officials have retreated. The event begins, and the fighters on tonight's card go through their warm-ups. I still have a few minutes before I need to do that, so I stay in my chair, my gym bag at my feet, and let the music dictate the flow of my thoughts.

"Sweet Child of Mine" begins playing on my iPod. Great song. Classic Guns N' Roses. I've listened to this playlist so many times in New Mexico that I've started identifying memories of Coach Jackson's gym with it. Workouts, long days of sparring, hours of individual coaching on Greg's unique style of mixed martial arts, which we now call Gaidojutsu—these are the things that have framed my life since I lost to Cantwell a year ago.

I think of my teammates. Keith Jardine has made an incredible effort to help me develop. So have Joey, Rashad Evans, and many others. Keith and Joey have nearly separated me from consciousness on several occasions during sparring rounds in our cage back in Albuquerque. They've done so much to prepare me for this fight. If I win, it will truly be a team victory.

One time, just before I left for Oklahoma City, Keith and I were sparring together, working on grappling techniques. Both of us were pretty smoked. It was late in the day, and we were breathing hard. As we wrestled, Keith accidentally blew a chunk of snot right onto my chest. We kept battling until the end of the round. But when it was over, Joey yelled over to me, "Hey Brian! You gotta big Keith snot on yer chest!"

I looked down and saw it clinging to me. "Oh," I said and wiped it on the mat. Then Keith and I went at it for another round as Joey, laughing with disgust, shouted at us, "Stooopid!"

That's one of his trademark sayings he busts out whenever something floors him, sort of like saying, "No way!" All of us had a good laugh at that little incident.

Keith has taught me to focus on the details. Every movement has a purpose for him. When he works with me, he shows me how to break down every technique to its most minute level. Then, we work at refining each component until it is absolutely flawless. He is an incredible training partner. The style the gym uses is very similar to the way officers plan their training in the Marine Corps.

Greg Jackson taps my shoulder. I look up and hear him say, "Let's start warming up in about ten, okay?"

"Roger, Coach."

It is time to begin my ritual. I turn the music off and tuck away my iPod in my gym bag. I fish around inside my bag until I find my wallet. With a deep breath, I extract the embossed card I've carried with me for the past two and a half years.

Make my lonely grave richer
Sweeter be,
Make this truly the land of the free
And the home of the brave.

I gave my life to save
That I might here lie
Eternally
Forever free.

I read the words that so often have filled me with unrelenting grief. Tonight, they bring me a sense of peace. I whisper them to myself one more time. There is finally acceptance here. For so long I had fought to deny and displace, when I should have just faced the truth. At the time, I didn't know how.

I look up and see Travis there beside me, goofy grin on his face, eyes bright and full of hell. I feel him alongside me like a physical presence. Even in death, the bond of loyalty we share cannot be broken. As always, he's got my back tonight.

Travis Manion was a man unafraid to stand for what was right.

He wrote those words on an index card while flying to Brett Harmon's funeral. Three years later, Joel Starret, Travis' wrestling coach at the Academy, read those words when he gave the eulogy at Travis' funeral service in the spring of 2007.

They return to me now, and I think of what they meant to Trav. For him, what was right was getting into the heart of the fight. He hated being stuck behind the wire on a base in Iraq during his first deployment. With so many of his friends and classmates out in harm's way every day, he felt cheated of his destiny. Doing what was right meant sharing the risks the men he loved were running. But that wasn't going to happen within the context of his battalion. When he returned from his first deployment, he tried to get a transfer to an infantry platoon. No luck. He was stuck in his supply billet without any chance of escape.

Then an opportunity came along. There was a need for Marine officers who were willing to embed with Iraqi Army units to help stand them up. They would carry on the fight long after American units had withdrawn from the country, so this program was critical to our ability to execute our exit strategy. Good men, good officers were needed. Travis didn't hesitate. He volunteered for the job and returned to the Middle East to lead Iraqi troops into combat.

He'd been gone almost six months when I heard from him via satellite phone. Teressa and I were planning a formal wedding, though we'd already been wed by a justice of the peace before I left for my second Iraq deployment. I had asked Travis to stand up for me. He was excited about it, and the timing looked like it would work out. He would be coming home just in time to join us and help us celebrate.

We chatted about his Iraqi troops. He'd come to love them as he led them out on daily combat patrols. They followed him everywhere and fought loyally by his side. If anything, Travis inspired such devotion in almost everyone around him. As we talked, I could tell how much getting into the fight meant to him. It was as if he had finally gotten the chance to live up to the responsibilities he had laid on his own shoulders. He would not be left behind after all.

In the final minutes of our conversation, I told him about my upcoming fight with Cantwell. As always, he was excited for me. "Remember, Brian, your heart is unbeatable. Bring that to every fight and you'll never lose."

A few days later, Travis was out with his boys, patrolling the streets of Fallujah. An insurgent cell ambushed his column and disabled one of his vehicles. In the middle of the fight, all he could think about was the safety of his men. He jumped out of his Humvee and raced through intense machine gun fire to try to save the Iraqi soldiers trapped in the stricken vehicle. A sniper took aim and killed him instantly.

His Iraqis loved him so much that they later honored him by naming the battalion's headquarters Combat Outpost Manion.

He lived the standard he set down on that index card in 2004. When the Marine Corps learned of his actions, Travis was awarded a Silver Star and a Bronze Star for Valor.

I hold the embossed card, reading the words again slowly. The locker room disappears. I see the funeral home where we said our goodbyes to Travis. Until I saw him there, I had been in complete denial. It had to have been a mistake, a screw up that sent the contact team to Trav's parents' door. I couldn't fathom life without Travis living it with me. So, I clung to false hopes all the way back to Pennsylvania. But the moment I came into the funeral home, there was no denying it anymore.

You with me, Trav?

I see him as clearly as I see Greg and George, Mike and John Bardis, my mentor and boss. Travis stands with them. He's my fifth corner man, the one who will always be there, in the octagon or out of it. I know this as surely as I know myself.

Know myself. Last year, I fought Cantwell and an identity crisis simultaneously. They both kicked my ass. Not now. Not tonight.

I tuck the card back into my wallet and place it back in my gym bag. It is almost time to start.

Who are you?

A year ago, I had no answer. Now, the question seems easy.

I am a Marine. In or out of the service, the Corps left an indelible mark on me, and I will always identify with it and feel a part of it.

Who are you?

I am a father, a son, a devoted husband.

I get to my feet. It is time.

What defines you?

A year ago, I would have said my performance in the cage. That's all I had after I left the Corps.

Not anymore. Fighting doesn't define me. The content of my character does. The values I cherish, the way I choose to lead my life, how I treat others. Those things define me.

Are you proud of who you have become?

Yes.

I think back to what I wrote during the flight to Brett's funeral. Should I have died in Iraq, Joel would have read it at my funeral.

"Brian Stann will be remembered as a loving son. He was a warrior and a man who never quit."

That's the answer right there. Define me as the man who never quit, whose warrior heart beat to the bitter end. And if I lose tonight and my long and wild ride in this sport comes to an end, I will never doubt that I left anything on the table.

All in?

Yeah. All in.

I strap on my gloves. George tapes me up. I go through my warm-up, striking pads, mentally studying my game plan. I get my heart rate up and start to sweat.

It feels glorious, even invigorating. I can't wait to get in the cage.

Remember, keep after his left side. That's his weakness. Hammer his left.

We head for the arena. It is time to fight.

CHAPTER TWENTY-NINE

The Passing of an Era

The convention center is packed tonight. The fans are in high spirits as they cheer and scream for their favorite fighters. We enter the arena and I climb into the cage.

Steve Cantwell is waiting for me.

Since our fight last August, our careers have gone in divergent directions. He fought his first UFC bout in December 2008 against a stubborn and determined opponent named Razak al-Hassan. At the end of the fight, Cantwell got him in an arm bar. Steve threw all his strength against Razak's arm until it broke at the elbow and bent almost ninety degrees backward.

He broke a man's arm in his UFC debut. After he did it, he bounced to his feet and celebrated as Razak writhed in agony on the mat. When interviewed after the fight, Steve and the reporter watched the replay together. "Watch it pop!" Cantwell said jubilantly. When Razak's arm broke, Steve declared, "That was soooo sweet, man! I've been waiting so long to do that!"

He took so much heat for those words that he later had to issue an apology. He called Razak to make amends, then offered him some advice on how best to recover from the injury.

He lost his second UFC fight against Luis Cane in the spring of 2009 in a unanimous decision. After we were matched up for this third fight, Cantwell publicly grumbled, "A lot of people have asked me if it is hard for me to get up for this fight, being that I worked Stann over so badly last time . . . it is my chance to show people how much better I've gotten than him." He later added in another pre-fight interview, "Brian Stann has one thing: a puncher's chance . . . I don't think he's shown that he's grown since our last fight. I have. So for him, I think it [the rematch] is a little early."

Cantwell doesn't think I earned this. Nor does he think I'm any different as a fighter. Fine. Let's get this going. We'll see what he says in the post-fight interviews.

We meet at the center of the cage, tap gloves. The bell rings and round one begins. Cantwell stays light on his feet and bobs his head. He waits for me to charge him, just like our last two fights.

Not this time, Steve.

I am a totally different fighter now. Gone are the days of my one-dimensional, brawling style. Coach Jackson and Coach Winklejohn have taught me to be tactical, to combine my speed and agility with my mind.

I stick with our game plan. John Brandis actually first noticed Cantwell's weak left side. To capitalize on it, John, Mike, and Greg developed a strategy to use that weakness to my advantage.

I was to keep moving and stay elusive. Whenever I could, they told me to slide laterally to my right and gain an angle against Cantwell's left. When I saw an opening, I was to blast forward, launch my attack, and then dash back out of the way to safety.

In the center of the cage, I see Cantwell waiting for me, so I slide right. He shifts and watches me warily. I wonder if he's surprised I'm not already trying to bang away on him.

I feint with a left-right combo, stepping forward at the same time to test Cantwell's reaction. He evades and tries to strike back but hits empty air. I've bounced out of range. We jockey for position. Cantwell's clearly not sure what to think of me. I'm certainly not doing what he expected. Movement. Maneuver. Agility. These are things that won battles in Iraq. Greg and Mike harnessed those combat lessons I'd learned and taught me how to apply them in the cage.

Mike tore down my footwork and started from scratch with me. Day after day for the past two months, he and I had worked on my lateral movement. He showed me how to stay on the balls of my feet, to keep bouncing while I made sure my weight was evenly distributed so that I could change directions quickly.

I use that agility training now to swoop in and deliver attacks on Cantwell's left flank. We joust and parry and thrust in the center of the cage until I suddenly explode forward and hit him with a left hook. I follow up with a right that he blocks, then I sweep my right leg into his left. The kick surprises the crowd, the announcers, and Steve's corner. I am not known for my legwork. I'm just the guy with the heavy hands and the huge heart.

Cantwell backs away and keeps his head bobbing. He sees an opening, bounds forward, and whiffs with a right jab. I counter-attack with a straight right of my own and catch him on the chin. We shadow box and maneuver for position. Then I come after him again, working his left side with a left jab combined with a kick to his lead leg again. I miss with the strike but connect with the kick.

The announcers are surprised at how the fight unfolds. "This is a different Brian Stann," one opines. "He's light on his feet . . . he's really showing some beautiful footwork here."

Props go to Mike for that.

I keep moving right, looking for openings to exploit. When Cantwell comes after me, I evade and close. Ducking down, I deliver an uppercut into his torso. Using my feet, I escape before Cantwell can counter-attack.

I work my way to the right again, Cantwell following. This time, he catches me with a jab that hits my face. He doesn't get away unscathed. Before he can react, I land another kick to his lead leg.

We circle left this time, until Steve charges at me. I uncork an overhead right just as he ducks and goes for a body blow. My fist grazes the back of his head.

Damn. If I'd landed that one, it would have rocked him for sure.

We dodge and weave around the cage. Again, I stick to the game plan and control the flow of the fight by circling right and searching for an opening. I see it again and explode forward with a left-right striking combo. Then I dash out of the way, leaving Steve to whiff air with his retaliatory blows.

He gets more aggressive and comes at me again. He lands a couple of punches, but I score a solid left hook. Then we're circling each other again.

Our last fight was a toe-to-toe brawl. This one is all about movement, position, and opportunity. I have to force myself to stay patient. A large part of me still wants to wade in with all guns blazing.

Instead, I rely on my discipline to stick with the game plan.

Steve tries to kick my face. I back away, circle right, then launch a counter-attack. I get him with another kick to the side of his lead leg. With about 2:10 to go in the round, Steve gives me a shot at a take-down. I charge in, duck low, and try to grab him around the midsection.

He twists out of it, and I don't waste time trying to force it. Staying low, I escape to the right again, forcing Steve to pivot in order to protect his left side. Hit and run, hit and run. I swoop in, land blows, take a few counters in return, then use my newly learned lateral movement to keep Steve on the move to defend that left side of his. I can tell this is starting to frustrate him. I think he expected anything but this.

With about a minute left in the first round, we trade vicious left hooks. Steve's glove tears open my upper lip, but at the same time I see that my own counter-punch got his attention. We back off and dance for position again.

We exchange more blows. I land another uppercut to his torso. He sneaks in another left. The rhythm's been established. Hunt and move, hunt and move, followed by a furious exchange, before one or the other of us backs off and the process starts again.

With fifteen seconds to go in the round, I surprise Cantwell with a kick to his left side. My shin strikes home just below his ribcage. Steve tries to deliver a shogun-like one-two kick combination right before the bell, but I'm able to back away and avoid the blows.

The round ends and I return to my corner. "Who won the round?" I ask Greg.

"You did! You did! You won it by far!" Greg says excitedly. He gives me my marching orders for round two as a trainer cleans up the cut on my lip from Steve's brutal left hook.

The bell rings. We emerge from our corners, bobbing and weaving, relying on movement once again. I land the first blow with another kick to Cantwell's lead leg. This time, I hit him below the knee. Instead of sliding right, though, I go left. Steve pursues until I see another opening and dart forward with a left that occupies his attention and exposes him to another kick to his lead leg. He's not even trying to block my kicks, though his corner men told him between rounds that he needed to do that. I don't think he's mentally prepared for the type of fight I'm bringing to him.

Slide left, dart right, go in low, and land an uppercut. Steve moves back and forth, totally reacting to my changes of direction. It allows me to pick and choose my moments to attack and helps me avoid his counter-blows. Time to try and take him down. I slide right again and edge back toward the cage wall, enticing him forward. Then, instead of slipping laterally again, I stay in place, bouncing on the balls of my feet. Steve sees opportunity and comes straight at me, fists flailing. I duck and drive forward, my shoulder slamming into his chest. I get my arms around him and bulldoze him toward the center of the cage. I try to grab the back of his legs to finish the take-down, but he backs out of it. As he does, I use my left leg to knee-kick him in the solar plexus. I score a glancing blow there, but my lower leg nails him in the crotch.

Oh God. Not that again.

Steve backs off and the ref keeps us separated until Cantwell recovers. From across the ring, I apologize to him. He nods to acknowledge it and we're back on again. Right away, Steve lashes out at me with a right kick that narrowly misses my crotch. He opens his arms and pauses, checking to see if he's connected. I let him know I'm fine, and we slap gloves and get back to it.

We exchange flurries, without scoring anything decisive. When I slip right this time, I see him focus on protecting his left side. I edge back left and let fly with a left kick that connects right under his ribcage. He comes straight at me and I stop him with a straight left that catches him full in the face. That was a brutal shot. Yet he doesn't even seem to notice it. My respect for Steve's toughness ratchets up a notch.

The next twenty seconds see both of us delivering kicks. Striking almost forgotten, we both go high, then low, then high again. I bound around, forcing Steve to keep moving after me. Then I see an opening. This time, I lead with a left hook that forces him to go defensive. He blocks it, but he doesn't expect my left foot to connect with his midsection.

I can see Steve growing frustrated. He tries to cut me off as I roll to the right. Every time he does, I snake in and hammer at him. He scores some counter-blows, but I feel the fight going my way. My confidence grows and fills me with renewed energy that blankets my growing fatigue. I feel lighter and quicker as I maneuver around him. I land several more kicks. He's still not trying to defend them. When he tries to catch me with a high kick to the face, I block it with my right arm.

The crowd, expecting to see a brawl, grows disappointed. Some start booing. The energy change in the arena seems to affect Cantwell. He suddenly drops his fists and calls out to me, "Come on, Bitch!"

I almost laugh. I've thrown him completely off his mental game. He thinks I'm running from him when I'm actually dictating the entire flow of the fight. Right then, my confidence surges. John Brandis, Coach Jackson, and Coach Winklejohn were spot on with our game plan.

I maintain my lateral movement. Steve stays in the center of the cage, not bothering to follow me this time. He looks tired. His movement seems a little slower. I drive in and punish him with a quick flurry, then bound backward before he can effectively counter.

Steve pursues half-heartedly. I can see the frustration boiling over again. Finally, he drops his fists again and cusses at me a second time. His footwork goes to hell and his fists are low, so I come at his left side again. Just as I give him a right hook, he ducks and swings back. We both fail to score, and before he can react, I'm out of range again, turning him left. He closes, I see an opportunity and try to hammer him with a left-right combo. He stands his ground and counter-strikes.

And then, I'm on the move. Steve looks beyond frustrated now. He's pissed off. He's getting hit with little opportunity to dish it back out at me. That is the key to Coach Jackson's fighting philosophy. Why get hit when you can use speed, maneuver, and agility to punish your opponent without retaliation?

I work around Cantwell's left again. He's a hair slower now, and I see my chance. I charge in low and hammer him with a quick left-right combo. He swings hard, but I duck under it and dance away. He starts to pursue, but his temper gets the best of him. He pulls up, drops his fists, and screams, "Fuck!"

So much for a poker face. Our game plan has thrown him mentally off balance. He can't gain control of the fight, and he can't land the strikes he needs to in order to catch up and win the fight. Instead of changing things up, he blows his stack. I notice, though, that he doesn't come straight at me, either.

I go for a take-down again, but he counters it. I manage to knee his upper body and score points while we grapple. He gets away, and we bob and weave around as the final seconds of the round tick off the clock. Suddenly, Steve lunges forward and gets his arms around my lead leg. He's going for a take-down. If he pulls it off, he could turn the tide and win the round.

I flash back to those days at the MACE, working with Travis on take-down defenses. He showed me how to defeat such moves five years ago. From that foundation, Coach Jackson honed and developed those skills, adding new wrinkles based on his Gaidojutsu techniques.

Steve presses me, but I use his own forward momentum to back away and keep him from getting a firm hold on me. Bounding on one foot, I spin in his grasp and tear away from him.

The round ends a few seconds later. As I cross in front of Cantwell on the way back to my corner, he screams, "BITCH!" I glance back at him. "Whatever."

Dude doesn't even know what's going on. But his coaches do. From across the cage, I can hear what they're saying. They look pissed—not at me—at him.

"You lost that round. You need to pick up this round," his coach tells him. Steve hasn't even reached his corner yet, forcing his coaches to come out into the cage to talk to him. He doesn't look ready to listen.

"You're not cutting him off. You're just following him," his coach tells him.

Exactly. I'm leading him all over the octagon, bending him to my will and forcing him to react to me.

"You gotta put it in your mind right now. Do you wanna win this fight? You're letting him pop-shot you to death out there. You gotta start landing some punches."

On my side, Greg and Mike are delighted. Greg tells me, "You got it, hands down, Brian. You got it, just don't start brawling, be smart."

The bell rings, and we come out for the final round. Cantwell gets aggressive and comes straight at me. It feels like a complete reversal of roles from our last fight. I dance around him, flaying him with quick jabs that don't land with devastating power but do score points. In return, he scores a couple of solid blows. For a while, the round is about even. He sneaks in a right cross that tags me on the chin. A few seconds later, I retaliate with a pair of right-left hooks to either side of his head. He goes defensive just long enough for me to slide away to the left unscathed.

He follows after me. I circle him around, slide left some more, then pause. He closes in. I don't see an opening, so I dart laterally to the right again. As he follows, I sense he's going to come in low at me. Sure enough, he ducks down and tries to work my upper body. I come over the top at him and connect. Then I'm on the move, darting out of range.

The clock ticks down. Cantwell grows more anxious and tries to get more aggressive. He momentarily catches me in a corner and delivers a stiff blow to my face. Before he can follow up that success, I use my feet to get out of range and lead him back out into the center of the cage.

He's landing more strikes now, even when I take the offensive. I've missed several chances to hit him, thanks to his head-bobbing elusiveness. In my head, I think we're almost dead even this round. If I did win round one, it won't matter. But what if I didn't?

Then it all comes down to this one. Right now, he's got to be ahead on points.

I've got to keep the pressure on Cantwell. I work him back and forth around the cage until I finally see another opportunity. He's just a hair more upright than usual. He's left his torso undefended. I explode forward and pound his upper body with a fierce uppercut followed with a straight left that connects with his face. Got him. He tags me with a left hook, but I pick up a point on that one.

Steve comes back hard and catches me with a couple of flurries. There are forty-three seconds left in the round. I think we're still dead even.

Suddenly, Cantwell comes at me and tries to take me down. I slip away, spin around, and stand him up against the cage wall. Before he can escape, I drive my knee into his chest. He gets away; I back up and lead him to the center of the cage. As he pursues, I nail him with a straight right.

He keeps coming, so I duck low and go for the take-down. Once again, he edges backward and breaks free. But this opens him up. I charge headlong at him, leading with a right uppercut, following with a left hook and another right before driving him almost to the cage wall and finishing the attack with a solid kick to his right side.

That may have just put me over the top. Only about twenty-five seconds left now. Cantwell comes at me, I don't see an opportunity, so I duck out of range. A few more seconds tick off the clock. Steve charges again. This time, I go for another take-down. He defends it beautifully, and we end up clenched in the center octagon. I hang onto him and work his upper body with my right until he gets away.

Eight seconds to go. He charges, desperate now. Then I make a mistake. As he comes for me, I go low, intending to strike his midsection. Simultaneously, he lashes out with his right leg, but misses. I lose my balance and fall back toward the cage.

He follows and hammers me with a right. I swing with my left and graze his head. Three seconds left. I press in and knee his midsection.

The bell rings. The fight is over. Who won the last round?

I go over to Steve to give him a congratulatory hug. He cusses at me again and pushes me away. I stare after him as he storms over to his corner, then shrug and walk over to mine. That may be his level of sportsmanship, but it will never be mine.

Greg Jackson comes up to me, shirt in hand. He's all smiles. "You did it Brian! You did it!"

The judges' scores have not been announced. That last round was too close for comfort, but I knew in my heart that I'd won.

Greg and Coach Wink also have no doubts. He bear hugs me and lifts me off the mat.

A moment later, we meet the ref in the center of the cage to hear the decision. Steve, who was probably just frustrated, comes up to me. He apologizes for his behavior and gives me a hug.

"Ladies and gentlemen, after three rounds we go to the scorecards," intones the announcer. "The scores are 30–27, 30–27, and 29–28. The winner by unanimous decision: The All American Brian Stann!"

Cantwell walks away, looking at once angry and dejected. The rubber match but mine. We'll probably never face each other again, though our careers have both been defined by our rivalry.

I savor the moment. At this level, victories of any kind are always hard won and hard earned. To beat

Steve Cantwell took a year of my life. I had to redefine myself as a fighter and at the same time figure out who I am. Now that I've done both, the future doesn't look so murky anymore.

Who are you?

I'm the guy who will never quit.

Long after my MMA career is over, that is a creed I can use to build a new life, with new challenges. Travis was right. Whatever you choose to do with your time here, if you want to make something of yourself, you've got to have the heart for the fight. Anything else will never be enough.

I walk away from the center of the cage. Coach Winklejohn waits for me in our corner with a huge grin on his face.

"Do you believe now, Brian?" he asks. He's still worried that I am saddled with that inferiority complex about my fighting skills. Not anymore. That monkey is finally off my back.

"Yeah, Coach. I believe."

Tonight I conquered another objective. In or out of the uniform, I am a Marine. Where my future lies, I don't know. I do know this: I'll always take the heat. I'll take the critics. I will live my life like the battle it is. Like Teddy Roosevelt's Man in the Arena, you must strive to be "the doer of deeds," to have heart for the fight.

Acknowledgments

To my mother, you have sacrificed so much your entire life to allow me the opportunities to live this journey. You have always been there for me when I needed you. I have told you this many times, and it still rings true: all that is good in me came from you. Thank you, and sorry for giving you so many sleepless nights through my life filled with adversity, combat, and fighting.

To my wife, for sticking by my side no matter what and bringing unconditional love and peace to a lifetime full of challenges. I loved you the minute I laid eyes on you, and now you have helped me with my greatest accomplishments to date, our daughters Alexandra and DeAnna.

To my family, from my sister to my crazy aunts, cousins, and uncles, thank you for always believing in me. Thank you for not laughing at my crazy dreams and aspirations. And most of all, thank you for being my biggest fans.

To George Lockheart, Richie Ferrel, Tony Moenich, Gary Hess, Mike Brown, and Jody Carter, thanks for all those long nights of training. Without coaches or a clue, we all won fights on sheer effort and heart. I will always remember those days as the best of my fighting career.

To my Marines, you gave me the defining moments of my life. I will never forget the days I was your leader and will cherish them always. I learned more from you than during any other period of my life. In the worst environment known to man, you were exceptional. For the rest of your lives you have nothing to prove to anyone. I love you, and it has been my greatest honor to lead you in combat.

To the families of Doug Champlin, Rene Martinez, Mike Brown, Willy Koprince, Jonathan Lowe, and Robert Gass. I am eternally sorry that I could not have done more for your sons, husbands, or brothers. Everything I do in my life is in their memory. I will honor them always. If there is ever anything I can do, please find me.

Thank you for the eternal support from all my Naval Academy brothers: Joey, Garret, Bryce, Dan, Donnie, Joel, Jimmy, Andy, Mike, and many, many more, thank you for always being there. For supporting me in great times and bad, you are the best friends any man could wish for.

John Bruning, I knew you were the right man for the job after five minutes. I didn't bother speaking to any other writers because I was looking for someone who was passionate and patriotic. I found plenty of both in you. You truly value the service of our men and women in uniform, and each time our country loses one of its warriors, your heart trembles with grief. Please continue to immortalize them with your writings as you have done for my Marines in this book.

John Bardis, thank you for believing in me and showing me a way to serve while out of uniform. You set an amazing example for everyone to follow. Utilizing our success for the greater good of our country and humanity is something I will continue to strive for my entire life.

Gabe Diana, Nate Smith, Joe Clemmey, Paul Habenicht, Lt. Col. Scott Leonard, Lt. Col. Joseph Shusko, Capt. John Cook, Col. Todd Desgrosseilliers, Col. John Love, Gunny

Johnny Marlow, Gunny Harmon, SSgt. James Robertson, and Sgt. Maj. Scotty Reeves. It was my distinct honor to lead, serve with, and follow each of you. I have learned a lifetime of lessons from each of you, and I would not trade a single second of our time together for the world. I owe you much more than I will ever be able to pay back. Each of you in your own way have inspired me and helped shape the man I am today and the man I hope to become. If you ever need me, please let me know. Semper Fidelis.

—Brian Stann

One meeting with Brian Stann up in the Portland area in the summer of 2008 was all it took to want to work with him on this book. We sat in a bar in Wilsonville, peanut shells strewn across the floor and tables, and ate dinner as fans came up and asked for his autograph. In those interludes when we were left alone, I saw in Brian a man of tremendous character and heart. They are the twin themes of his life and became the pillars upon which we crafted his memoirs. As a Marine, a fighter, and a man, Brian represents the best of us. In an age where sports figures more often than not seem to be cautionary tales and not role models, Brian has chosen to remain humble, modest, and focused on his wife and daughters. So to you, Brian, I say thank you for giving me the opportunity to help share your amazing story and life with our readership. It has been a tremendous joy to work with you.

To my agent, Jim Hornfischer: in a shark-filled business you've been a friend, not just a professional associate. Through the ups and downs of the last year, I found that without you, the writer's life becomes a chore instead of a passion. You're the buffer between the two. Getting to work with you makes me eager to get to the office every morning and regret having to head home for the night. Thank you for all that you've done for my family, for my career, and for me personally. Someday soon, I'll be coming to Austin for that drink.

To Richard Kane and Steve Gansen: thank you both for your patience and consummate professionalism. More importantly, thank you for believing in Brian and his story.

At the end of August 2009, I was en route to see Brian during the final stages of his pre–Cantwell 3 training camp in New Mexico. I'd decided to make a road trip out of it and had thrown my laptop, camera gear, and poncho liner into the right seat of my Pontiac. I set out for the Southwest but only got a few hours out of Portland when devastating news reached us. One of the founding members of our nonprofit organization, the 973rd Civilians on the Battlefield, had joined the Oregon National Guard upon graduating from high school. On the 28th of August, a roadside bomb took his life and the life of his truck commander, Sergeant Earl Werner.

Specialist Taylor Marks was a special young man. I recruited him into the 973rd, saw him grow and achieve with every drill weekend we supported. He babysat my kids; come prom time I let him borrow my GTO to impress his date. Before he left for Iraq, Taylor had become a member of my extended Oregon family.

When news of his death reached me on the road, I had to cancel my trip to see Brian. Our group met in my office, grieving like we had never experienced. But that first night, something extraordinary happened. When we went to visit Taylor's family, they greeted us with singular warmth and love. By the time we left the house that evening, I knew that this was a blow we would survive, thanks to their grace. So, to Michelle and Courtney, I want to say thank you for your love and support. Without it, I would never have found the strength to finish this book.

To the 973rd—Ox, Mark (your kittens are still here, come pick them up), Aaron, Joey, Ben, Andrew, Joe, David, Allison, Jones, Patti, Robbie, Kyle, KK, Spencer, and Mike: your encouragement and example paved the way. Thank you for setting the standard so high. That level of professionalism is what I try to match with every book project I take on. Whatever success I have as a writer is yours as well. You guys are my Oregon family.

To Denice, Andy, Bob, Becca, and Brenda: you guys took great care of me and kept me fueled for the ongoing marathon. Your friendship is treasured.

Bob and Laura Archer are another reason why I can function as a writer. You guys not only are the best animal docs in Oregon, you're also the best landlords. Thank you for the space you've given me in your extraordinary and historic building. I can think of no finer place to write.

Finally, I need to thank Eddie, Renee, and Jenn. I know I drive you guys nuts with my crazy schedule, my catnaps in the afternoon, and my late-night writing sessions. I know we've missed out on a lot of time together these past months. I hope when you finish Brian's story, you will see the value in it and understand the sacrifice we have all shared to see it through to the end. Your understanding and support helped make it happen. And I do appreciate you finding Vol for me whenever I need my squirrel-tailed, orange muse to give me inspiration. Thank you for being so loving and selfless.

—John Bruning